From The Women's Press Ltd
34 Great Sutton Street, London EC1V 0DX

Lis Whitelaw is a writer and teacher. She has published short stories in *The Reach* and *Pied Piper* (Onlywomen Press), a number of articles including 'Lesbians of the Mainscreen' (Gossip 5) and translations of contemporary Icelandic poetry. She lives in Kent.

Lis Whitelaw

The Life and Rebellious Times of Cicely Hamilton

Actress, writer, suffragist

The Women's Press

First published by The Women's Press Limited, 1990
A member of the Namara group
34 Great Sutton Street, London EC1V 0DX

British Library Cataloguing in Publication Data
Whitelaw, Lis
The life and rebellious times of Cicely Hamilton: actress, writer, suffragist
1. Acting. Hamilton, Cicely, *1872–1952*
I. Title
792.028092

ISBN 0–7043–4225–1

Typeset in 9/11pt Times by MC Typeset Limited, Gillingham, Kent
Printed and bound by Cox & Wyman, Reading, Berks.

In memory of Rosemary Manning

Contents

Acknowledgments

I would like to thank all those people who have helped and supported me during the researching and writing of this book. Sibyl Grundberg, Alix Adams, Cherry Potts, Rosemary Auchmuty and Sheila Jeffreys have all made an important contribution in their own special and particular ways. David Doughan of the Fawcett Library generously shared his enthusiasm and expertise and Joe Mitchenson and Richard Mangan of the Raymond Mander and Joe Mitchenson Theatre Collection provided much useful material. I am very grateful to Sir Leslie Bowers, Cicely Hamilton's literary executor, for his interest, to Mrs Angela Findlater for allowing me access to her late husband's research on Lilian Baylis and to Michael Bott of the University of Reading Library for help in tracing many of Cicely Hamilton's letters. Jen Green has been a most sympathetic editor and she, Rosita Boland, and Ros de Lanerolle at The Women's Press have done much to make the process of publication as painless as possible. Finally, throughout the time I was writing this book, I was sustained by the love, support and encouragement of Rosemary Manning; it is very sad that she did not live to see it published.

For permission to quote from copyright sources I have to thank: The Bodley Head for quotations from Lucy Boston's *Perverse and Foolish* and Evelyn Sharp's *Unfinished Adventure*; Hamish Hamilton for quotations from Elizabeth French Boyd's *Bloomsbury Heritage*; David Higham Associates for quotations from Victoria Glendinning's *Vita*; Random Century Group for quotations from Andro Linklater's *An Unhusbanded Life*; Virago Press for quotations from Margaret Llewelyn Davis's *Life as We Have Known It*,

Sylvia Pankhurst's *The Suffragette Movement* and Ray Strachey's *The Cause*; A P Watt Ltd for quotations from H.G. Wells' *The New Machiavelli*; The Harry Hansom Research Center, The University of Texas at Austin for quotations from letters from Cicely Hamilton to Lillah McCarthy and Elizabeth Robins.

Every effort has been made to find copyright holders; I apologise for any error or omissions in the above list and would appreciate being notified of any corrections or additions.

Introduction

When I set out to write this book I intended it to be a straightforward biography in the new tradition of feminist biography, offering an account of Cicely Hamilton's life and work and an analysis of her writing and thus making known the achievement of a remarkable woman whom I considered had been most unjustly neglected. I had chosen to write about her for two reasons: firstly because she was herself a very interesting and unusual woman and secondly because she had participated in so many major events of the twentieth century. I believed that by discovering what she felt and thought about two world wars and the campaigns for peace that they brought into being, the fight for women's suffrage and the changing role of women in society, and the many other social and political questions with which she concerned herself throughout her life we might gain a better understanding of twentieth-century history from a woman's point of view.

It turned out not to be that simple. In the course of my research I have discovered a great deal about how easily women disappear from history – even women who were well known in their own day, and how, very often, consciously or unconsciously, they help to bring about their own invisibility. As a result this book draws attention to the problems I have encountered in writing it. I have deliberately not papered over the cracks to produce a seamless narrative, but instead pointed out the gaps and silences, for these are as much a part of Cicely Hamilton's life as it has come down to us as the facts and the photographs. By being aware of the omissions we can also become aware of the social climate in which women like Cicely lived and the effect that has had on what we know of their lives. Armed with that knowledge, we can try to ensure that later generations do not suffer the same invisibility.

Nancy K. Miller has written, 'To justify an unorthodox life by writing about it is to *reinscribe* the original violation, to reviolate masculine turf.'[1] Cicely Hamilton's life needs no justification from me or from anyone else, but Miller is right in saying that accounts of lives as unorthodox as hers present a challenge both in themselves and in their telling. Accounts of women's lives, when they have been written at all, have, at least until the most recent wave of feminism, tended to polarise women's experience. Women have been presented either as successful in their personal lives or as achievers who have compensated by success in the public sphere for their failures in the private domain. In the former case the subjects have almost always been wives and mothers and in the latter they have usually been spinsters or childless women. Until the last ten years or so the only biographies of women that have been written have been those of extraordinary women – rulers or distinguished figures in the world of the arts or of public affairs – and we have learned of the lives of other women only in relation to the lives of men, as wives, mothers, lovers and muses. Personal fulfilment has been set against public achievement and the subtext has always been that the former is more important for women than the latter. Feminist biographers can and must protest against what Miller has called 'the available fiction of female becoming'.[2]

In writing Cicely Hamilton's life I have set out to show that there is another pattern of 'female becoming' – one that has, until recently, been ignored so totally that its omission looks suspiciously like suppression. This version shows that women can, do and always have lived rich and fulfilling lives without men and that friendship and love with other women has sustained and nurtured many of the most creative and successful women of the century as well as many others whose lives we are only now beginning to discover.

The treatment of love and friendship between women in conventional biography has tended to be presented in one of three ways, or has sometimes drawn on a mixture of all three. If a woman is known to have been sexually involved with another woman the presentation of their relationship may be deliberately designed to titillate the reader; all the most distasteful examples of this have been written by men. Heterosexual women biographers tend to fall into a particular trap when writing about women who may have had lesbian relationships; they give details of possible lovers, in some cases quote what might be construed as love-letters, and then at the last moment pull back from following their own evidence to its logical conclusion, offering an explanation as to why, in spite of everything, they do not believe that their subject was a lesbian.

In the third category are the biographies of well-known lesbians like Radclyffe Hall and Gertrude Stein where the nature of their relationships can be in no doubt. In these cases they are depicted in a very stereotyped way and their partnerships are often described in terms of patriarchal marriage at its most conventional. Often such overt lesbians are discussed in terms of the abnormality of their psychology so that their way of life cannot be seen as something that women might choose voluntarily. It is only recently that biographers, usually women, have written honestly and straightforwardly about the lives of lesbians.

There is a discussion in this book of Cicely's sexuality, but rather than restrict the discussion of whether or not she was a lesbian I have expanded it to include the political implications of thus defining a woman who lived in the past. In the discussion I have paid particular attention to Cicely's friends and colleagues and to her relationships with them since I believe that the analysis of communities of women such as that in which Cicely lived and worked is central to our understanding of the lives of women-oriented women of the past. There is no doubt that her friends were of crucial importance to Cicely herself.

In the more distant past women's friendships differed from men's in that whereas men had the chance to support one another as they set out to conquer new challenges, women's role denied them the opportunity to do that for one another in the public sphere. In the past century or so that has changed; women have helped each other to dream ambitious dreams and supported each other as these dreams become a reality. Carolyn Heilbrun has written,

> The sign of female friendship is not whether friends are homosexual or heterosexual, lovers or not, but whether they share the wonderful energy of work in the public sphere. These, some of them hidden, are the friends whom biographers of women must seek out.[3]

Cicely's life offers a good model of this kind of female friendship since her friends were, for the most part, the women with whom she worked. As she entered new spheres of activity she made new friends among the women already working in them and so, by the end of her life she had friends among women who were involved in a wide range of public, political, social and artistic activities. These friendships sustained her and once she had become friendly with someone the relationship seems to have lasted for life.

It is, sadly, not only friends who are hidden in the existing material about Cicely's life; the research for this book has been a process of fleshing out the barest of bones. The basic source of information on Cicely herself has been her autobiography, *Life Errant*, which must be one of the most uninformative autobiographies ever written. When someone decides to write an autobiography they make certain decisions about how they wish to present themselves and these decisions may depend on a number of factors, both personal and public. *Life Errant* was written when Cicely was in her fifties in the 1930s and reflects both her own feelings about her past and the mood of the times. One of the most stimulating and enjoyable periods of Cicely's life was the time when she was involved in the campaign for the vote and yet the account of it in *Life Errant* is restricted to some anecdotes about the campaign, a bare list of the organisations with which she worked and a somewhat prolonged account of one of the less creditable episodes of the campaign, the Albert Hall riot of 1908. It was only when I turned to articles that Cicely had written and speeches that she had made at the time that I became aware of what the suffrage campaign had really meant to her. The accounts of her fellow-campaigners revealed what she had meant to them. It may be that, by the 1930s, she had become ashamed of the very outspoken attacks on men and patriarchal society that she had made in the 1900s and as a well-known public figure did not wish to remind her readers about that phase of her past.

Life Errant is a very selective account of her past; time and again she plays down her achievements and her enthusiasms. To some extent this can be attributed to middle-class English reticence and to a genuine humility which was, apparently, very characteristic of her. But the reader is also aware of being kept at a distance; that there are parts of her life which she firmly intends to keep private. Although writers of autobiography in the 1930s were on the whole far less prone to revelations about their private lives than their modern counterparts, *Life Errant* is unusually silent even about major events in Cicely's life. In the book she mentions that she was parted from her mother very early in life yet gives no indication of the circumstances or of the effect it had on her. This reticence extends to the way in which she writes about her friends, restricting herself to factual anecdotes about those of them who were well known. At least two of the women who were, on other evidence, among the closest of her friends, Elizabeth Abbott and Elizabeth Montizambert, are never referred to at all.

If there had been plenty of other material upon which to draw for information the limitations of *Life Errant* as a source would not have mattered but this was not the case. Most of my information has come from Cicely's own published work: books, articles, reviews, and from what people wrote about her in articles, their own autobiographies and interviews. The few letters that remain are random in their preservation and while helping to fix events and put them in context they rarely give any insight into the private woman. There are no private papers, diaries or letters to Cicely from her friends. This leads one to the inescapable conclusion that she was either very careless and did not worry about how she appeared to posterity or that, on the contrary, she was very careful and destroyed them – or someone else destroyed them for her. Indeed, Cicely herself destroyed material, one can only guess at her reasons – it may have been no more than a simple desire to preserve her privacy beyond the grave, but it may have been that the nature of her private papers was such that she regarded their contents as compromising. The most likely reason why she might have felt this was that they revealed an intimacy with other women which might, by the 1950s, have been seen as unacceptable. Before the influence of Freud and the sexologists, most notably Havelock Ellis, had made itself felt in Britain close relationships between women had, on the whole, been regarded as a perfectly natural part of life. Once the public became fully aware of the possibility that two women who lived together might not merely be friends but that they might have a sexual relationship – and they did become aware in the wake of the prosecution for obscenity in 1928 of Radclyffe Hall's novel *The Well of Loneliness* – women's friendships came under scrutiny as never before. Cicely may well have preferred not to submit her relationships to this kind of scrutiny.

In the face of such self-censorship the biographer has an even greater duty to try to reconstruct a woman's life as it was really lived rather than acquiesce in the way in which she was forced to present it. In trying to do that I have worked from the position that our current understanding of women's relationships may form a guide to the nature of women's relationships earlier this century. Those who have been less reticent than Cicely have provided enough clues to show us that our own emotional lives can provide us with a reliable understanding of the feelings of women who lived and worked in women-centred environments two or three generations ago. One must, of course, beware of ignoring the historical context – the constraints were different and so were the practicalities of their lives – but we may surely take leave to question whether some things ever really change out of all recognition.

The hardest part of writing the biography of a woman whose life is recorded almost entirely in public utterances and printed works is to catch the tone of voice, the laughter. We are all very aware that interviewers misrepresent their subject and that professional journalists are often forced to write what someone wants to hear. This can sometimes obscure the biographer's sense of her subject but I have become increasingly convinced that the woman who emerges, albeit hesitantly at times, from all these words is a woman who was fighting many of the battles that we are still fighting today and who offers one 'fiction of female becoming' to those who come after. She can, ultimately, be best summed up in her own words:

> Here and there – and only here and there – are human beings who do not need editing to be interesting; who cannot be affected, cannot be conventional, who are simply, straightforwardly themselves.[4]

One

Born in a Barracks

The account of Cicely Hamilton's childhood and family life contains, like other parts of her life, some unexplained mysteries; it is incomplete and, inevitably, the records that do exist tell us far more about the male than the female side of her family.

She was born Cicely Mary Hammill on 15 June 1872, the first child of Denzil Hammill and his wife Maude Mary Florence, née Piers. Cicely was born at home, 15 Sussex Gardens in Paddington, London. Her parents had been married in October 1870 at Weymouth in Dorset where her father, a captain in the 75th Regiment, the Gordon Highlanders, was stationed. The wedding had taken place in the handsome eighteenth-century parish church of Saint Mary's in the part of the town properly called Melcombe Regis, and the curate had officiated. According to the marriage certificate both Denzil Hammill and Maude Piers were residents of Weymouth at the time of their marriage so it is possible that they had met as a result of Denzil's posting to the town.

Cicely's family on her father's side was solidly middle-class; her grandfather, John Hammill, was a barrister who had been called to the Bar of the Inner Temple in 1832. He became a boundary commissioner, determining the boundaries of newly created boroughs in 1835 and five years later was appointed commissioner of bankruptcy in Liverpool. In the July of 1840 his eldest son Denzil was born at New Brighton, Cheshire and the family stayed there until 1847 when John Hammill became stipendiary magistrate at Worship Street Police Court in London and they moved to 34 Sussex Gardens, Paddington. When he was old enough Denzil

Hammill was sent to school at Westminster and in 1856 his father wrote applying for him to take the entrance examination for the Royal Military Academy, Sandhurst. In his letter of application, designed to prove how suited his son was to a military career, John Hammill mentions two cousins who had fought at Sebastopol in the Crimean War and also refers to one of his ancestors, Colonel Hugh Hammill, who had, five generations before, raised a regiment at his own expense and defended Londonderry, for which he had been thanked by the King and Parliament.

The normal route by which one became an army officer in those days was to purchase a commission and it is clear that John Hammill intended his son to do this after attending Sandhurst. Denzil Hammill passed the entrance examination for Sandhurst and spent the time before taking up his place travelling in France and Germany, learning the German language and studying the military systems of both countries, but in December 1857 his father was forced to admit that he could not afford to purchase the desired commission. He had had money in the Borough Bank in Liverpool which had collapsed and he therefore requested that, in view of the fact that the army was expanding in order to deal with the Indian Mutiny, and in the light of his own career of public service, his son should be given a commission without purchase. The request was granted and in September 1858, eight months after joining the army as an ensign, Denzil Hammill set sail for India. He missed the Mutiny but this was the beginning of a distinguished military career.

Cicely's father was based in England for most of the first ten years to her life and for much of that time the family seems to have lived in London, although they were in Weymouth when a second daughter, Evelyn, was born in 1873 and again in 1880 when Lieutenant Colonel Hammill, as he was by then, commanded the regimental depot. Cicely had fond memories of life in the army barracks in Weymouth, high on the hill known as the Nothe, looking out over the harbour and beyond towards France. Friends in later life often felt that her army background made it difficult for her to be completely unambiguous in her condemnation of war and the military; the memory of the barrack square at Weymouth and the image of her burly, much decorated father in full Highland regimentals clouded her normally clear vision.

Inevitably we know less about Cicely's mother since details of the lives of women of her generation rarely find their way into public records. Cicely wrote in her autobiography that her mother came from an Irish family in County Westmeath and it is likely that they were at least members of the landed gentry. The evidence for this lies in an incident which Cicely herself recorded – her discovery that the head of the family in the 1800s paid the highest damages of any co-respondent in a divorce case heard in Dublin in the whole of the nineteenth century. Divorce at that time, difficult and expensive as it was, tended to be the prerogative of the upper classes. It was probably as a result of this burden on the family fortunes that the Piers side of the family became as impecunious as the Hammills.

Cicely's mother Maude remains a shadowy figure, although we know she was much loved by her eldest daughter. Cicely's love for her mother was tinged with a constant fear of separation and loss:

> Life without my mother could not be borne, and I made up my mind that, if she were to die, I would go to the kitchen for the carving-knife and give myself a stab just where I could feel my heart beating.[1]

It is possible that Maude Hammill travelled with her husband, leaving Cicely behind in the care of her nurse, Eliza, and that these early separations gave rise to Cicely's childish plan.

For much of her early life Cicely had a solid if impoverished middle-class childhood and before she was four she had taught herself to read:

> My father was amusedly proud of his small daughter's accomplishment, and one day he carried me down from the nursery, sat me on the luncheon table, and bade me display it to a couple of brother officers; the performance beginning with extracts from *Red Riding Hood* and going on to a paragraph in *The Times* with which I wrestled phonetically, to the encouraging applause of my audience.[2]

From this time on books became Cicely's chief delight but also another source of anxiety and fear. Her reading seems to have been largely uncensored and the effect of the more violent kind of fairy tale on what was probably already a very vivid imagination was at times most disturbing. It gave rise to a rather strange and lifelong habit:

> I still sleep o' nights with the sheet wrapped round my head like a

> hood; an adaptation of my youthful practice of covering not only my head but my face with the bed-clothes – covering it tightly and tucking myself in, to hide the awful company of ghosts from sight, and make sure there could be no gap or loophole to give entrance to a spectral hand.[3]

Despite the underlying anxiety which seems to have dogged Cicely from infancy, she clearly felt herself much loved, by her mother, by her nurse Eliza and by her two aunts, Amy and Lucy Hammill, who played a very important part in her later childhood. Like all children Cicely lived mainly in a world of women but unlike most children she early felt an intense loyalty to her own sex. She herself traced many of her ideas and feelings about women and about marriage back to her relationships with these women when she was a small child. When she was about six – and determined to become a railway guard – she came across slighting references to spinsters for the first time and was deeply indignant:

> Of the four women whom I greatly loved, only one, my mother was married; the others were my dear aunts Lucy and Amy, and my nurse the beloved Eliza. They were not failures – my best-loved friends – and I would not have them called so.[4]

In the manner of the times Maude Hammill had two more children in rapid succession, Evelyn and then John, known as Jack, in 1875. The fourth member of the family, Raymond, arrived in 1879. Cicely did not like the look of the newborn Jack and when she was first taken to see him she hit him in the face. She maintained that this was not because she was jealous of him but simply because he was so ugly, and even as an adult she preferred to have nothing to do with very small babies. She was similarly appalled by the sight of a child being breast-fed and needed reassurance from Eliza that she herself had been bottle-fed. Such intense early dislike of babies and their habits has no obvious explanation in her childhood but it may have influenced her later attitude to motherhood and child-rearing, particularly her refusal to sentimentalise the image of motherhood as something sacred.

More immediately distressing for Cicely, however, was the disappearance of her mother from her life. This is the first of the mysteries about events in Cicely's life and she herself gives no indication of what happened. In her autobiography she wrote simply, 'The parting from my mother came early in life, but it was a parting whose finality was not recognised at the time.'[5] The most obvious explanation is that Maude Hammill died while away from her children for some reason, but her death is not registered in Britain nor does it appear in the records of British subjects who died abroad. Other explanations are also possible and Cicely's reticence about the cause of her mother's disappearance might suggest that there was some shame attached to it.

It is hard to be certain whether her use of the word 'parting' rather than 'death' signifies that Maude Hammill did not die or whether it is simply a euphemism typical of the period. If she did not die she may have left her husband and returned to her family in Ireland or she may have been committed to an asylum. Either of these possibilities would have been sufficiently socially unacceptable at the time to explain Cicely's reluctance to discuss the matter.

The only other mention that Cicely makes of her mother in her autobiography is when she refers in passing to a meeting which she had as a young woman with an old friend of her mother's who was a deaconess. It seems rather unlikely that if Maude Hammill had behaved scandalously such a woman would have stayed in touch with her family. Cicely's almost total silence on the subject is in keeping with her reticence about her private life but it may also have been hard for her to discuss such a terrible event because of the traumatic effect it had had upon her. Whatever may have happened to her mother Cicely had, by the age of ten, embarked on one of the grimmest periods of her life.

In 1881 Denzil Hammill left England for Egypt and set out on the military campaign which was to bring him great distinction. It is possible, although unlikely, that his wife went with him to Egypt and died there. The British Army was sent to Egypt to strengthen the power of the ruler, the Khedive, and in so doing protect the very considerable British interests in his country. It was particularly important to maintain access to the Suez Canal, which was vital for Britain's communications with the eastern parts of her Empire, especially India. The French were also involved, not least because they managed the canal, even though the British government was the major shareholder. In August 1882 the Gordon Highlanders arrived at the port of Alexandria and joined the forces occupying the isthmus at the head of the canal in order to protect the railway and the water supply. The British took Tel-el-Kebir and the rebellion against the Khedive collapsed. Lt-Col. Hammill commanded the 1st Battalion, the Gordon Highlanders, throughout the campaign and was mentioned in dispatches. In November 1882 he was made a Companion of the Order of the Bath and also honoured by the Egyptians for his part in the campaign. The Gordon Highlanders stayed in Egypt until 1884 when, again under Denzil Hammill's command, they were sent to Sudan to relieve the garrison of Tokar. During the fighting of the Nile campaign, the culmination of which was the attempt to relieve General Gordon at Khartoum, Denzil Hammill was twice mentioned in dispatches, decorated three times and awarded the brevet of Colonel in May 1884. This meant that he held the rank of full Colonel in the army rather than in his regiment and it was a recognition of his distinguished service during the campaign. When he left Egypt in October 1885 he was promoted to the honorary rank of Major-General.

While their father was behaving like an archetypal Victorian hero in the deserts of Egypt and the Sudan, his children were fighting a very different battle at home in England. When he had left for Egypt Denzil Hammill had boarded them out with a family in Clapham. This was a very common practice at the time for middle-class families whose father was serving abroad. Cicely was later to describe the four years she spent in Clapham as the unhappiest of her life and at one point she became so desperate that she tried to kill herself. She had read somewhere of a successful suicide in which the victim had drowned himself in a mere basinful of water and so she tried to do the same with the basin from her washstand. Cicely was only ten when she attempted to kill herself but as the eldest she felt a great sense of responsibility for her younger siblings. Since she was only a child herself she was powerless to protect them and in the end suicide seemed the only way to draw attention to their plight: 'If I drowned myself, there would be an inquest and the police – in whose omnipotence I had absolute confidence – would find out that we were not being kindly treated and things would be better for the others.'[6]

Cicely remained proud all her life of her attempt to help her brothers and sister and certainly her action was, in the circumstances, both brave and unselfish. One can only guess at the sense of desperation which drove her to it but the experience must have made an impression which lasted for the rest of her life. Presumably when her plan failed she had no alternative but to go on putting up with the feelings of despair and hopelessness that had prompted it.

It is tempting to see Cicely's early experience as *de facto* head of the family as having shaped her attitude to individual responsibility. Throughout her life she felt responsible for the welfare of others. This showed itself both on a personal level – she supported various members of her family financially for most of her life – and in more public ways. Her social and political commitment can be seen as part of the same attitude to life: a desire to improve the lot of those around her, regardless of what it cost her in time and effort.

There were two particular causes of the Hammill children's misery; the attitude of their foster mother – and the food. As the woman with whom they boarded had children of her own she discriminated against the Hammill children, who experienced the desolation of being second-best in everyone's affections, and denied the comfort of adults for whom they came first. As a small child Cicely had felt herself protected and loved by her mother, her aunts and her nurse; the contrast with the bleakness of the Clapham household must have been heartbreaking. Their foster mother does not seem to have taken account of the fact that the Hammill children were suffering all the distress associated with separation from both their parents and that the youngest, Raymond, was only three years old. As a result of their parents' attitude the children of the family felt at liberty to join in the persecution of the Hammills, thus adding to their misery.

The final straw, for Cicely and Jack in particular, was the food. Cicely throughout her life enjoyed good food and her discriminating palate had been developed by her mother's skill as a cook. It was therefore a special torment to be required to finish every mouthful on her plate when the food was gluey rice or thick white snakes of macaroni; to be made to stay at the table and somehow force down the disgusting mess. The harsh discipline at meals was symptomatic of something which Cicely came to call the 'Stepmother' mentality; the jealousy women feel for children other than their own whom they have none the less to care for. Later in life Cicely resented deeply the idea that motherhood was the great justification for women's existence; she knew from bitter experience that it did not always bring out the best in women. The punitive atmosphere in which she lived for four years must have been especially distressing to a child like Cicely who, even when living in a loving and secure environment, had been prone to anxiety and nightmares. Cicely did not regard herself as a pessimist – she enjoyed life too much for that – but another effect of her years in the Clapham household was that it was hard for her to believe that events would turn out to her advantage, and good fortune was always unexpected. It is hardly surprising that in later life she avoided travelling to Clapham whenever possible.

The household did, however, have one compensation – the library; so when she left in 1885 on her father's return to England she was very widely read in history, biography and literature, even if she had received next to no formal schooling. One reason why Cicely had received so little education was lack of money; in many middle-class families education for daughters was not considered important and therefore was a convenient economy to make if money was short. Her father's family had lost much of their money through mismanagement of a family trust by their solicitor and so her father had to manage on his army pay which, by the time he retired in 1885, was £328 10s per annum. It is not at all clear why he resigned his commission when he did; he was only forty-five and at the peak of his career. Perhaps he thought he could make more money in some other occupation. In 1886 he converted his pension to a lump sum but there is no record of how he earned his living until mention of his death in 1891 when he was Vice-Consul at Bonny in West Africa. Cicely says that his return to England in 1885 was only temporary, so he may have been in the consular service throughout that period or have been involved in some sort of overseas trading venture. Whatever he did he does not seem to have prospered financially since Cicely was aware throughout her time at school of being far less well off than her fellow pupils.

When he returned from the Nile campaign Denzil Hammill took his children to live with his sisters Lucy and Amy in Bournemouth and their aunts continued to give them a home until they all, at a very early age, set off to make their own living. Her aunts provided Cicely with the straightforward affection and security which she had so missed during her time at Clapham and she remained close to them until their deaths. Although Cicely would probably have preferred to go to school in Bournemouth she was offered a place at a boarding school where the headmistress was prepared to educate her for very substantially reduced fees and so, for the first time in her life, the freckle-faced, red-headed thirteen-year-old was plunged into the company of other girls her own age and confronted with all the constraints of boarding school life.

The school to which Cicely was sent was in Malvern, Worcestershire – one of those towns which, partly because of its reputation as a health resort, became full of schools catering for children of every age, boys and girls alike. Many of the smaller establishments which were there in the nineteenth century have ceased to exist, Cicely's school among them, but education remains one of the staple industries of the town. Cicely's education had been so erratic that when she first arrived she was put with children of nine, but her miscellaneous reading and native intelligence ensured that by the end of her first day she had moved up to the appropriate group for her age.

By the time Cicely went away to school there had been something of a revolution in the education of girls but it does not seem to have touched the establishment in which she was being educated. The traditional education of girls had emphasised the development of accomplishments such as music and drawing, in addition to literature, some history and a smattering of French. By the 1860s women such as the legendary Dorothea Beale of Cheltenham Ladies' College and Frances Dove of Wycombe Abbey and St Leonards were offering girls a far more academic education. Intellectual endeavour was encouraged and the classics and mathematics which had long formed the basis of the curriculum in boys' schools now became available to girls as well. Cicely's friend and contemporary Margaret Haig, later Lady Rhondda, described her schooldays at St Leonards as 'gloriously happy' – the combination of intellectual and physical freedom and the chance to make close friendships with girls of her own age delighted her. Margaret Haig's relationship with Miss Sandys, her housemistress, was clearly important, helping her to become aware of the possibility of 'combining public esteem with personal charm'.

Girls from a school like St Leonards would have been prepared to go on to one of the recently founded women's colleges. The first of these, Girton at Cambridge, had opened its doors in 1869 and by the 1890s there were also women's colleges at Oxford and London Universities. Women were not awarded degrees at Oxford until 1920 or at Cambridge until 1948 but they could follow the same course of study as men and take the degree examinations. London, in keeping with its more radical nature, allowed women to receive degrees as early as 1878.

Cicely's education seems to have followed a more traditional pattern. She shone at English and history but had considerable difficulty with some other subjects. Music was a special case, as far as Cicely was concerned. When she discovered that playing the piano meant an hour of practice every day in an icy, unheated music room she decided that it was an accomplishment she would rather do without and set about proving to her teachers that she was a total musical dunce:

> The more they taught me, the more hideous the effect on the ear; I couldn't hear the difference between wrong notes and right, I gave the same value to quavers and semi-breves, and my fingers hit the keys straight as pokers.[7]

In later life Cicely was surprised by the fact that she felt no guilt at this sustained deception since she was normally a truthful and conscientious child. She concluded that at the time it was a piece of play-acting and as such seemed to her childish conscience to be very different from telling lies.

She developed a taste for more conventional sorts of acting too. Plays in French were a regular feature of school life and, despite the difficulty of learning long speeches in a foreign language, Cicely relished these dramatic opportunities. Even better were plays in English, and in one production of *As You Like It* Cicely happily doubled the parts of Touchstone and Orlando. She does not tell us how she managed in the final scene when both characters are on stage together. Acting was one of her few real pleasures at school. On the whole she spent her time longing for the holidays and for some semblance of the family life of which she had enjoyed so little. Perhaps because she had come late to school life and also because of an innate preference for a more solitary kind of existence, she greatly disliked community life. She was popular with her school-fellows, not surprisingly if the sense of fun and mischief which so delighted her adult friends was part of her character as a child, and she was on good terms with her teachers – but this was not enough. She hated the regimentation, noise and lack of privacy of school life and longed to be left alone to read and think her own thoughts. Cicely later described her childhood as 'unhappy and frightened' and boarding school probably did little to make it any happier. The separation from her brothers and sister must have been hard to bear for a child who felt so responsible for them during the four years at Clapham, and separation from her aunts must have made her fear that they would disappear in the same way as her mother had done.

Matters were made worse by the fact that while most of her fellow pupils came from prosperous middle-class homes her family was always extremely hard up. Girls did not wear school uniforms in those days and Cicely's dresses were often shabby and well-worn and the replacements might well be hand-me-downs: 'Well do I remember the query "Is that your new dress?" with the accent on the "new"; showing that traces of previous wear had been spotted by a sharp-eyed schoolfellow.'[8] As an adult, Cicely was careless of her appearance but teenage girls tend to be conformist and she felt the taunt keenly. School at Malvern was not all unpleasant. Apart from the acting, lectures on history and literature from a French master who also encouraged her writing were a bright spot in her week and with characteristic individualism she became a fluent reader of French by working her way unaided through the many melodramatic volumes of Eugene Sue's *Le Juif Errant*. Independent and dogged effort was typical of Cicely's approach, even as a girl. Even so she was not sorry to leave Malvern and, just before she was seventeen, a cousin of her father's – better off than the rest of the family – offered to pay for her education in Germany. For the first six months of her stay her fees were paid for her but after that she had to make her own way by speaking English to her fellow pupils. She had had to fend for herself emotionally very young; now she had to be independent financially as well.

The school was in Bad Homburg, then a fashionable spa frequented by English visitors in the summer. Cicely did not enjoy school any better just because it was in Germany but at least in Bad Homburg she was occasionally taken out to lunch or dinner at one of the smart hotels by friends of her family who were staying in the town. Such treats encouraged her interest in good food and as a result of the time she spent in Germany Cicely developed another taste she never lost – for beer, unusual in a middle-class woman of her generation. The main purpose of her stay in Bad Homburg was to improve her German and that was certainly achieved; she became fluent and remained so all her life. Her linguistic skills proved very useful when, as an impoverished actress and writer, she was able to augment her income by translation work. The experience of living abroad as part of another national community gave Cicely great insight into the character of other nations and peoples which she used effectively in her writing. It also gave her a special understanding of and affection for the German people, which she never lost. Many English people of her generation and background were familiar with German and the Germans and it was to add yet another dimension to the horror that they felt more than twenty years later at the outbreak of World War I.

In 1890, at the age of eighteen, Cicely left school and was launched into the world to make her own living as a pupil-teacher. Despite her own reticence on the subject, her childhood experiences must have marked her deeply. Although she came from a middle-class background her family was always poor and she realised early on that her father, no matter how impressive a figure he cut, was not a good provider. He was probably rather remote from the lives of his children and the family as such had ceased to function by the time Cicely was about ten. Since we do not know what happened to her mother it is difficult to be sure what effect her disappearance had on Cicely. It seems that, in the face of such unhappiness and disruption, her sister and aunts became very important people in her life. She continued to share a home with Evelyn till 1929 and was always in close touch with her aunts; the remaining part of her family was central to her happiness. Once Cicely ceased to tour as an actress she moved only twice and both houses she lived in were in the same street. It is tempting to see her resolute 'staying put' as a reaction against the many different places she had to live in as a child. Later, from a secure domestic base, she came to enjoy travelling all over Britain and Europe but her home was always very important to her. Indeed much of the way she lived her life as an adult can be seen as a response to the difficulties of her youth; her sceptical attitude towards men and marriage; the centrality of women in her life and her reluctance to move house are all easily explained in terms of earlier experiences. And is it stretching credibility too far to suggest that her preference for a solitary way of life, her apparent failure to share her life with an intimate partner, were the result of a fear of loving anyone too much? She had adored her mother and her mother had deserted her – perhaps she never took the risk again.

When their father died in 1891 Cicely was nineteen, and the three older children were forced to make their own way in the world. Her self-reliance in later life was surely the result of her early exposure to the harsh realities of earning her own living while still comparatively young. Not for her the sheltered domestic life more usual for women of her class, waiting at home arranging flowers and doing fancy work until a suitable young man proposed marriage. Jack was sent to Canada, where he lived a wandering life, riding boxcars as he moved from job to job. Like Raymond, who was still too young to leave school in 1891, he ended up in Australia. Evelyn was living in Germany as an au pair when her father died and was forced to come home and find work as a nursery governess. So Cicely's fate was no harsher than theirs – she just resented it more.

The work that Cicely could do was limited by her qualifications – and she had none except a high standard of conversational German and a very eclectic range of reading. Her education at the school at Malvern had not equipped her to go on to university, even if there had been the money to pay the fees, and without a degree there was no hope of teaching in one of the better girls' schools. She would probably not have been happy there anyway; the spirit of total dedication and absorption in the life of the school would not have suited her as a teacher. Her unwillingness to take other people's ideas on trust and her extreme dislike of influencing people to her own way of thinking would not have fitted in well with an environment where the personalities of the teachers had a crucial effect on the students' attitudes to the subjects they taught and where the teachers themselves were often in thrall to a headmistress of powerful and commanding personality. In the circumstances it better suited her sense of grievance to work in a school where she could feel completely discontented with her lot.

The school in the Midlands where Cicely ended up as a pupil-teacher may very well have resembled the one described by the writer of children's books, Lucy Boston, in her autobiography. Of her private school of forty girls in Southport, she remembered:

> The teaching in the school was very simple: for arithmetic we learned the multiplication tables and weights and measures. For history we learned by heart the dates of all the kings and queens of England, one dynasty a week. For literature we learned a simple poem such as Wordsworth's 'Daffodils' . . . the bulk of the class seemed simply to sit through every lesson without the slightest interest or effort . . . None of these girls was going to earn her own living. They saw no point in learning. They were there to be kept out of mischief till they grew up.[9]

Lucy Boston comments of the two pupil-teachers that they were 'really schoolgirls with their hair up'. Cicely was probably just that and she hated her job. Later she described herself as 'a discontented, sullen young creature, strongly conscious of her grievance against fate.'[10] Not only did she hate being forced to continue her life in the confines of another institution, worse still she was not able to follow what she considered her true vocation – the theatre. Teaching itself held no charms for her:

> Except for some practical or immediate purpose I seldom want others to agree with me or think as I do, while a good teacher, I imagine, must desire to persuade and convert. I like my ideas and thoughts for themselves, not because they are approved by other people; I like playing with them and seeing where they lead me.[11]

She adds that one of her friends once observed that she only really liked an idea which she alone held and everyone else disagreed with: 'as soon as it was shared by half a dozen other people I ceased to be interested and went on to something else.'[12] Independence of thought was one of Cicely's hallmarks throughout her career in public life and she probably developed the characteristic early. It is really another aspect of her self-reliance; she thought things out for herself because she had no one to ask and her wide and eclectic reading probably meant that some of her ideas were rather eccentric for a young woman.

In her autobiography Cicely remarks that 'Youth, if I may judge by my own experience, is an over-rated epoch; a season of frequent disappointment . . .',[13] adding that life improves considerably as one gets older. Her youth had certainly not lived up to whatever hopes she might have had for it; it had not been the carefree Golden Age beloved of the poets but after some time as a teacher Cicely could stand it no longer and, with a few pounds she had saved, set off to London to try her luck in the theatre.

It was a major change from being a pupil-teacher in the Midlands to becoming an actress in London and Cicely must have been a very bold young woman even to contemplate it. The theatre had never been a respectable profession, especially for a woman. 'Actress' was used as a euphemism for 'prostitute' well into the twentieth century and kings and aristocrats had, since the time of Charles II, traditionally found their mistresses from among the ranks of the theatrical profession. By the early nineteenth century the theatres had ceased to be respectable places of entertainment for the middle classes; they had become associated with drunkenness and dissolute behaviour but by the 1860s their rehabilitation had begun. In 1865 Marie Wilton, who was married to the actor Squire Bancroft, took the lease on a run-down theatre in the Tottenham Court Road and transformed it into a place where middle-class audiences could watch pleasant, undemanding plays in congenial surroundings. She established a trend and the great actor-managers of the Victorian theatre, Wyndham, Tree and, above all, Henry Irving wooed the bourgeoisie with naturalistic drama, rewritten Shakespeare, historical plays and melodrama. The seal was finally set on the profession's respectability when Irving became the first theatrical knight in 1895. The naturalistic plays, especially those known, from their drawing-room settings, as 'cup and saucer' dramas, required actors with an understanding of how to behave in polite society. This opened the way for middle-class women and the 1860s were the first time they entered the profession in any number.

It may have been a growing trend but families were not usually at all happy about their daughters wanting to become actresses. When Eva Moore, a contemporary of Cicely's and a fellow suffragist in later life, told her father, a strict Victorian paterfamilias, that she was going on the stage:

> The expected tornado swept the house, and the storm broke and the thunder of my father's wrath rolled over our heads . . . So my mother wept, and my father washed his hands with much invisible soap, ordering me never to darken his doors again.[14]

It was easier for Cicely to take the risk of becoming an actress because she did not have parents to worry about, but even so she changed her name from Hammill to Hamilton at this time 'in deference to the lingering prejudice of an elder generation, not from any wish of my own'.[15] It was probably her aunts Lucy and Amy whose sensibility she was trying to protect; she was fond of them and would not have wanted to distress or embarrass them.

Cicely said that her experience of acting at school was responsible for her decision to go on the stage. It seems likely that she had enjoyed the chance it offered her to give rein to the more exuberant side of her nature after the narrowness of the years in Clapham and, to judge from her behaviour in later life, she liked making people laugh. Her sympathy for and interest in human beings in general, which is later so apparent in her writing, are qualities which she considered essential for an actor and she hints in her autobiography that she also enjoyed the opportunity for self-discovery that acting afforded her. A desire for adventure and excitement may also have contributed to her determination to make a change. Even as a child she had envied the variety of opportunities open to boys and a career as an actress was one way out of the restricted life which was the norm for women. She may have found it somewhat easier to take the risk than many women would have done since she had been forced to be self-reliant from an early age but she was under no illusions about how hard her new career would be.

Cicely was not, so she claimed, good-looking in a conventional way and so she knew that she would probably be unsuitable to play *ingénue* roles, the obvious parts for a woman of her age. There are no surviving photographs of her from this stage of her career so it is impossible to assess how accurate her judgment on her appearance was. When she was older people meeting her for the first time commented with admiration on her red-gold hair and beautiful grey eyes, and photographs taken when she was in her thirties show a strikingly handsome woman.

There is an interesting paradox in Cicely's character in that she appeared in some ways to seek security to compensate for the unhappiness of her childhood – living in the same street throughout her adult life for instance – and yet on the whole was restless and exploratory, always looking for a new challenge and reluctant to restrict herself to any one project for too long. Her move from teaching to acting was typical of her determination to live life to the full – in defiance of convention if necessary – and of her recognition that there was often a price to be paid for self-fulfilment.

At this period there were no drama schools – anyone wanting to go on the stage tried their luck with theatre managers until someone offered them work. It was harder for Cicely than it was for young women with more conventional or obvious charms: while her contemporary, Violet Vanbrugh, was found her first job by Ellen Terry, Cicely had to make her own way, which she did with dogged determination. When she could not find theatrical work she resorted to minor journalism, translation and the writing of short stories for some of the many magazines which flourished at the time, but she remained determined to become an actress. By sheer persistence and after appearing a few times in suburban theatres she was offered a character role in a play by Henry Arthur Jones which was touring the provinces, and from then on she worked almost entirely in touring companies.

In the days before the cinema, the theatre and the music-hall were the sole commercial sources of popular entertainment and even quite small towns had theatres. Repertory companies had not yet developed and so these theatres depended for their programmes on the succession of touring companies which crossed and re-crossed the country. The touring companies were divided into numbers one, two, and three tours and fit-up companies, and each type of tour had its own beat. The number one tours played the major provincial cities and twos the smaller towns, threes the most minor theatres, while the fit-up companies played in towns without a theatre at all. They brought with them all the paraphernalia of an ordinary theatre, including the proscenium arch, and fitted it all up in any building large enough to accommodate it. They played in corn exchanges, municipal baths and assembly halls of all kinds. Cicely's first job was in a fit-up company. The staple of the fit-ups was melodrama, especially the kind of spectacular melodrama in which rocks crushed the villain as he was about to hurl the virtuous heroine from a towering precipice. To an audience as yet unfamiliar with the way the cinema could present such scenes, plays like this were still exciting but with the advent of 'the pictures' they disappeared, their spectacle suddenly tame beside cliffhangers like *The Perils of Pauline*.

It was not an easy life on the road; the usual starting salary for an actress was £1 a week and find all your own clothes – about the same as for a young woman typist but with none of the security. Fit-up companies usually only played in the smaller towns for one or two performances and so they were constantly moving on, constantly looking for somewhere to stay. In her autobiography Cicely recalls the desperation which drove her finally to ask at the local police station if they could rent cells for the night. An amused inspector sent out some constables to persuade local people to give them a bed. This incident happened in Armagh where local residents may have been reluctant to take in actresses as lodgers because, as devout nonconformists, they were suspicious of the women's morals. In larger towns there were established theatrical landladies with whom all the touring companies stayed but in smaller places the actors had to take pot luck. Despite the nomadic life there was a strong sense of camaraderie within the profession and Cicely always enjoyed a wait at Derby:

> Where every train that ran into the station had its labelled theatrical carriages attached and where theatrical specials were shunted and assembled and divided. As each train came in you hurried up to read its labels, and hail any member of the company with whom you had previous acquaintance; and there would be

> five minutes' talk on the platform or – if the wait were long enough – an adjournment to the refreshment-room.[16]

The companies were very hierarchical in organisation and there was a recognised route which an actress took from walk-on to leading lady. If she was not leading-lady material she might become what was known as a 'heavy' in melodramas, as Cicely did. The 'heavy', often played by an older woman or a character actress, was usually responsible for betraying the heroine into danger or in some other way bringing about events in which the leading characters suffered. Cicely seems to have played character and 'heavy' roles almost from the beginning of her career despite the fact that she was only in her early twenties. Hers was quite an elevated position within the company and it entitled her to share a railway carriage with the leading lady when they were travelling. Cicely may not have relished this enforced intimacy but, together with the brief meetings with friends and acquaintances on railway stations, it did something to counteract the essential loneliness of life on tour. Lena Ashwell, who first produced Cicely's play *Diana of Dobsons*, found touring quite terrifying:

> It was the first time that I had been quite alone on tour, entirely on my own and the rooms in which I found myself filled me with terror. As there was no key or lock, I barricaded myself with all the furniture I was strong enough to move, and then I was afraid to sleep.[17]

In the early days at least Cicely could rarely afford a room to herself; in order to survive on £1 a week it was necessary to share, often with two other actresses. At times her old longing for solitude coupled with all the other hardships must have made her wonder if she was not paying too high a price for her adventurous new life.

The touring companies of which Cicely was a member were mostly too insignificant to be noticed in the professional journals such as the *Stage* and *Era* so there is very little record of the plays in which she appeared at the beginning of her career. By 1897 she was in the company run by Edmund Tearle, a member of a famous American theatrical family whose cousin Godfrey, later Sir Godfrey Tearle, was an eminent contemporary of Cicely and appeared in some of her plays. Edmund Tearle preserved some of the old barnstorming traditions of Shakespearian acting which had already been abandoned by more sophisticated performers. During her time with Tearle Cicely played a range of Shakespearian parts, which suggests that she had reached a status beyond that of a mere bit player: Gertrude in *Hamlet*, Emilia in *Othello* and a Witch in *Macbeth*. For this she was now paid £2 and still had to find all her own clothes. This was always a problem, especially in costume dramas, and sometimes meant that she had to raid her savings, put by for when she was out of work.

> I have never been clever with needle and scissors and, in my years on the stage, the clothes problem was sometimes a nightmare. I remember the straits to which I was put when the Tearle company staged a version of *The Three Musketeers* and I was cast for the Queen – queens are horribly expensive to dress. How I went through my dress-basket wondering what I could make do? and how much of my savings I should have to draw out of the Post Office?[18]

In Tearle's company the versions of Shakespeare's plays which were performed often differed markedly from what Shakespeare actually wrote – characters were written out to reduce the size of the cast and other characters given new speeches to cover the omissions. None the less Cicely learnt a great deal about handling an audience from playing 'emotional scenes to a Saturday Tyneside audience – which had come to the theatre with plenty of beer in it, and brought nuts to crack through the show'.[19] On Saturday nights they always played *Richard III* or *Othello* – the villainy and violent action appealed to the audience and they were roles which Tearle relished and which, if he was in the mood, he acted very well. One of the non-Shakespearian plays in which Cicely appeared with Tearle's company was *The Christian's Cross*, one of the company's notable successes. The play, adapted from Cardinal Wiseman's novel *The Church of the Catacombs*, is about the trials of the early church which was a popular subject at the time – the combination of religion and fine historical costume appealed to contemporary audiences. The play probably provided Cicely with her first role as a saintly woman – a type of part with which she became associated later in her career. She may well have played Agnes, the widow of a Christian martyr with all the virtues of a Roman matron who, at a time when Christianity is forbidden in Rome, openly professes her faith and after declining to save her life by marrying the Prefect is executed for her beliefs. The play is melodramatic with a number of violent and gory murders and ends with an Apotheosis in which the martyred centurion Sebastian is borne to Heaven by angels. The mixture of piety and violence was well received. The play opened at the Theatre Royal, Portsmouth, and was seen in Chester and Langton before coming to the Surrey Theatre in Blackfriars, Lambeth, one of the many outer London theatres of the time which have since disappeared. As the list of venues shows, this company was more substantial than some of those in which Cicely had worked: these were quite major theatres.

Records exist for only one other play in which Cicely appeared during this phase of her career – *The Gamekeeper*, 'a new play by Herbert Pearson McPherson and Florence Marryat'. Cicely appeared in the first tour of the play which began at Brighton Aquarium in May 1898. The venue suggests a rather less prestigious company than Tearle's, forced to fit itself into a town already full of companies which had taken the better theatres. Once again the character Cicely played was a woman of principle, this time one who gives up the man she loves, Ralph, in order that he may preserve his reputation and marry the woman to whom he has become betrothed. The play is full of disguise, trickery and finally violence as the gamekeeper of the title murders his faithless wife who has been about to marry Ralph while posing as a French lady of quality. Reading a melodramatic play like this, totally devoid of characterisation and with action its only virtue, it is easy to understand why Cicely finally became disillusioned with life in a touring company. Even for a woman as stage struck as she was the limitations of the material must have placed a severe strain on her enthusiasm.

The hazards were by no means only artistic; if the manager was unscrupulous and had insufficient financial backing the company might be left stranded with its wages unpaid while the manager disappeared rather than face his creditors. Bad luck could strike even reputable managers and one production in which Cicely was playing the female lead had very poor audiences in a small town near the Welsh border, leaving the manager unable to pay either the wages or the fares which would get the company to the more lucrative venues of the South Wales coalfield. In this case Cicely lent the manager £2 from her tiny savings and thus enabled the tour to continue. Their fortunes soon improved and the manager was able to reimburse Cicely and pay the cast.

Cicely had not enjoyed a particularly sheltered life up to this point. Emotionally and materially it had been hard but, until she went on the stage, it had been lived within middle-class boundaries. Now travelling around the country she was brought face to face with the harsh realities of life for a woman on her own. This was the beginning of her development as a feminist. She is very reticent about her own sexual and emotional development but in the theatre she saw a great deal of the relationship between the sexes and was not impressed with what she observed. Sometimes her own livelihood was threatened:

> Twice in the course of my life on tour I was thrown out of work to make room for a manager's mistress; no fault was found with the playing of my part, but it was wanted for other than professional reasons, and therefore I had to go.[20]

The association of the theatre with sexual immorality was a problem for many women working in the profession who were seen as fair game by the 'stage-door johnnies'. Cicely does not record any experiences of her own but one of her contemporaries was sent a series of obscene post cards and May Whitty was accosted by a man who accused her of being, 'A female cad . . . And I've no time for female cads.'[21] Cicely's education as a feminist was beginning during this period of her life and she gradually became aware that men's attitude towards women affected their working lives as well as their private ones:

> To a much greater degree than men women are engaged by their employers for reasons which have no connection with fitness for their work; because they have the right shape of nose, the right shade of hair, or a particularly pleasing smile.[22]

This was particularly true of actresses of course, and Cicely's friend, the American actress Elizabeth Robins, observed wryly, 'What was wanted of women of the stage was first and mainly what was wanted of women outside – a knack of pleasing.' Later when Cicely had become a feminist, she often attacked the emphasis on women's sexual attractions to the exclusion of other, to her more important, qualities; her experience of the theatre, where a woman's appearance is part of her professional stock-in-trade, must have done much to shape her attitude on this issue. In later life she flouted conventions of female appearance very determinedly – presumably as a reaction against the restrictions which had been placed upon her during her career as an actress – and feminist actresses today are still concerned with challenging the view that actresses should conform to stereotyped ideas of female attractiveness. Cicely began at this time to understand the importance of money in relationships between men and women and especially how the assumption that women did not need to work and that they could, if they wished, be kept by their father or husband, undermined all women's attempts at independence by discriminating against them financially. She observed that there was a popular misconception that in the theatre men and women were paid equally. This idea was based upon the salaries of the stars who were paid according to their popularity rather than their sex; Ellen Terry earned as much as £40 a week even before she became a major star through her work with Irving at the Lyceum. In Cicely's experience women were always paid less than men, often as little as half, even in a revue chorus where their work was both more important and more strenuous. Furthermore the professional expenses of actresses were far heavier than those of actors:

> In companies (such as Edmund Tearle's) which ran costume plays, clothes would be provided for the men of the cast, the women often had to find their own – and if their dresses were not suitable, the management looked at them askance.[23]

If the life of actresses was hard, that of working-class women was much harder and Cicely saw their poverty at close quarters for the first time as she lived in cheap lodgings in order to survive on her own meagre salary. The plight of one of her landladies particularly moved her: a widow living in an industrial town in Lancashire, this woman was trying to keep herself and six children on a tiny wage as a cleaner which she supplemented by letting out two rooms to 'theatricals', charging them 10 shillings a week for room and service.

> . . . morning by morning, long before it was light, I would hear my landlady shuffling downstairs and out into the street, for a couple of hours' hard cleaning and scrubbing of office floors before she came back to give the children their breakfast and pack the elder ones off to school. Then her lodger's breakfast and

> her lodger's room to straighten – with an eye to keep on the two youngest children, not yet of an age for school . . . A little hunted woman who, so far as one could see, never, from morning till evening, had a moment of rest and good comfort. I used to shiver in my bed when I heard her going out in the six o'clock cold, remembering how thin was her shawl.[24]

Cicely was able to alleviate her landlady's immediate distress slightly by giving her one of her own winter coats, but as she watched the woman's struggles to bring up her family and observed how hard it was to raise and control six children, she began to think about the desirability of birth control, which at that time was unavailable to working-class, and indeed most other, women. Later in her life Cicely became a passionate advocate of birth control and she traced her commitment to the cause back to her landlady in Lancashire:

> If I have a bee in my bonnet the name of that insect is birth-control; the right of men and women (but especially of women) to save themselves suffering, spare themselves poverty, by limiting the number of their children. When I met the little woman I doubt if I had heard of birth-control; but, when, in after years, I was brought into contact with those who preached its doctrine, their arguments were backed by the memory of her struggle with poverty . . . That was the ounce of bitter fact that outweighed many pounds of sweet theory on the beauty and glory of motherhood.[25]

There was plenty of evidence for the sufferings of women who had had to bear too many children on too little money. One woman wrote to the Women's Co-operative Guild in 1914:

> My grandmother had over twenty children; only eight lived to about fourteen years, only two to a good old age. A cousin (a beautiful girl) had seven children in about seven years; the first five died in birth, the sixth lived and the seventh died and the mother also.[26]

Another woman, who had had seven children and two miscarriages while living on an average wage of 30 shillings a week felt very strongly that men were to blame for the sufferings of women in pregnancy:

> I do wish there could be some limit to the time when a woman is expected to have a child. I often think that women are really worse off than beasts. During the time of pregnancy, the male beast keeps entirely from the female; not so with the woman; she is at the prey of a man just the same as if she was not pregnant. Practically within a few days of the birth, and as soon as the birth is over she is tortured again.[27]

Cicely may not have been fully aware of the grimmer details of such women's lives but she was certainly beginning to question the sentimental notions of marriage and motherhood which were so widely promulgated and which contrasted so sharply with the reality she saw all around her. More and more she began to see that many of women's problems could be traced back to men. At the moment she was too busy earning her living to make any use of her new-found understanding but in a few years she would put it all into her great feminist work *Marriage as a Trade*. But now she decided that the time had come to change her career.

Two

My First and Most Glamorous Love

Cicely spent about ten years in touring companies and gradually became convinced that she was in a rut. Her aim, like that of any aspiring actress, had been to appear on the London stage and all her hard work in the provinces was bringing her no nearer to that goal. She had passed her thirtieth birthday without any notable professional success and so she decided to break away from touring altogether in about 1903. Cicely was hard-working and determined and certainly not one to give something up just because it did not live up to her expectations, but neither was she prepared to waste her effort on stale projects when there were new possibilities to be explored. She had wanted so much to be an actress that she must have felt some disappointment when she was forced finally to give up the dreams she had once had, but as ever she was realistic about the need for change. She attributed the decline of her theatrical ambition not only to a lack of professional success but also to the fact that she was outgrowing the need, so strong in her youth, to perform:

> . . . acting, that intensely personal art, makes its strongest appeal in youth, the most personal season of our lives; a formidable percentage of the human race feels, in its youth, an urge towards self-expression in acting – an urge that, in most cases, dies down as youth is left behind.[1]

The theatre remained important to Cicely for the rest of her life. Many of her friends were actresses and she always felt a special affinity for theatre people, enjoying the shared familiarity with a glamorous and rather secret world. She went on doing quite a lot of acting on a casual basis but the days when she thought of herself primarily as an actress were over. During her time on the road Cicely had already been doing some journalism and translation; as her ambitions as an actress waned she determined to make a living as a writer instead.

From the beginning she aspired to writing plays but even in the late 1890s and early 1900s when there were so many theatres and touring companies it was not easy for a beginner to have work accepted, so for the time being at least Cicely had to accept a compromise as she had at the beginning of her theatrical career. No matter how elevated her aspirations she had first and foremost to earn a living. She wrote chiefly for cheap periodicals, mainly those aimed at younger readers. She had no illusions about the quality of her output – 'sensation was their keynote'[2] – and the stories usually featured bandits, adventures in wild and unknown territory and crimes which were solved by the young detective heroes. It was not how she would have chosen to start off as a writer: 'The serial story was my worst, most exhausting problem; it was the editorial rule that each instalment must finish on a note of excitement that would leave the reader guessing till the next week's number came out.'[3]

Sometimes she tried to write more romantic fiction, aimed at the women's market. At that time there was a large number of weekly papers full of undemanding fiction which was, then as now, readily consumed by a vast female public hungry for a little emotional excitement. D.C. Thomson of Dundee alone published six different titles; *Red Letter, Weekly Welcome, Girls' Weekly, Red Rose, Home Weekly* and *Weekly Companion*. This was, however, a type of story with which Cicely herself felt no sympathy; already her awakening feminist consciousness and her innate dislike of excessive emotion made her a most unsuitable writer of romantic fiction: '. . . the sugary treatment required of me – the utter sloppiness of the admired kind of heroine – was apt to produce a mental nausea which sent me back to my bandits and detectives with a sensation that was almost relief.'[4]

Hack writing did at least provide a slightly better income than acting had done. In the days when Cicely was working as an actress her sister Evelyn seems to have earned her own living, but even before Cicely became successful as a writer she seems to have supported Evelyn. Her income was enough to enable the two sisters to take occasional holidays abroad; Paris, where Cicely had a bad attack of measles as soon as they arrived, Switzerland, Holland and Belgium. Cicely always worried about money, presumably because she always had so little of it, but she was generous, even if her account of the pleasure of spending on others is somewhat self-deprecatory:

> I wonder, by the by, if there is any experience much more pleasurable than the moment when the human being whose life has hitherto been a process of spare and grind and making ends just meet finds himself, for the first time, in a position to spend money on others? As usual with our poor humanity, the impulse to such spending is not wholly altruistic; in most cases, I doubt not, there is something of swagger and something, also, of personal delight in the exercise of unfamiliar power. Be that as it may, I have not forgotten the happiness of entering one of Cook's offices . . . and asking for two return tickets to Switzerland, two tickets I had paid for with my earnings.[5]

While her tales of bandits and detectives were paying the bills, Cicely's real energy was directed towards writing plays. Her ambition now was to become a good dramatist; where once she had hoped to appear on the London stage herself, now she dreamed of seeing her plays performed there.

At the beginning of the century there were still very few women playwrights and such was the prejudice of the critics that the manager Otho Stuart considered it necessary to warn Cicely that if her play appeared under her own name it would inevitably be unfavourably reviewed. Within a few years this had changed significantly, with Cicely herself in the vanguard, but in 1906 when her play *The Sixth Commandment* was performed at Wyndham's Theatre the name of the author was given simply as C. Hamilton. (This has since led to some confusion over the authorship of the play and it is often attributed to Cosmo Hamilton, a prolific contemporary male playwright.) In her autobiography Cicely claims to have forgotten where the play was first performed and to have kept no copy of it, a clear enough indication that she did not, at a later stage of her career, regard it very highly. Broadly speaking her judgment was correct, but the play was very typical of its time and was obviously considered worth a West End production. One reviewer described it as 'sensational' and another as 'grim' but that was to be expected of the one-act melodramas which formed curtain-raisers for the full-length plays, the main attraction of the evening. Their function was not unlike that of the old 'B' movies – warming up the audience before the main feature. They were a relic of the time when an evening at the theatre consisted of a range of entertainment, not merely a single play.

The sixth commandment is, of course, 'Thou shalt not kill', so the audience would have known at once that the play was about murder. The play opens with Johannes, a woodcutter, and his wife Anna weeping over the child they have just buried. They have robbed and killed a woman traveller in order to feed this child. Johannes' brother, Martin, appears and reveals that he is no longer a soldier; he is seeking to avenge the death of his beloved, who has been murdered nearby as she was on her way to join him. Johannes realises that they are the murderers. When Martin goes upstairs to sleep Johannes says:

Johannes: It is his life or ours.
Anna: Then better ours.

The curtain falls.

Like most melodrama the play lacks characterisation; the plot alone carries it. Cicely had acted in many melodramas in her time and knew the ingredients necessary to make them work effectively. The piece was first performed as *The Traveller Returns* at the Pier Theatre, Brighton, in May 1906 and when it came to the West End in September the same year it was the curtain-raiser to *Peter's Mother*, a play by the very successful novelist and playwright Mrs Henry de la Pasture. Many years later Cicely was to be a colleague of Mrs de la Pasture's daughter, who had anglicised her name to E.M. Delafield, on the feminist journal *Time and Tide*.

The London production of *The Sixth Commandment* gave Cicely the confidence to continue writing plays. She confessed to an inability to believe in the value of her own work and wondered if it was a result of her 'unhappy and frightened' childhood. She wrote, 'I am apt to expect very little of life – certainly I never count on success',[6] but she persevered with her full-length play in the intervals of writing pot-boilers. The result was her first and greatest success – *Diana of Dobsons*.

Diana of Dobsons was first performed in February 1908, at a time when the theatre was enjoying great popularity among all social classes. In London in 1901 there were forty-two music-halls and thirteen theatres licensed by the London County Council and a further forty-four theatres where plays had to be licensed by the Lord Chamberlain before they could be performed. This responsibility of the Lord Chamberlain, of vetting plays to make sure they did not offend public opinion or received morality, was only relinquished in 1968. The Lord Chamberlain's ideas about what was acceptable were rather limited and as a result both Shaw's *Mrs Warren's Profession* and Ibsen's *Ghosts* were denied a licence and could for a time only be seen in performances by private stage societies. The playwright's attitude to his or her subject was not taken into account – the mere presence of prostitution or syphilis in a play was enough for the Lord Chamberlain to deem it indecent. Despite such constraints the theatre flourished. In the West End a seat in the stalls cost 10s 6d while the gallery cost 1s. In the suburbs, at the Brixton theatre, the stalls cost 2s and a gallery seat cost 4d. At the time a clerk might earn £2 10s a week, while a labourer earned about 30s.

The theatre at this time was sharply divided between 'high-brow' and 'low-brow'; in the West End and the major theatres of the provincial cities predominantly middle-class audiences watched well-made plays in three acts, Shakespeare and the spectacular productions of Henry Irving at the Lyceum. Elsewhere, in the provinces and suburbs, the staple fare was melodrama and the style of acting was still declamatory, very different from the restrained tones of the West End. Many of the plays seen in the West End were what were known as 'cup and saucer' dramas: plays set in a limited upper-class social world which were beautifully dressed and elegantly acted. Working people only appeared in farce or as comic relief and usually spoke in a particular kind of stage cockney. William Archer, who did much to encourage a major change in this state of affairs, wrote:

> The English playwright concerns himself exclusively with the manners and the emotions of the idle rich. The life of the doctor, the lawyer, the schoolmaster, the journalist, the clergyman, the clerk, the tradesman, the peasant is no less seriously studied on the German stage than the life of the baron, the millionaire or the guardsman.[7]

When ideas from the continent reached England, however, it was not the standard West End plays that they influenced, but rather more advanced playwrights. The most influential European playwright was the Norwegian Henrik Ibsen, whose play *A Doll's House* had been given a private reading in 1884 by Eleanor Marx and her lover Dr Aveling and performed by the actress Janet Achurch and her husband Charles Charrington in 1887. Here was a play that dealt with real issues: the right of a woman to act according to her own code of morality even within marriage, a woman who finally rejects the stifling prison which the Doll's House of bourgeois marriage has become. For the first time in living memory morality was seriously debated in the theatre and the critics, with the notable exception of Shaw, hated it. What Ibsen's plays introduced was the concept that drama set in contemporary society could be about ideas and could question and explore the accepted norms of society and its morality and probe deeply behind the façade of bourgeois respectability. Actresses loved Ibsen's plays because they offered interesting, challenging parts which bore some relation to their own lives and because it was 'such glorious actable stuff', as Elizabeth Robins called it. This was all the more welcome because:

> There is not one play on the London stage at the present time which takes any account of women except on the level of housekeeping machines or bridge players – the actual or potential property of some man, valuable or worthless as the case may be.[8]

This was written over twenty years after *A Doll's House* was first seen in London so it is obvious that Ibsen's influence was very slow to reach the commercial theatre. Some playwrights, however, did see the possibility of a new realism and the chance of a new freedom to debate issues which was not evident in the standard West End fare. Although Cicely never acted in one of Ibsen's plays she cannot fail to have been aware of the debate about his work. Her own writing was not directly influenced by Ibsen but she began her career as a dramatist in a theatrical atmosphere which had been significantly altered by his presence.

Modernity was seen as a positive virtue in every sphere of Edwardian life and the theatre was no exception. The idea that a playwright could explore theories on the stage was new and exciting to a generation of playwrights that included Shaw, Barrie, Galsworthy, Maugham, Henry Arthur Jones and Granville Barker. Plays became more realistic and the protagonists were as likely to be shop-workers or doctors as dukes and duchesses. In time the 'new drama', as it was known, became as set in its ways as that which it had replaced and the concern with 'issues' became as limited and repetitious as the earlier society drama. Sometimes writers attempted to appear modern in spite of rather than because of their subject matter. Henry Arthur Jones, a very popular playwright, was particularly limited; all his plays have a similar theme – the unmasking of hypocrisy. As A.E. Wilson recorded:

> Anthony Ellis in *The Star* considered one of his plays '. . . in which a great parade of profundity disguised a sentimental melodrama tricked out elaborately to resemble a problem play – a description which might have been applied to many of Jones's pieces.[9]

Even if the 'new drama' initially had little impact in the West End, groups of writers, directors and actors were experimenting with all kinds of progressive plays, both home-grown and imported from Europe. As far as the commercial theatre was concerned the Court Theatre, later the Royal Court, under the management of Otho Stuart and with Harley Granville Barker as director, was the mecca for new playwrights. Many of Shaw's plays had their first performance there and both Cicely's play *How the Vote was Won* and Elizabeth Robins' *Votes for Women* were put on there. The Court was the first London theatre to run on a 'repertory' basis, which made it possible for plays by new writers to be put on at matinées while a piece by a better-known writer performed in the evening covered the costs. Later some of the same management and directors put on similar seasons at other London theatres, including the Duke of York's, the Royalty and the Haymarket. Cicely acted in plays which were part of these seasons and some of her own plays had matinée performances there as well.

Another result of the desire for experimentation in drama was the proliferation of private stage societies dedicated to the production of interesting new works. As they were private societies they did not need a licence and could therefore put on works which would not have found favour with the Lord Chamberlain. The best known of these organisations was the Stage Society but Cicely was chiefly associated with the Play Actors; all the actors were members of the actors' trade union, The Actors' Association, and it was a useful way for actors working in the provinces to bring themselves to the attention of London managements. The *Stage*, writing after Cicely had enjoyed her first success, was warm in its praise:

> The Play Actors have progressed considerably since they started. . . . In the course of their progression they have produced many welcome plays, 'discovered' more than one new dramatist, the most notable of course being Miss Cicely Hamilton, and best of all have drawn managerial attention to the interpreters of the plays, in many cases with very favourable results.[10]

It is clear that although, before the success of *Diana of Dobsons*, Cicely was forced to earn her living by literary hack work she was very much involved in the more innovative side of the London theatre and this undoubtedly had an influence on the kind of play she wrote.

It is perhaps not surprising that Cicely offered her first full-length play to one of the first of the actress-managers – Lena Ashwell of the Kingsway Theatre. They must have moved in the same theatrical circles, although Lena Ashwell had been far more successful than Cicely and was already a star. Lena Ashwell's speciality as an actress was 'errant women', of which there were many in the plays of the period. In her autobiography she wrote:

> I am the great criminal of the stage, I have broken all the commandments, I have committed all the crimes in the calendar. One day I shall write a book – it will be a very small book – and it will be called 'Crimes I have not committed'.[11]

Lena Ashwell was not, however, satisfied with acting in plays produced and directed by others. Like a number of other actresses she wanted greater control over her career and saw the only way to achieve this was to manage her own theatre. In October 1907 she took the lease of Penley's theatre in Great Queen Street and renamed it the Kingsway. Her stated intention was to alternate plays of serious interest with comedies and to encourage the work of new playwrights. Her partner in the management was Otho Stuart, who, by coincidence, had accepted Cicely's first play *The Sixth Commandment*.

Lena Ashwell chose the plays to be performed at the Kingsway with an eye to good parts for herself. The Kingsway's first production *Irene Wycherley* had provided her with a fine dramatic role of the kind in which she excelled: *Diana of Dobsons* was to provide her with a very satisfying piece of comedy. The play opens in the dormitory attached to a large drapery store where the shop assistants have to live as well as work. One of them, Diana Massingberd, an impoverished doctor's daughter, receives a letter which tells her that she has been left £300 and at once decides to pass herself off as a widow and enjoy all the pleasures life has to offer. While staying at an expensive hotel in Switzerland she meets a young ex-Guards officer, Victor Bretherton, who appears to fall in love with her and who is urged by his matchmaking aunt to propose. When he does so Diana reveals her true situation and accuses him of wanting to marry her for her money. After a fierce argument, in the course of which Diana says that Bretherton would be incapable of keeping himself solely by his own labour for six months, Diana storms out and goes back to England with all her inheritance spent. The last act is set on the Embankment where Diana, now down and out, meets a young man whom she recognises as Bretherton. Stung by what Diana said to him when they parted, he has been trying to prove himself worthy of her by earning his own living for six months. He too is down and out but he has not 'thrown in the sponge' and still has his private income to fall back on, although he has not touched it during the past six months. He proposes to Diana again and after some initial hesitation she accepts him.

The play was an immediate and continuing success; on the opening night it received nine curtain calls and Cicely herself was cheered and applauded. It ran at the Kingsway for 143 performances in 1908 and was revived for a further 32 in 1909, a revival Lena Ashwell justified in the programme on the grounds that it had been withdrawn while it was still 'in the heyday of its success'. The play was certainly an important source of income for the Kingsway management, both from the London production and from the provincial tours which continued for years. Lena Ashwell herself played Diana on the first tour and three other tours were travelling the country at the same time. The play also received seventeen performances at the Savoy Theatre in New York. According to Frank Vernon, the Kingsway 'lived on *Diana of Dobsons* and died when the momentum of that hybrid play, that compromise of old with new spirit passed away'.[12]

Vernon's comments draw attention to something very important about the play – the way it combines sentimental comedy with satire; social comment with melodrama. In an interview printed in the *Sphere* before the play opened Cicely said, 'Although I take a great interest in the social and industrial questions of the day, in so far as they affect women generally, I had no serious purpose in writing *Diana of Dobsons*.'[13] She went on to hope that 'the story may prove interesting to the general public, who do not know as a rule much about the lives of shop-girls and the want of consideration with which some of them are treated by their employers'.[14] She claimed that she had been as interested in contrasting the characters of Diana and Bretherton as in any social issues. Lena Ashwell, who played Diana, described the play as 'very, very light comedy indeed' although 'the authoress can hit hard when she likes, and some of the scenes are written in a spirit that can only be described as exceedingly sarcastic and satirical'.[15]

Many of the reviewers, and the play was reviewed very widely indeed, commented on Cicely's gift for dialogue and her well-developed sense of theatre. Presumably, as with so many actresses turned playwright, her years of performing other people's lines gave her a real awareness of what would and would not work. The *Sphere*'s critic wrote 'the whole thing is shaped with an instinct for the stage which Miss Hamilton knows from experience from the standpoint of an actress'.[16] Despite Cicely's disclaimer of any serious purpose in writing the play, reviewers fastened on to its topicality. The *Era* wrote '[the play] is produced quite apropos of the agitation against "living in" and of the cry for female suffrage' and added, 'it has the great advantage of striking what is practically new ground for dramatic cultivation'.[17] It is indeed here that the play's originality lies and here that Cicely reveals how much she is a writer of her time. Plays which tackled social issues, the so-called 'problem plays', were all the rage, and as a member of the Play Actors she had been involved in a number of experimental dramas. Her sense of what could be presented on stage, the way in which it could be used as a forum for ideas, had been expanded by the progressive elements in the theatre while the basic plot elements she uses remain those of traditional comedy or melodrama. Some reviewers criticised Cicely for giving:

> . . . a suggestion of handling a big theme, of the play being something more than a pleasing stage entertainment, that never comes to anything. The first act made me think that the living in

> system and all its evils were to be tackled and that we were in for a big play.[18]

Others did not mind the mention of a whole range of issues, even if they were not explored in detail. *The Times* reviewer was surely right to recognise that:

> The sufferings of overworked shop-girls . . . the discomforts of the living in system, the employer's point of view, the essential antagonism between the struggling breadwinner and the idle rich, the 'unemployed' problem and its difficulties are all treated seriously . . .

while the play remains, 'A bright little comedy, novel in subject and fresh in treatment.'[19]

In their pre-production interviews both Cicely and Lena Ashwell seem to have been so afraid of scaring off potential audiences that they played down the more serious aspects of the play. By this stage of her life Cicely had already become, to use a modern expression, politicised, and she had already embarked on the analysis of the relationship between men and women that she published as *Marriage as a Trade* in 1909. *Diana of Dobsons* is not a sustained piece of agitprop but throughout the play there are telling comments on a wide range of social issues. It is hard to tell what effect they had on a contemporary audience – some reviewers thought the indictment of the idle rich rather harsh – but to modern ears they do not sound like the words of a woman who had no serious purpose in writing her play. True she sweetens the pill with humour and as the reviewer of the *Pall Mall Gazette* observed, 'Humour, however, like charity covers a multitude of sins; and it was for the sake of the laughter in it that "Diana of Dobsons" had so hearty a welcome.'[20] The play sets the position of workers and that of the idle rich in opposition. When Mrs Whyte-Fraser – one of the guests staying at the same hotel as Diana in Lucerne – complains that people who earn their living are 'so aggressively unornamental', Diana replies:

> I am rather inclined to think that there are great difficulties in the way of being useful and ornamental at the same time. Strictly speaking we of the ornamental class are not useful and the useful class – the class that earns its own living and other people's dividends is seldom decorative.[21]

Cicely's main attack on the idle rich – and doubtless as a woman who had always earned her own living it was one that came from the heart – occurs in the scene where Diana refuses Captain Bretherton's proposal and denounces him as an adventurer and a parasite. He indicates that he would marry her despite her lack of money were she not a shop-girl.

> *Diana*: . . . I cannot understand how you and your like have the impertinence to look down on me and mine? When you thought I had married an old man for his money, you considered that I had acted in a seemly and womanly manner – when you learnt that, instead of selling myself in the marriage market I have earned my living honestly, you consider me impossible.[22]

This emphasis on the dignity of women who earn their living prefigures much of Cicely's later writing during the suffrage campaign but while she may regret that women have to live off men she is positively vitriolic about men who live off women:

> *Diana*: You were ready and willing and anxious to run after me, so long as you believed I had money in the hope that I should allow you to live upon that money
> *Bretherton*: Diana – Mrs, Miss Massingberd!
> *Diana*: It's true – and you know it – (*rises*) and what is that may I ask, but the conduct of an adventurer? You are far too extravagant to live on your own income – you are far too idle to work to increase it – so you look round for a wife who is rich enough to support you in idleness and extravagance. You cannot dig, but to sponge on a wife you would not be ashamed.[23]

It is such elements of forthright social comment which make the play much more than a mere romantic comedy. Elements of the play's structure also set it apart and these elements were seen at the time as important innovations. The opening act, which exists to show the realities of the life that Diana is only too happy to be leaving, is effectively a prologue to the main action and such prologues were very much the fashion in experimental drama at the time. The prologue caused considerable comment for its daring realism in showing the shop assistants preparing for bed. The dormitory actually has beds in it and the young women remove some of their garments and slip into nightgowns during the course of the scene. This was seen as very daring at the time (although it would not startle a modern audience at all). Only the *Stage* disliked the scene, criticising it as: 'a cheap expedient, all the more wanting in taste . . . because there is not dramatic significance to justify it'.[24] The setting of the final act on the Embankment was also seen as innovative, although one or two reviewers commented on the extreme improbability of Bretherton's being prepared to live as a tramp in view of his behaviour earlier in the play. Instead of the lovers coming together in some respectable setting they celebrate their engagement with tea and 'doorstep' sandwiches from a nearby coffee stall. At this time it was still unusual for a West End actress to appear on stage looking anything other than elegant and stylish, especially in the denouement. To judge from photographs of the original production, Lena Ashwell managed to look fairly convincing in her grubbiness and dishevelment.

It is hard for a modern theatre-goer to see what all the fuss was about, so completely have the conventions of the 'New Drama' become those of the contemporary theatre. At the time it was still unusual for a shop-girl to appear as the heroine of a play, so unusual that the interviewer in the *Sphere* felt it necessary to ask Lena Ashwell how she liked playing the part. Lena Ashwell's rather snobbish reply is very much of the period: 'I am only a saleslady in the first act, you know and I like my part immensely . . . Although Diana is a shop-assistant, she is a girl of good family but left by her father's death absolutely penniless'.[25]

In writing *Diana of Dobsons* Cicely was not breaking down so many barriers as her contemporaries supposed. She had skilfully blended elements of traditional West End theatre, of the experimental drama and of the problem play to produce a cocktail which won both popular and critical acclaim. A consummate woman of the theatre, she found a formula which enabled her to display both her talent for writing witty dialogue and her social concern; she did not do it again with such unmixed success until *The Old Adam* in 1926. None the less she deserved the acclaim, even the plaudit of the *Evening News* reviewer, 'Miss Cicely Hamilton is the best woman dramatist we have had these many years.'[26]

The success of *Diana of Dobsons* was important for Cicely because it established her reputation as a writer. She was offered commissions to write what interested her and was able to give up the writing of weekly serials. She did not, however, make the sort of money from *Diana* that she should have done. Without the benefit of an agent or any other adviser she accepted a down payment of £100 instead of royalties which would have brought in thousands. In her autobiography Cicely makes it clear that she bore no grudge against the Kingsway management and blames herself for her lack of shrewdness. But Lena Ashwell clearly had the matter on her conscience: she mentions in her autobiography that she had been criticised for the financial deal over *Diana* and attempts to vindicate herself by saying that she shared the post-tax value of the film rights with Cicely. In any event the two women remained friends; Cicely's early life had made her surprisingly tolerant of the whims of fortune. As far as she was concerned she had more money in a lump than ever before in her life and that was enough. And besides there were other compensations:

> . . . And in the afternoon I got on a bus and went all the way to Liverpool Street; for this reason only, that my chosen bus had *Diana of Dobsons by Cicely Hamilton* advertised along the top. *Cicely Hamilton* was writ very small, and in all probability few who saw the advertisement noticed it; but I noticed it and that it was that mattered.[27]

It may have been the success of *Diana* which launched Cicely's next one-acter into the West End. *The Sergeant of Hussars* had already been seen twice in matinée performances with Cicely herself playing the part of Jeanne. The matinée on 25 June 1908 was given by the Play Actors as a benefit for the Actors' Association. In October 1908 it ran for fifty-nine performances as the curtain-raiser to the revival of *The Lyons Mail* at the Shaftesbury Theatre. This was a revival by Henry Irving's son of his father's great success. The *Sergeant of Hussars*, set during the German invasion of France in 1870–1, is another melodrama which ends in death. The reviewer in *The Times* called it 'a powerful little play . . . the dénouement of which is based upon one of the longest-armed coincidences of our experience.[28]

Another result of Cicely's new-found success was that she became involved in campaigning on behalf of writers as a member of the Society of Authors, an organisation with which she remained associated for the rest of her life. In November 1909 she agreed to sign a letter from the Society which was opposed to the office of Lord Chamberlain and his censorship of plays. This letter was probably in support of the recommendations of a Parliamentary

Joint Select Committee that it should be optional to present a play for licensing and that the Director of Public Prosecutions could indict a theatre manager if an unlicensed play was deemed indecent. In spite of her willingness to sign, Cicely was unsure whether the recommendations would make much difference even if they were adopted – which they were not:

> I must admit that I am not furiously against the censorship. I quite see the illogical nature of the office; but I can't help feeling that it is less the objection of the censor than the timidity of the ordinary theatre manager and his backer which hampers what is called 'the play of ideas' and I don't think you will lessen that timidity by thrusting the entire responsibility for the production of such a play on to these not very courageous persons.[29]

Cicely was now sufficiently well known for her signature to such a letter to be sought after; after all the struggles that must have been a special kind of satisfaction and one that set a trend – she was an enthusiastic correspondent to newspapers for the rest of her life. And with solid success behind her she was preparing to move outwards from the world of the theatre to the world of politics.

Three

Far More than Wives and Mothers

For Cicely the suffrage campaign marked both her entry into public life and her willingness to admit the importance to her of other women. Until now her life had been one of struggle, hard work and often unhappiness and isolation. Before the suffrage campaign the only companion she mentions is her sister Evelyn; once she began working for the cause she was surrounded by comrades in arms, friends and admirers – a network of like-minded women who valued Cicely for herself and for her particular contribution to the campaign.

As far as I have been able to determine, Cicely's first public involvement with the suffrage campaign was her participation in what became known as the 'Mud March' of February 1907. This had been organised by the National Union of Women's Suffrage Societies (NUWSS), the oldest of the suffrage societies and dedicated to achieving the vote by constitutional means: petitions, pressure and reasoned argument. This organisation had its origins in the National Society for Women's Suffrage which had been very active from 1870–90 under the leadership of Lydia Becker. It had existed in its current form since 1891 and was now led by Millicent Fawcett, the sister of Elizabeth Garrett Anderson. The NUWSS set out to show that women were as deserving as men of higher education, medical careers and the vote. Their argument was based on the contention that women had now demonstrably become fit to enjoy these privileges. No appeals were made to natural justice, nor to the idea that women could offer something different from or better than men. For a long time they had seemed quite willing to tolerate the slow progress of the cause and not to rush matters, although this does not mean that they were not dedicated and vigorous campaigners.

This was not, however, the style of the Women's Social and Political Union (WSPU), led by Emmeline Pankhurst and her daughter Christabel. The WSPU, founded in 1903, initially aimed to enfranchise women on equal terms with the men who qualified under the 1884 Reform Act, i.e. 'those who paid rates and taxes, as owners, occupiers, lodgers'. Although the Pankhursts were originally members of the Independent Labour Party (ILP) and Mrs Pankhurst had founded the Union with the specific intention of recruiting among working women, the property qualification caused them to be accused of concern only for rich women. The WSPU had proposed to the Labour Party at its annual conference in 1905 that the party should adopt women's suffrage as part of its policy. In the event the party preferred to support adult suffrage – the vote for every adult, male and female – a policy which fighters for women's suffrage distrusted, fearing that when put to the test the 'adult suffragists' would abandon the women's side of their cause – as had happened before with the Chartists – and compromise in order to achieve full manhood suffrage. For its part the Labour Party argued that the vote for women on the basis of the 1884 Reform Act would help the Conservatives and do nothing to enfranchise the working class. Without Labour Party support any prospect of success for the WSPU's campaign seemed to fade into the unforeseeable future. But Christabel Pankhurst had no intention of letting this happen.

On 13 October 1905 Winston Churchill, Liberal candidate for North-West Manchester in the forthcoming general election, held a public meeting at the Free Trade Hall in Manchester which was to be addressed by Sir Edward Grey, a leader of the moderate Liberals. Christabel Pankhurst and another WSPU supporter, Annie Kenney, attended and during questions Annie Kenney asked Churchill, 'If you are elected, will you do your best to make Women's Suffrage a Government measure?' Churchill did not reply and Christabel Pankhurst then held up a banner which read 'Votes for Women'. This provoked uproar but the women continued to heckle and were finally thrown out of the meeting. Outside Christabel Pankhurst, having previously given warning that she was about to do so, spat at a policeman. Technically this constituted assault and she and Annie Kenney were arrested. The magistrate fined them and when they refused to pay sent them to prison,

Christabel Pankhurst for seven days and Annie Kenney for three.

This was the first direct action of the suffrage campaign and revealed Christabel Pankhurst's great talent for staging stunts which attracted publicity and at the same time appealed both to women's desire for dramatic action and to their enthusiasm for martyrs to the cause. It is somewhat ironic that both Grey and Churchill were in favour of women's suffrage and it was only Grey's belief that the issue would not become one of party politics that had prevented him from intervening and giving Christabel Pankhurst the response she had wanted. None the less, Christabel's imprisonment inspired many women to become involved in the suffrage struggle; they felt that she had issued a challenge and if they really cared about women's rights they had to take up that challenge. As Helena Swanwick, a dedicated campaigner, put it, 'It bludgeoned my conscience.'[1]

By the autumn of 1906 the WSPU had established itself in London and had made itself visible through a campaign of militancy. In January 1906 it began a concerted campaign against the newly elected Liberal government in an attempt to force it to include women's suffrage among its measures. In April members disrupted a debate in the House of Commons with shouts and a shower of leaflets from the gallery. This action earned them the name, first used by the *Daily Mail*, of 'suffragettes'. Direct action, lobbying, public meetings and above all spectacularly stage-managed demonstrations became the hallmark of WSPU activities.

All this militancy made the more sedate tactics of the NUWSS seem tame and ineffective and so they determined that they too would hold an open-air demonstration – for the first time. It was timed to coincide with the opening of the next session of parliament and the NUWSS hoped to achieve publicity as the militant societies had done but by more peaceful methods which would ensure that they did not alienate potential supporters. Three thousand women marched through mud, slush and fog from Hyde Park Corner to the Exeter Hall in the Strand, led by Lady Frances Balfour, Lady Strachey and Mrs Fawcett. Forty years later Cicely remembered it fondly:

> One of my good memories of forty years past is of tramping muddily in our first procession – organized by the National Union of Suffrage Societies and displaying banners designed and embroidered by members of the Artists' Suffrage League.[2]

The march was widely reported in the press for at this time it was a great novelty to see women of all social classes walking together in public, from the titled ladies leading the procession through the professional women, who probably made up the largest contingent, to the women manual workers from the industrial north. Many of the middle-class women found appearing in public in this way a considerable ordeal, but having survived it once they were prepared to do it again and large-scale processions became an accepted part of the suffrage campaign. As Ray Strachey, a historian of the campaign and the daughter-in-law of Lady Strachey observed:

> The vast majority of women still felt that there was something very dreadful in walking in a procession through the streets; to do it was to be something of a martyr, and many of the demonstrators felt that they were risking their employments and endangering their reputations, besides facing a dreadful ordeal of ridicule and public shame. They walked, and nothing happened. The small boys in the streets and the gentlemen at the club windows laughed, but that was all. Crowds watched and wondered; and it was not so dreadful after all . . . the idea of a public demonstration of faith in the Cause took root.[3]

It is hard to believe that Cicely would ever have been daunted by marching; indeed her published accounts of later marches suggest that she revelled in the experience.

It is not clear exactly when Cicely began to do more for the cause than simply marching in processions and writing about them for the press; it is likely that, at least until after *Diana of Dobsons* was produced, she was simply too busy making her living. She belonged to the WSPU 'for some months' and during this time played her part in the campaign of harassment of Liberal ministers – it was WSPU policy at this time to ensure that none of them ever spoke in public without being heckled about the vote. She admits in her autobiography that she did this, but adds characteristically:

> I never persuaded myself on these occasions, that I was doing anything to further the cause of Free Speech; on the contrary, I knew I was preventing Free Speech on the part of my opponents and behaving as I did in order to make myself objectionable.[4]

Apart from heckling, much of Cicely's early active participation took the form of speaking at suffrage meetings. Despite initial reluctance she became a very popular speaker and did a great deal of public speaking for the rest of her life, both for the vote and later, after World War I, for a variety of other causes, political and literary. Organisers of suffrage meetings were always on the lookout for new speakers – there were so many meetings that it was often hard to satisfy the demand – and when Cicely, by asking a question from the floor, showed herself to be reasonably articulate she was pounced on at once and asked to speak at an open-air meeting the following day:

> I thought that she mistook me for someone else, and began to explain that I couldn't possibly – I had never made a speech in my life and I shouldn't know how . . . 'Nonsense!' she retorted, 'You can speak quite well if you like – what were you doing just now?' And to my terror, next day I found myself standing on a chair in Battersea Park, addressing an audience which – much to my relief – was neither very large nor greatly interested.[5]

One reason Cicely gives for the frequency with which she was used as a suffrage speaker is that *Diana of Dobsons* had made her known to the public; this would suggest that she joined the WSPU some time in 1908.

An anonymous contributor to *Time and Tide*, in a profile of Cicely published in May 1923, described her in her role as a suffrage speaker:

> At that time she had sacrificed her individualism to the extent of adopting the conventionally feminine style of dress with which leading agitators for the vote strove to convince a hostile society that they were neither unwomanly nor eccentric. There she was on the platform trying with doubtful success to look like an ordinary woman, thoroughly domesticated. It was obvious that she was listening with some impatience to the speech which preceded hers. (It must be confessed that Cicely Hamilton is not a good listener at any time.) Now it is the turn of the woman with the shock of reddish-gold hair, the pale mobile face and pale greenish-grey eyes. She lets them have it! She is a nervous excitable speaker. Her platform manner is atrocious – fidgety, restless, too deprecating one minute, too assertive the next, but what she says is witty and wise, practical and well-reasoned.[6]

Cicely was rather scornful of the idea that suffragettes should dress in a womanly fashion; her own style of dress is perhaps best characterised as 'tailored' when she was in her thirties, declining into 'shabby-eccentric' as she grew older. It amused her that:

> There was no costume code among non-militant suffragists but in the WSPU the coat-and-skirt effect was not favoured; all suggestion of the masculine was carefully avoided, and the outfit of a militant setting forth to smash windows would probably include a picture hat.[7]

The WSPU wished to avoid the suggestion that women who wanted the vote were anything other than entirely ordinary and they sought above all to refute the accusation, seen all too clearly in cartoons of the time, that campaigners for the vote were 'men in petticoats'. Cicely for her part had decided at an early age that she did not much care what anyone thought about her appearance. She admitted that 'for several years of adolescence and young womanhood I did conscientiously strive to make myself attractive to the male,'[8] but she only did so for as long as she considered marriage a possibility. Once she had decided that it was not for her she stopped making the effort and found that "I felt friendlier towards my male fellow-creatures once I had realised I didn't care a button as to whether or not I resembled their ideal of womanhood."[9]

Cicely considered that Mrs Pankhurst's preference 'real or politic' for conventionally feminine dress: 'is no doubt one of the reasons why her followers have woven around [her] a legend of womanly gentleness and charm – a legend that hardly does her justice'.[10] Cicely admired Mrs Pankhurst for her determination and powers of leadership and saw no reason why womanliness, as measured by male standards, should come into it at all. Indeed she was delighted that young women had shown they could be as rowdy as young men. This breaking out from conventional roles was all part of her vision of the changes that women could bring about by their campaigning. The contradictory position of the WSPU which preached militancy while wishing to preserve womanly appearances disguised the truly radical nature of the campaign for the vote and obscured the fundamental changes that Cicely and others like her hoped this revolution would bring about.

The comparative narrowness of the WSPU's official vision (there were of course many within its ranks who shared Cicely's point of view) may have been one reason why Cicely left it. But there were also other, possibly more compelling, ones, including the character of the WSPU leadership. The personalities of Emmeline Pankhurst and her daughter Christabel dominated the Union and since they had annulled the constitution in 1907 they had a free hand to dictate policy. Aided by Mr and Mrs Pethick Lawrence, who organised the financial and practical side of affairs, and supported by passionately loyal lieutentants such as Annie Kenney and Flora Drummond – known as the General – the Pankhursts, mother and daughter, were adored and obeyed implicitly by their followers. Cicely had a deep distrust of charismatic leaders and although what she wrote about Mrs Pankhurst in 1935 was, it is true, coloured by an awareness of what such leaders had done and were doing all over Europe, the doubts must surely have also been there at the time.

> It was an interesting phenomenon, the militant suffrage agitation; even more interesting than I realised at the time. For it was the beginning – the first indication of the dictatorship movements which are by way of thrusting democracy out of the European continent. Not the Fascists but the militants of the Women's Social and Political Union first used the world 'leader' as a reverential title; and the *Führer-prinzip*, the principle of leadership, was carried to something like idolatry by the wearers of the purple, white and green. Emmeline Pankhurst, in this respect, and on a smaller scale, was forerunner of Lenin, Hitler and Mussolini – the leader whose fiat must not go unquestioned, the Leader who could do no wrong.[11]

Some writers, usually male, have written slightingly about the adulation of Emmeline Pankhurst in terms of schoolgirl 'crushes' and adolescent enthusiasm. Undoubtedly there was a great spirit of excitement among women, brought together for the first time to work for a cause which they hoped and believed would transform every aspect of their lives. The commentators seek to diminish the importance of the suffrage movement in much the same way as contemporary opponents did by suggesting that the suffragettes were unwomanly and, by implication, lesbian. Devotion to a woman's cause and to a woman leader is depicted as childish and unnatural behaviour. No other major force for political change has been written off in these terms, because there, of course, the participants have largely been men. In her analysis Cicely gives due weight to the movement and rightly points out that such uncritical support for a leader has not been confined to women. Her preference, hardened by the experience of the 1930s into something like an obsession, for the operations of the individual conscience over the actions of mass movements, may have caused her to judge Mrs Pankhurst harshly when she was writing her autobiography, but the grounds on which she accords the suffragettes a serious, if rather sinister, significance in the history of twentieth-century European political movements is characteristically unexpected. Later in life she saw the suffrage campaign in a different light and more readily acknowledged the importance of its role in the emancipation of women, but she never revealed whether she thought that in this instance the ends justified the means.

The suffrage campaign was Cicely's first practical experience of politics. Until then it had all been theoretical, 'derived from the reading of books and newspapers, and occasional lectures, mostly of a Socialist type',[12] and some of the political realities came as a considerable shock to her. Early in her career as a public speaker she was addressing a small suffrage meeting in front of an invited audience. In the course of her speech she made a statement which she regretted almost as soon as she had uttered it. When taxed about it during question time she 'promptly replied that the remark had been made carelessly – it was rather a silly thing to say'. The response took her completely by surprise:

> There was a moment of silence while I felt a little awkward, and then the whole meeting burst into applause and the chairman began to laugh, 'I've never heard a speaker say that before,' was his comment . . . Looking back, it seems to me that I must have been somewhat simple-minded when I entered the suffrage movement; I was well on in my thirties, I had read a good deal and been interested in public questions; yet it came as a shock to me that a shiftiness which would have been thought contemptible in private life was permitted – expected on the platform.[13]

Amusing as this incident appeared at the time, it made a deep impression on Cicely. While retaining her commitment to the suffrage cause, she began to have doubts about unquestioning participation in political campaigns and unthinking obedience to political leaders. Her reservations about what she called 'Organisation Man' became more pronounced after she witnessed a riot of suffragettes at the Albert Hall when Lloyd George was speaking.

In December 1908 the Women's Liberal Federation organised a meeting at the Albert hall, the purpose of which was to demand that the Liberal Government put a bill before Parliament granting women the vote. Up until this point the government had given indications that it believed in votes for women but because of a Cabinet split was unwilling to introduce the measure into the House of Commons. The resolution before the meeting was:

> This meeting, speaking on behalf of the Liberal women of England, Wales and Scotland, claims from this Government as a measure of justice long overdue the Parliamentary enfranchisement of women.[14]

Inevitably a great many suffragettes planned to attend the meeting and the organisers had asked the leaders of the WSPU to restrain their members from their usual practice of heckling Cabinet Ministers so that Lloyd George, Chancellor of the Exchequer and principal government speaker at the meeting, could be given a hearing. The WSPU committee refused to give such an undertaking unless Lloyd George assured them in advance that 'immediate action by the Government is contemplated'. In an exchange of letters Lloyd George refused to indicate in advance the content of his speech, adding,

> interruptions during the course of the delivery of that speech will simply be a piece of gratuitous annoyance to a speaker who will be doing all in his power to advance the cause which you profess to have at heart. If your friends choose to accept the responsibility of preventing a Cabinet Minister for the first time delivering an address in support of Women's Suffrage the responsibility must be theirs.[15]

In her reply Mabel Tuke, Secretary of the WSPU, replied that '[The Government's] continued refusal to enfranchise women – a refusal for which you as a Cabinet Minister are jointly responsible – forces women to adopt militant tactics.'[16]

The battle lines were clearly drawn up. According to the account of the meeting in the WSPU paper, *Votes for Women*, Lloyd George managed to speak for nearly three hours, admittedly with interruptions, without giving any new undertaking from the government. Time and again he was interrupted with cries of, 'Give us the message', but in fact there was no message to give. His bland reassurance that he was in favour of votes for women, his lengthy enumerations of women's achievements and his assertion that they fully deserved enfranchisement were by no means adequate for an audience containing women who had suffered the hardships of imprisonment in the second division (the category normally reserved for dangerous and violent offenders). In the end all he said was that the Prime Minister 'had pledged himself to bring in an electoral Reform Bill', but not until he was ready to go to the country at a general election – which was not yet.

The equivocation in Lloyd George's speech, and the great length at which he managed to say very little, provoked considerable anger among his audience, many of whom heckled vigorously. But this anger was greatly exacerbated by the violence with which the protesters were treated. The *Manchester Guardian*, in its report of the event commented:

> Not only did the stewards perform their apparently self-appointed task of throwing out interrupters with a promptness which gave the chairman no opportunity of intervening, but in many instances they did so with a brutality which was nauseating and the audience played up to them.[17]

The whole scene was one of anger and of often gratuitous violence against women. Cicely describes how,

> Looking down on the amphitheatre from a first tier box, one saw orderly rows of decent human beings break up into struggling knots and groups whereof the centre was a woman, up on a chair and shouting something inaudible at the platform till her neighbours pulled her down.[18]

The occasion made a lasting impression upon her:

> It was not the first time I had been at an angry meeting, though never, I think, at one quite so angry . . . . The brawling men and women, the mobs that surged round them – I knew that if you could get them away from their causes, away from their crowds, they would be perfectly decent individuals. Yet gathered together in the Albert Hall, they were violent, they were brutal, they were

> crazed . . . And the reason for their violence, their lack of control, was crowd-life, overpowering sense of membership.[19]

In some ways what she saw that day coloured her political thinking for the rest of her life. Watching the riot in the Albert Hall she became convinced of the moral danger that lurked in any organisation, not matter how lofty its ideals. For her Mazzini summed it up when 'he said that if he had done for himself what he had done for Italy, he should be accounted a scoundrel'. Many years later Cicely wrote:

> Is there any form of the life collective that is capable of love for its fellow – for another community? Is there any church that will stand aside that another church may be advantaged? . . . You and I are civilised as man and man; but collectively we are part of a life whose only standard and motive is self-interest, its own advantage. A beast-life morally, which demands from us sacrifices, makes none itself . . . That's as far as we've got in the mass.[20]

From this time on Cicely wrote extensively about the effect of the immorality of collective life on human society and what she saw during and after World War I and again in the 1930s only confirmed her in her convictions, 'but it was in contact with the politics of pre-war days that I first began to realise its ugly moral possibilities'.[21] Given the significance to Cicely of the Albert Hall riot and the disgust she felt at it, it would not be surprising if this was the moment when she abandoned the WSPU in favour of the Women' Freedom League (WFL), whose militancy did not take the form of mass meetings.

The WFL had broken away from the WSPU in October 1907 in a dispute over party politics and democracy. The policy of the WSPU was to oppose the government candidate in every election, regardless of the candidate's personal position on women's suffrage. This meant that they tended more and more towards the Conservative Party in their sympathies, even though the Pankhursts were still members of the Independent Labour party. Although the WSPU had acquired a distinctly bluish tinge there were none the less members who combined staunch and active support for socialism with their suffrage activities. Notable among these was Charlotte Despard, passionate campaigner for social justice, member of the

Irish ascendancy and, rather embarrassingly for both of them, sister of Sir John French, who was later to become commander of the British Expeditionary Force in 1914. He was already a very high-ranking officer in the British Army, which ensured that his sister's activities were much remarked upon in the press. Mrs Despard was an active member of the ILP and had become disturbed, like some others, by the political direction the WSPU was taking. She became spokeswoman for a group which bound itself not to do anything which might work against Labour's interests and in particular not to work in any by-election in which a Labour candidate was standing. The leaders of the WSPU took this as a challenge to their authority but there was in reality little that ordinary members, or even members of the Executive like Charlotte Despard, could do to influence the Pankhursts and their allies the Pethick Lawrences. Although the WSPU had a constitution, it did not operate in practice and Mrs Pankhurst and her daughters, both of whom were paid organisers of the Union and who made up the so-called Emergency Committee, effectively ran things as they wished, controlling expenditure and determining tactics. When critics argued that control of the Union should be more broadly based, Mrs Pankhurst announced that the annual conference would be abandoned and the constitution annulled. When Charlotte Despard questioned the authority upon which this was done and sought an opportunity to question the Union's political alignment, Mrs Pankhurst replied blithely that she alone was responsible. She announced that a new organisation, the NWSPU, had been formed; that a new committee would be elected by those present at the Emergency Committee meeting and that the new committee would have to sign a pledge which stated: 'I endorse the objects and methods of the NWSPU and I hereby undertake not to support the candidate of any political party at Parliamentary elections until women have obtained the Parliamentary vote.'[22]

Charlotte Despard refused to sign and said she would wait until the pledge had been approved by the conference. Those who still adhered to the constitution duly held a conference in October 1907 and demanded the return of funds, literature and offices currently held by the Pankhursts but rightfully belonging to the WSPU – which they considered themselves to be. Charlotte Despard, who had been elected chair of the organising committee, argued that the desire for revenge, which would hinder the aims of the suffrage movement as a whole, should be subjugated to the greater good of the cause. Accordingly the constitutionalists left the Pankhursts in undisputed possession of all the Union's assets and, six weeks later, also ceded the name WSPU to them without a fight. To avoid confusion they called themselves the Women's Freedom League, and their chair was Charlotte Despard.

The style of the WFL was as different from that of the WSPU as Charlotte Despard was from Emmeline Pankhurst. Despard's social and political goals determined the character of the League to a very great extent. Widowed in her forties, she had put her energies and her considerable private wealth into alleviating the effects of poverty in the inner London districts of Wandsworth and Nine Elms. She had funded clinics, set up young people's clubs to keep them off the streets, and helped individuals whenever their needs were brought to her attention. Most unusually for a late-Victorian philanthropist, she lived among the people she helped, not in a 'settlement' like those set up in the East End, but in an ordinary working-class house in Wandsworth Road. As a Poor Law guardian – one of the few official appointments open to women at that time, and one which a number of eminent suffragists had held before becoming involved in the campaign for the vote – she stirred her male colleagues out of their complacent lethargy and forced them to recognise the suffering and degradation which the neglect and corruption of those administering the workhouses inflicted on the inmates. As a school manager she argued that children who were hungry and permanently underfed were incapable of benefiting from even the most rudimentary education.

For her, as for many women, the great attraction of the campaign was, 'True love of comrades, strenuous cooperation of those who have realised union means strength, [and] a firm faith in a fair vision of the future.'[23]

Under Mrs Despard's somewhat chaotic chairing – she had an objection to authority so fundamental that she refused either to take the lead in discussion or to rule other speakers' irrelevant comments out of order – the scope of the WFL was far wider than that of the WSPU. At the League's first conference Mrs Despard told the members, 'Our cause is not only votes for women but the binding together of all womanhood with human rights.' She laid great emphasis on the need for economic equality in the workplace and in the home: 'It is indeed deplorable that the work of the wife and mother is not rewarded. I hope the time will come when it is illegal for this strenuous form of industry to be unremunerated.'[24]

This was a sentiment with which Cicely was entirely in agreement, as she was with Charlotte Despard's description of the claim of the male worker to be paid more than his female counterpart as fostering 'the fatal error that women are and ought to be economically dependent on men'. The League highlighted the brutal anomalies of the employment of women in sweated labour, placing particular emphasis on the chain-makers of the Black Country because by participating in the campaign for women's rights they were, in Charlotte Despard's words, symbolically breaking the chains 'which woman has forged around her own consciousness from the moment she permitted herself to be the instrument of man's pleasure'. Many of their activities, far beyond the simple issue of the vote, highlighted the double standard applied by the law and by public morality to women. They drew attention to the fact that it was only prostitutes and not their clients who were charged in court and for a long time the WFL newspaper, the *Vote*, had a column which contrasted the punishments handed out by the courts for crimes against property and for crimes against women. One example, in the issue of 3 July 1914, was:

> The Glasgow News (June 22 1914) reports the case of a miner charged . . . with beating his wife until her face was like pulp, and there was not a bone in her body which did not ache. Sentence: fined 7 guineas, or 40 days imprisonment. The same paper reports the case of a young man charged . . . with stealing from a house a purse, five pawn tickets, two keys and 35s 7d in money. Sentence: Twelve months imprisonment.

Another aspect of the injustice of the legal system which the WFL highlighted was that women were tried by an all-male judiciary under laws passed by a legislature in whose election they had had no say:

> A few members of the League attended each court, and when a woman was placed in the dock the members rose and in turn protested against the trial of women by men alone and by laws exclusively made by men. The protest made, the members quietly left the court.[25]

The WFL considered themselves a militant society but on the whole they preferred other tactics than the mass demonstrations favoured by the WSPU. The stunts they staged were none the less often very striking. At the opening of Parliament in 1909, Muriel Matters scattered leaflets over London from a balloon, and on another occasion chained herself to the grille of the Ladies Gallery in the House of Commons. The grille had obviously been considered necessary to protect MPs from women deprived of the vote; in order to remove Miss Matters it was necessary also to remove the grille – it was never replaced.

Perhaps the action of the League which had the most impact on those who saw it was the picket of the House of Commons, which lasted from 5 July to 28 October 1909, a total of 14,000 hours. The picket began spontaneously when Asquith, the Prime Minister, refused to receive a deputation from the League to protest at his failure to accept a petition (to the King) from the WSPU. The women waited to catch him as he left the Commons but he eluded them and so they remained there until the end of the parliamentary session, a constantly changing, silent vigil of women who impressed all who saw them except, it seems, the politicians. H.G. Wells described the scene:

> All through the long nights of the Budget sittings at all the piers of the gates of New Palace Yard and St Stephen's Porch stood women pickets and watched us reproachfully as we went to and fro . . . There were grey-haired old ladies there, sturdily charming in the rain; battered looking ambiguous women; north country factory girls; cheaply dressed suburban women; trimly comfortable mothers of families; valiant eyed girl graduates and undergraduates; lank hungry creatures who stirred one's imagination; one very dainty little woman in deep mourning, grave and steadfast, with eyes fixed on distant things. Some looked defiant, some timidly aggressive, some full of the stir of adventure, some drooping with cold and fatigue. I had a mortal fear that somehow the supply might halt. I found that continual siege of the legislature extraordinarily impressive – infinitely more impressive than the feeble-forcible 'ragging' of the more militant section.[26]

Asquith continued to refuse to see them and when they began to picket Downing Street as well he had them arrested. Charlotte Despard was among those arrested and in a letter to *The Times*, drew attention to the fact that by refusing to receive the petition, Asquith was denying women the use of the only constitutional right they had.

The activities of the WFL would appear, at least with hindsight, to have been more considered for their effect than the more spectacular mass meetings of the WSPU where sheer force of numbers was often deemed sufficient in itself. The WSPU events were also designed to create great surges of emotion among the participants while the WFL concentrated more on impressing the spectators.

The League had a much broader geographical base than the WSPU, with a particularly strong following in Scotland, and it put far more effort into recruiting outside London. But in rural districts Mrs Despard and her volunteers often met with hostility, obscene language and even violence: they were stoned viciously in Maidstone, and at times had to be rescued by the police. The aggressive response of people in rural communities illustrates the extent to which men felt threatened by the prospect of women's emancipation, particularly since they had far less contact with independent women than did the men of cities or large towns.

The chivalry which was supposed to characterise men's behaviour to women was notably absent on such occasions. Cicely, in a number of her writings, claimed that men's chivalry towards women was of little value. It was, she claimed in her essay 'Man', 'a dole or payment for submission in other directions and if a woman stands up to men it will be withdrawn'. Even on a day-to-day level it was conditional: 'He . . ., if we don't look too much like suffragettes, has frequently been known to offer us his seat on a train.' When women stepped outside their allotted sphere they were fair game. In the same essay Cicely offers an explanation of why many men were so appalled by suffrage campaigners:

> Don't, *don't*, DON'T try to obliterate the caste distinction between the sexes! Be dependent; because we can look down on the dependent. Don't be sensible; because it is difficult, even impossible to despise the sensible person. For if you are independent, if you are sensible, if we can no longer look down on, despise you, you will have deprived us of one of the sweetest pleasures that life has to give – the consciousness of inborn superiority.[27]

For the working men who attacked the suffrage campaigners, who were at or near the bottom of class-ridden Edwardian society, women were the only people they could look down on: no wonder they fought with such fury to maintain the status quo.

In view of the amount of violence to which they were subjected it is hardly surprising that an argument was put forward within the WFL that violence was an inappropriate weapon for feminists to use; that it was of its very nature a male type of behaviour. Both Teresa Billington-Greig and Charlotte Despard argued that true feminism was hampered by the use of militant tactics and that women were only mimicking the behaviour of their oppressors by using them. In response to this argument the League and its affiliated organisations found a variety of alternative methods of attracting publicity for the cause, and it was in this area that Cicely made her greatest contribution.

In her autobiography, *Life Errant*, Cicely discusses her involvement with the suffrage campaign with some enthusiasm but plays down the extent to which she worked for it. This may be explained by the fact that *Life Errant* was published in 1935 when Cicely's concern was much more with world peace than with feminism even though she remained a member of various feminist organisations throughout her life. The way in which Cicely describes receiving her notification of the right to vote shows how her priorities had been changed by World War I:

> What use was the vote as a weapon against German guns, submarines and Gothas? The problem of the moment was to keep ourselves alive, and while a people is engaged in a life-and-death struggle, it is apt to lose interest in matters which yesterday were of sufficient importance to raise it to a fury of dispute . . . I remember – how well I remember – receiving the official intimation that my name had been placed on the register of the Chelsea electorate. I was in Abbeville at the time, and, as the post arrived, a battery of Archies began to thud; an enemy airplane was over taking photographs. I remember thinking, as I read the notice, of all that suffrage had meant for us, a year or two before! . . . and that now, at this moment of achieved enfranchisement, what really interested me was not the thought of voting at the next election, but the puffs of smoke that the Archies sent after the escaping plane.[28]

This tendency to play down the importance of the suffrage campaign is to be found in autobiographies written by a number of Cicely's contemporaries in the 1930s. Militant feminism was out of favour and feminists seem to have been reluctant to discuss it in any detail. Later, during and after World War II, Cicely's attitude to the importance of the suffrage campaign had softened somewhat and she was prepared to accord it a significance similar to that which she had given it at the time. In the extract just quoted she makes out that the campaign had just been about the vote but elsewhere, even in *Life Errant* itself, she is quite clear that it was about a much wider range of issues. Speaking in a radio broadcast on 2 April 1943, the twenty-fifth anniversary of the granting of the vote, she stressed that all women were caught up in the struggle and that it was not only about the vote but, more importantly, about social justice. According to Cicely different groups hoped for different things from it; some for equal pay and others for the reform of the family. She added, in a rather sardonic tone, perhaps unsurprising considering that she was speaking during the second major war of her lifetime, 'Some optimists there were, doomed to disappointment, who saw it as an antidote to the combative spirit, which would sweep away the outworn idea of militarism when women cast their peaceful vote.'[29]

But even if the vote could not achieve that: 'How I saw, how I see the suffrage agitation was part of the process of getting into masculine heads, and some feminine heads, that women were far more than wives-and-mothers.'[30] Cicely concluded her talk by admitting the importance to her and to all women of the campaign for the vote:

> In many ways the world of today is considerably less civilised than the world I was born into but with regard to the position of women I have seen betterment all along the line. Some of that at least we owe to enfranchisement.[31]

In the context of celebrating the granting of the vote it was easier for Cicely to admit its importance than it had been when she wrote her autobiography and it is reassuring to find her, nine years before her death, once more proud of the cause into which she put so much energy as a woman in her thirties and early forties.

In her autobiography Cicely plays down her involvement in the suffrage campaign so thoroughly that it has taken fairly exhaustive reading of suffrage memoirs and journals, and indeed of national and theatrical newspapers, to establish just how important a figure she was. She makes a point of saying, 'My militant activities were of the slightest; I was not of those who wore honourable badges in token of a Holloway martyrdom'[32] – by which she means that she did not get sent to prison in Holloway gaol. Yet her activities were wide-ranging and probably far more influential than those of the pillar-box arsonists and Regent Street window-breakers. This reticence is characteristic. Her friend Elizabeth Abbott, writing after Cicely's death, emphasised her humility, implying that that quality kept those who did not know Cicely from recognising her true greatness. Cicely herself always admitted that her unhappy childhood meant that she grew up unable to believe in herself or her own abilities:

> . . . my frequent reaction towards any newly-completed manuscript is a sense of failure, humility, and even shame; and the reaction is sometimes so acute that I refrain from reading the completed work before I dispatch it to its destination – lest I be tempted to consign it not to the post-box but to the flames.[33]

Her early unhappiness gave Cicely a very determined and self-sufficient streak and it also produced a capacity for loyalty and dedication, to people and to causes, which found its first and perhaps fullest expression during the suffrage campaign.

Cicely's view of woman's role in society was central at this time to all her political activity and she retained a characteristically independent analysis of the real reasons for the campaign. She was more than willing to fight shoulder to shoulder with other women, but under no circumstances was she prepared to dissemble about her reasons for doing so:

> . . . there were, I had reason to know, a good many ardent workers in 'the Movement' who regarded me and my views with considerable suspicion; chiefly, I suppose, because I never attempted to disguise the fact that I wasn't wildly interested in votes for anyone, and that if I worked for women's enfranchisement (and I did work quite hard) it wasn't because I hoped for great things from counting female noses at general elections, but because the agitation for women's enfranchisement must inevitably shake and weaken the tradition of the 'normal woman'. . . My personal revolt was feminist rather than suffragist; what I chiefly rebelled against was the dependence implied in the idea of 'destined' marriage, 'destined' motherhood – the identification of

> success with marriage, of failure with spinsterhood, the artificial concentration of the hopes of girlhood on sexual attraction and maternity.[34]

This radical analysis, which Cicely expounded in greater detail throughout her career as a suffrage speaker and writer, was in fact shared by many workers for 'the Cause' but few proclaimed it as openly as she did. It was, however, the subtext to the whole campaign and it was surely this unstated aim which attracted the violent hostility of so many men. They were threatened, not so much by women gaining the vote as by the assertion of an alternative set of values and aspirations by which women could live.

Cicely had become aware of the injustice inherent in the relations between the sexes at a very early age, questioning, even as a child in the schoolroom, the idea of womanly virtue as extolled in the story of the Rape of Lucrece:

> Loathing was comprehensible and disgust and outraged modesty – but that she should feel herself called upon to die for the guilt of another . . . I became a feminist on the day that I perceived that – according to the story – her 'honour' was not a moral but a physical quality. Once that was clear to me my youthful soul rebelled – it was insulting to talk of 'honour' and 'virtue' in a woman as if they were matters of chance – things which she possessed only because no unkind fate had thrown her in the way of a man sufficiently brutal to deprive her of them by force.[35]

This kind of feminism did indeed have little to do with gaining the vote; it called into question every aspect of the relations between the sexes, and while Cicely may not have been militant in the suffragette sense, she was certainly radical in her analysis of the effect male supremacy had upon society in general and on women in particular. Although the suffrage campaign has, at least in popular history, been portrayed simply as a struggle for the vote, many of the most ardent campaigners saw it as an opportunity to challenge all aspects of male supremacy. The vote was important only in so far as it would give women a foothold in the institutions, still totally male-dominated, through which men obtained and held on to their power. Feminists like Cicely were sceptical about the difference that the enfranchisement of women would make – and history has amply vindicated their scepticism. For Cicely the campaign was about men's abuse of sexual power in all its manifestations and about women's right to sexual, economic and political self-determination. In an article published in August 1912 in an American weekly journal, the *Literary Digest*, Cicely describes her gradual realisation that she did not fit into the patterns for women ordained by the existing male-devised system. When 'six or seven or so' she was filled with 'envy and resentment' over the 'preferential treatment and superior prospects of the human boy'.[36] As she wrote in *Marriage as a Trade*,

> . . . our small hearts bore a secret grudge against Almighty God that he had not made us boys – since their long thoughts were our long thoughts, and together we wallowed in cannibals and waxed clamorous over engines. For them, being boys, there might be cannibals and engines in the world beyond; but for us – oh the flat sameness of it – was nothing but a husband, ordering dinner and keeping house.[37]

Her personal dislike of the effort involved in making herself attractive to men in order to catch a husband led her 'to ask myself how far I and the other women of my acquaintance were really and honestly in want of the things that we had been told from our childhood were what we ought to want'.[38]

Eventually Cicely was able to formulate a political explanation of her feelings about her role in society, based on her own experience as a woman who did not in any way conform to the expected pattern – and not always from choice.

> Thus long before I had learned to dispute, in so many words, the proposition that woman's place is in the home, I knew that women situated as I was could not stay at home unless they wished to starve . . . and [this helped] in no small degree to develop me from a mere rebel, conscious only of personal misfit in the scheme of things, to a fully fledged feminist – that is to say a woman who understood that her sense of misfit and restiveness was not peculiar to herself, but the characteristic of a repressed and restive class.[39]

At the core of Cicely's feminism was a fierce rejection of the stereotypes of womanhood, enforced by the need of women to support themselves by marriage. Once women recognised that their most crucial connection with men was an economic one they were, she argued, free to shape their lives on the basis of that recognition. And they could choose, as Cicely herself had chosen, not to bother with men at all. If they did not need them as sources of economic support they did not need them as partners, and Cicely developed this argument most comprehensively in her influential and entertaining book, *Marriage as a Trade*.

Four

On Strike against Tradition

Although Cicely's initial involvement with the suffrage campaign was as a public speaker, she soon realised that while many women could stand up and address an audience, far fewer had her talent as a writer – a talent which could be put to good use. Also, as she admitted in *Life Errant*, her enthusiasm for appearing at endless public meetings was limited:

> it was bad enough to make a speech myself – always on the same subject, trying hard to think of something new to say; but even worse was the necessity of listening to all the old arguments as put forth by your fellow orators.[1]

After the success of *Diana of Dobsons* in the early part of 1908 she became a well-known figure in literary and theatrical circles and spoke more than ever at meetings. Thus it was that her idea for the founding of the Women Writers Suffrage League (WWSL) reached an enthusiastic collaborator – Bessie Hatton.

> One night Miss Hatton was at the Dramatic Debates where she heard Miss Cicely Hamilton speak on the suffrage. She was immensely struck by her earnestness and the power she exercised over the small audience, which was composed largely of 'Indifferents'. The next day she wrote to Miss Hamilton and said how much she had enjoyed her speech. She received a prompt reply in which was expressed the desire to found a Women Writers Suffrage League, 'If only someone would undertake the

> secretary-ship.' This wish was immediately fulfilled by Miss Hatton.[2]

Bessie Hatton came from a literary family – her father Joseph was an author and journalist – and had originally established her reputation as a writer of romantic fairy stories, described by one critic as having a 'happy atmosphere of Hope, Youth, Dreams and Love ever in the major key'. She was a committed suffragist and devoted a great deal of time to working for the cause, sitting on innumerable committees. Her greatest contribution to the work of the League was probably as an organiser; she was famed for her tact, which was most necessary when dealing with such a variety of members, many of whom were used to organising matters to suit themselves. It is probably fair to say that Cicely was quite unsuited to the day-to-day running of an organisation like the WWSL; her concern was with the large gesture and the striking public event. Without Bessie Hatton she and the many like her in the League would have been denied the platform which it provided for them and for the cause.

With the founding of the WWSL and, later in same year, its sister organisation the Actresses' Franchise League (AFL), Cicely found the means by which she could most effectively contribute to the struggle for the vote. The League stated that its object was 'to obtain the vote for women on the same terms as it is or may be granted to men. Its methods are those proper to writers – the use of the pen.'[3] Thus it made it quite clear that, as an organisation, militant demonstrations were outside its scope, although many of its members remained in the WSPU which, of course, did believe in militant action. For many writers though, Cicely among them, this was a much more congenial way of campaigning. This kind of political activity changed the way suffragists saw the world and other women; as Cicely put it:

> The sense of a common interest, the realisation of common disabilities have forced [woman] into class-consciousness and partisanship of her class . . . Most important of all, the knowledge of each other and the custom of necessity of working side by side in numbers is bringing with it the consciousness of a new power – the power of organisation.[4]

In the period before the outbreak of World War I a great number of women were making their living by writing fiction, by journalism and, to a far lesser extent, by writing poetry and plays. Writing had traditionally been the most acceptable creative activity for women, other than the necessary female accomplishments, and was one that fitted in more easily than some with domestic commitments. As Cicely's experience showed, it was by no means an easy way to make a living but it was one to which middle-class women often resorted, frequently through lack of training for any alternative. Even Charlotte Despard had written romantic three-volume novels with titles like *Chaste as Ice, Pure as Snow* and *Wandering Fires* in the early years of her marriage, putting into them all the passion which had no other outlet. At this time a great number of serious periodicals, both weekly and monthly, also published fiction and non-fiction and provided a market which has now almost entirely vanished.

The suffrage agitation brought these women together, giving them a chance to celebrate and perhaps also to bemoan their shared experience as writers and women, as well as campaign for the vote. The range and number of WWSL activities demonstrate how ready they were to meet, talk, entertain each other and enjoy their shared identity of purpose. The League attracted some of the most distinguished writers of the day; Mrs Belloc Lowndes was an immensely popular novelist and became a vice-president of the WWSL, as did Alice Meynell. Mrs Meynell was a poet so much to the taste of the Edwardians that at one point she seemed likely to become Poet Laureate. In the event John Masefield, an 'Hon. Man Associate' member of the League, got the job instead.

It was important that the League attract such well-known figures because 'it was thought that a society headed by the names of some of the cleverest women writers of the day might form another good reason for the granting of the Suffrage to women'.[5] This position places the League closer to the constitutional societies such as the NUWSS which campaigned for the vote on the grounds that women's achievements were now equal to men's, measuring them, of course, by male standards. For many members of the League, Cicely among them, it was not necessary to prove women's right to the vote but even so the presence of these *grandes dames* of English letters did ensure favourable publicity and help to imprint on the public mind the idea that many women of distinction were as concerned about the vote as their less famous sisters. The League was pledged to help all other suffrage societies whether militant or constitutional, so there was room within it for a wide range of political opinion; Elizabeth Robins, for instance, the League's first president, remained a committed member of the WSPU. In a speech delivered to a WWSL 'At Home' on 4 May 1909 she told her audience what she saw as the special contribution that writers could make, not only to the cause of suffrage but to a better understanding of women generally. Citing among other books in the tradition of Mary Wollstonecraft's *Vindication of the Rights of Woman*, Cicely's *Marriage as a Trade*, Robins said: 'We must have known that one of the most important, most indispensable services to Social Reform would have to be undertaken by the writers'[6] and she saw clearly how it was to be achieved:

> The magnificent platform work being done from various centres must be supplemented and further spread about the world through the medium of the written word. I don't mean by frankly propagandist writing (though I am the last to deny the importance of that) but even more valuable is, I think, the spirit of fairness and of nobler thinking about women, a spirit which both men and women writers are able in a thousand ways to illustrate and justify.[7]

Mindful of the power of men's pens as well as women's, the League had a number of 'Hon. Men Associates' as they were called, among them some very distinguished writers. Two of these, Israel Zangwill and Laurence Housman, worked tirelessly and very publicly for the cause, contributing plays and a positive flood of articles and after-dinner speeches.

In a later speech to the League, in May 1911, Robins was very specific about how, in her opinion, women had been ill served by writers in the past:

> My complaint is that not enough has been made of such traces as history preserves of significant lives lived by women . . . When we read the pages of such chroniclers as I have in mind, we see again and yet again that the fine work the woman did was an offence – for which she is made to pay by gross intrusion into her private life, and by misleading accounts of some detail which the intrusion revealed. What is there in such biographies to inspire you and lead you on? Everything rather to lame the spirit and drive you back into obscurity. Yet these literary outrages should

> rather call upon women to take possession of this field themselves.[8]

Robins cited Mrs Gaskell's *Life of Charlotte Brontë* as a good example of what can be achieved when one woman writes about another, adding that it was 'also a fine example of literary friendship'. Men, she said, even well-intentioned ones, were embarrassed by writing about women, considering the task unworthy of them. Little has been written about women, and what there is is 'poor stuff'. This then gives women writers a marvellous opportunity to write about women as they really are:

> The Great Adventure is before her [woman]. *Your* Great Adventure is to report her faithfully. So that her children's children reading her story shall be lifted up – proud and full of hope. 'Of such stuff,' they shall say, 'our mothers were! Sweethearts and wives – yes, and other things besides: leaders, discoverers, militants, fighting every form of wrong.

Cicely's belief that women writers would enjoy belonging to an organisation where they could use their talents for the cause and also meet socially to discuss matters of mutual interest was soon proved correct. As a writer herself she knew what a lonely occupation it could be and rightly suspected that she was not alone in finding a new and exhilarating camaraderie in the suffrage campaign. The WWSL held monthly 'At Homes' where members and their guests had tea and then listened to speeches and where suffragist literature was sold. The League could call on a distinguished array of speakers, and attendances were large. In common with the other committee members Cicely was involved in the organisation of these events and she was also a popular speaker. With her wide range of contacts in both the literary and theatrical worlds she may well have used these occasions to bring together writers and actresses who could be persuaded to collaborate on suffrage plays and other projects which supported the cause and to attract new members for the WWSL. The most useful function of the 'At Homes' was probably the opportunity they provided for extensive 'networking', and Cicely seems to have been very active in this side of the WWSL's activities.

In May 1909 Cicely was one of the speakers at an 'At Home', together with Elizabeth Robins, part of whose speech has already been quoted, Margaret Wynne Nevinson, Evelyn Sharp and Israel Zangwill: the members must have had a considerable taste for speeches to sit through so many. These speakers were some of the most active members of the League and they also worked directly with other suffrage organisations; Elizabeth Robins and Evelyn Sharp with the WSPU and Margaret Wynne Nevinson with the WFL. These three women were in some ways quite typical of the better-known members of the WWSL; they earned their living by writing, usually combining journalism with fiction or some other literary activity. They were also very socially and politically aware and were involved in causes besides the campaign for the vote.

Elizabeth Robins was an American, an actress who had been one of the first to recognise the possibilities that playwrights such as Ibsen gave to actresses seeking more demanding and interesting roles. She had secured the English performing rights to *Hedda Gabler* and starred in the play in 1891. After she left the stage she found that writing was an alternative way to make a living and produced a considerable quantity of fiction as well as innumerable articles and pamphlets. She wrote a suffrage novel, *The Convert*, based on her own experience of the WSPU and intended to publicise the suffrage cause. She also wrote a play, *Votes for Women*, first produced in 1909 and the forerunner of the many propagandist plays which members of the WWSL wrote during the campaign. In it there is a great set-piece scene of a suffrage meeting in Trafalgar Square. It is a bold piece of theatre, skilfully using a large crowd to voice arguments against women's rights while the platform speakers present some of the most important arguments of the campaign. Elizabeth Robins was an experienced woman of the theatre and had a very shrewd idea of how to make her deeply held political beliefs palatable to an audience.

Evelyn Sharp, the sister of the folk-song collector Cecil Sharp, had earned her living as a writer from the time she left school, supplementing her income with fees from teaching private pupils. Her family greatly disapproved of this independence but she quite soon achieved success when her first novel was published by the Bodley Head and she became a regular contributor to the *Yellow Book* – at the time one of the most notorious literary journals, largely because of its association with Oscar Wilde and Aubrey Beardsley. Like many other suffragists, she saw that the denial of the franchise meant that women were also denied a whole range of other human rights. In her autobiography Evelyn Sharp refers to the close bond between women who have fought together which lasts throughout their lives, even if they never mention it, to each other or to anyone else:

> With one's fellow suffragettes the tie, only sometimes an intimate one, was nevertheless unbreakable. You have a different feeling all your life about the woman with whom you evaded the police sleuth and went forth to break windows in Whitehall or to be mobbed in Parliament Square or ejected from a Cabinet Minister's meeting. Probably when you meet again in after life you talk about everything on earth rather than the suffrage movement; but the memory is there . . .[10]

Evelyn Sharp was imprisoned for her suffrage activities a number of times and in August 1913 was arrested while the WWSL delegate at a conference protesting at the 'Cat and Mouse' Act. This Act was passed in 1913 when there was growing public protest at the forcible feeding of suffragettes who were on hunger strike. Under the Act, hunger strikers were released on licence when they became dangerously ill and were then rearrested once they had been nursed back to health. Many women, however, managed to evade rearrest. Unlike most suffrage campaigners, Evelyn Sharp refused to undertake war work and was one of the founders of the Women's League for Peace and Freedom. Throughout her life she worked for human rights and world peace within a variety of organisations. A woman of great energy and commitment, she had a rather odd link with her friend and colleague Margaret Wynne Nevison – after Margaret Nevinson's death, when Evelyn Sharp was in her fifties, she married her friend's widower, the distinguished radical foreign correspondent Henry Nevinson.

Margaret Wynne Nevinson had enjoyed a fairly free and easy childhood in a Welsh-speaking High Church vicarage. She learned Latin and Greek but although she longed to go to Cambridge she realised she would never be able to afford it. After travelling and teaching she married Henry Nevinson and moved to Whitechapel, to one of the settlements where middle-class people lived in order to do social work among the poor of the East End. Later, unsure of how much good they were doing, the Nevinsons moved to Hampstead where Margaret became frustrated by the sense of sacrificing her literary ambitions for marriage. She wrote for journals and became a member of the Kilburn Board of Guardians administering the workhouses. This provided her with material for her one-act play, *In the Workhouse* which shocked audiences and critics (particularly critics) when it was first performed in 1911. One critic was so horrified that he refused to 'degrade' the actresses by naming them.

This play was 'written for a propaganda purpose to show up the abominable anachronism of the law of couverture,[11] the hard position of married women and the advantage a clever woman can take of the laws apparently made for the punishment of virtue and the maintenance of vice.'[12] According to the law of couverture a wife has no independent civil rights, as is illustrated here by the forcible confinement of a respectable married woman in the workhouse. In this production Cicely played one of the 'bad uns', whose position is contrasted favourably with that of the honest wives.

During the suffrage campaign Margaret Nevinson was very active in the WFL, speaking at outdoor meetings, including the ones in Hyde Park which could often turn violent, and travelling with the suffrage caravan. She joined the WWSL early on and noted in her autobiography that 'our meetings always drew distinguished audiences'.

Around the time that Cicely and Bessie Hatton were founding the WWSL, mass demonstrations were being organised in London by the WFL, the NUWSS and the WSPU. Speaking in February 1908 the Home Secretary, Herbert Gladstone, had effectively challenged the campaigners for the vote to prove that the majority of women supported their cause. In what must be seen as a very provocative speech, he said that political campaigns reach a stage when mere argument is not enough. In the course of his speech he commented, 'men have learned this lesson and know the necessity for demonstrating that *force majeure* which actuates and arms a government for effective work'. Harking back to the great demonstrations of the Chartists in the early nineteenth century, he added:

> It will be found that people . . . assembled in their tens of thousands all over the country . . . Of course it cannot be expected that women can assemble in such masses, but power belongs to the masses, and through this power a government can be influenced into more effective action than a government will be likely to take under present conditions.[3]

This was a very inflammatory statement for a Home Secretary to make and all branches of the movement resolved to show him just what large crowds of supporters they could muster.

The first great demonstration of 1908 was that organised by the NUWSS in which the WFL also took part. The 1907 'Mud March' had made an impact largely because it presented the new and shocking spectacle of women marching in public; this time the effect had to be achieved by other means. The NUWSS decided to create an impression by staging a large-scale demonstration with thousands of women arriving from all over the country by special train and marching together in a spectacular procession with 'nearly a thousand beautiful banners and bannerettes, each different, each wrought in gorgeous colour and rich materials'. The Artists' Suffrage League designed and executed banners for professional, local and other organisations which drew on the particularly 'womanly' skill of art-needlework which was enjoying a considerable revival at the time.[14] The whole purpose of the procession was to make apparent both to the government and to the general public, that women had dignity and importance in the world and to attract public support for the cause by demonstrating it. It was for that reason that the block of women doctors and graduates in their academic dress were such an important part of the procession; they showed a public, who were vaguely aware that women could now take degrees at some universities, that these women were not like the 'half-human monsters' of popular myth while at the same time symbolising all the other advances women had made in public life, still without being granted the vote.

The writers had an important part to play in all this, not only as marchers but as reporters and publicists. Cicely wrote about the march for the *Daily Mail* and celebrated the excitement women felt at participating:

> . . . the force of a womanhood conscious of its own individuality, conscious of latent capacities and eager, fiercely eager, to develop them – a womanhood that declines to see life henceforth only through the eyes of men, and will take upon its own soul the responsibility for its own actions.[15]

The WWSL walked under a banner designed for them by Mary Lowndes, described by Lisa Tickner as 'the most energetic and influential of all artists working for the suffrage campaign,'[16] and worked by Mrs Herringham of the Artists' Suffrage League. It was made of appliquéd black and cream velvet and depicted a black crow surmounted by a quill with the word 'Writers' above it. During the march it was carried in turn by Cicely, Evelyn Sharp, Sarah Grand – a distinguished writer and sometime president of the League – Beatrice Harraden and Elizabeth Robins. Behind them other League members carried banners commemorating the Brontës, Jane Austen, Elizabeth Barrett Browning and Josephine Butler, famous for her campaigns for the rights of prostitutes. The march contained between ten and fifteen thousand women and took an hour and a half to cover the distance between the Embankment and the Albert Hall, where it culminated in a mass meeting which also celebrated Mrs Fawcett's forty years' work for the cause. The impact of the march was considerable and there was much comment in the national press but it was largely overshadowed by the tremendous gathering on 21 June in Hyde Park organised by the WSPU. The account in *The Times* the next day shows the impact of the event:

> Its organisers had counted on an audience of 250,000. That expectation it certainly fulfilled, probably it was doubled: it would be difficult to contradict anyone who asserted that it was trebled. Like the distance and the number of the stars, the facts were beyond the threshold of perception.[7]

Despite the size of the meeting it had little political impact; Herbert Gladstone and his Cabinet colleagues were not as easily influenced as they had claimed they would be. It was obvious that the fight would have to continue on as many fronts as possible.

In mid-December 1908 a new organisation, closely associated with the WWSL, came into being – the Actresses' Franchise League (AFL). Its membership was even more distinguished than that of the WWSL; many very popular stars were present at the inaugural meeting including Ellen Terry and the comedienne Mrs Kendal from the older generation of actresses, and Decima and Eva Moore, Violet Vanbrugh and Lillah McCarthy from among current favourites. Telegrams of support were read from Sarah Grand, Pinero, J.K. Jerome and others to a packed audience of 400 actresses, actors and dramatists. Despite the fact that the membership of the League was exclusively female, it was considered a good idea on this occasion to have a man in the chair – the actor-manager Forbes Robertson. The two main speakers were Cicely and Evelyn Sharp. According to the account of the meeting in the theatrical journal the *Stage*, Cicely addressed the meeting 'with no little humour' although she also spoke 'with great feeling of the many ways in which women are necessarily placed at a disadvantage in life'. She added the story of a speech made by an anti-suffrage speaker at a meeting she had attended surreptitiously. This woman had asserted that a woman's place was at home consoling her husband; 'Miss Hamilton failed to see why a husband should need "incessant" consoling and thought too that there might be a difficulty in the way of some women fulfilling their mission in life as consoler should they not happen to possess a husband waiting at home to be consoled.'[18] The audience, many of whom also lacked husbands, loved it. The League had three aims:

1. To convince members of the theatrical profession of the necessity of extending the franchise to women.
2. To work for women's enfranchisement by educational methods.
3. To assist all other Leagues wherever possible.

Cicely and Elizabeth Robins were among those who were both actresses and writers and were therefore eligible to serve on the committees of both Leagues.

It was not uncommon in the late nineteenth and early twentieth century for political meetings to be enlivened by musical interludes and recitations and initially the members of the AFL provided such entertainments at suffrage meetings, making a particular speciality of monologues in which a woman told how she converted her husband or friends to the cause. They were usually comic but the comedy, while mainly at the expense of the anti-suffragists, was also often achieved by making the speaker an archetypal cockney 'character' of a type still prevalent in the theatre at the time. Thus the middle-class writers and audiences, while often citing the hard lot of working-class women in their platform speeches, were oblivious to their patronising attitude to working-class women in their performances.

In a play written by Beatrice Harraden and performed by the AFL, *Lady Geraldine's Speech*, one of the characters remarks, 'And quite apart from anything to do with the vote itself, it is so splendid coming in intimate contact with a lot of fine women all following different professions or businesses.'[19]

This pleasure was one that Cicely felt very strongly and one of the most intimate and long-lasting relationships of her life started at this time as a result of her involvement with the AFL; that with Edy Craig and her lifelong partner Christopher St John (Christabel Marshall). The house the two of them shared with the painter Clare 'Tony' Atwood at Smallhythe in Kent was for Cicely a place of escape from the pressures of work and London. The atmosphere of shared hard work and agreeable, if somewhat chaotic, domesticity, was very different from Cicely's own life at home in Chelsea and it was sufficiently inaccessible to provide her with a wonderful excuse to decline speaking engagements once she was there. In a letter to Evelyn Sharp she explained: '[we are] three miles from a light railway which eventually takes you to the South-Eastern. It takes four hours or so to do the fifty or sixty miles from London.'[20]

Edy Craig was the daughter of one of the greatest and most popular actresses of the day, Ellen Terry, and had started her theatrical career at the Lyceum where her mother starred with Henry Irving in spectacular productions of Shakespeare and non-classical plays. She had started out as an actress 'but I was always too near the best not to realise my own limitations'. Her real talent was as a designer, especially of costumes, and this talent she brought in abundance to the AFL. Her early experience working with Irving's company had developed her skills in ways which were especially useful in the makeshift conditions under which AFL performances often took place:

> Women often suffer from many disadvantages in their training, but curiously enough, for that very reason they make better emergency workers than men . . . They get there somehow, when a man, who had had a better chance of training, will refuse to undertake anything that has to be undertaken quickly.[21]

Christopher St John had taken her surname at the time of her conversion to Catholicism as a sign of her devotion to John the Baptist and she felt better suited by a male rather than a female first name. She had first met Edy when she called on Ellen Terry backstage at the Lyceum and from that day she was, in her own words, the 'devoted slave' of both mother and daughter. After some initial hostility on Edy's part they became inseparable and set up house together when they were both in their twenties. Chris, as she was generally known to her friends, aspired to be a writer but supplemented her income by working as secretary to Lady Randolph Churchill. Later she was able to support herself by a mixture of reviewing, journalism and fiction writing.

Edy Craig was totally committed to the suffrage campaign, belonging to eight suffrage societies, 'and when I think, when one considers all the cause means, one cannot belong to too many'. Edy Craig was good-looking, not as beautiful as her mother but with a grace and style of her own. Her ringing voice and fine posture were frequently commented upon, and her commanding presence fitted well with her determination to do things her way, with no room for compromise. She attracted loyalty and devotion from her many friends and admirers but this did not stop her having ferocious disagreements with those who thwarted her plans. Humour did usually manage to creep in in the end. Cicely was an amused participant in one of her more spectacular arguments, with the committee of the AFL. At the previous meeting: 'there had been something of a first class row; Miss Craig in the view of those present, behaving most unreasonably and, despite objection on the part of the majority, insisting on her own way'.[22] Cicely was instructed by the committee to write to her friend 'pointing out the error of her ways', and she agreed to do it:

> The idea tickled me; I knew my Edy well enough to be fairly certain that, if she had made up her mind to any course of action, the committee's rebukes would have no effect on her – so it could not matter what I wrote on its behalf.[23]

Cicely duly wrote the letter and when she called in to see Edy the next day found her friend planning a reply. When asked about the letter, Cicely readily confessed to having written it.

> 'Well,' said Edy cheerfully, 'as you've helped the committee with their insulting letter, it is only fair that you should help me to answer it. You just sit down and write it before you go.' And write I did, to Edy's enjoyment and my own.[24]

Cicely continued to write both sides of this ferocious correspondence for some time until they thought the joke had gone far enough and she confessed to the committee. Luckily they saw the funny side of it and the quarrel was allowed to lapse.

There was something about Edy Craig which encouraged Cicely in pranks of this kind. Edy's boundless self-confidence, born of a childhood in which, in the absence of a father – '[women] were of far greater importance from the age of three up' – seems to have emboldened Cicely and perhaps this was the first time she had found such a congenial companion. It was certainly true that, for the first time in her life, she did not have to worry so much about her income and her career; she was free to give rein to the energy and humour which her writing shows was always present. In May 1910 she and Edy Craig were giving performances with the AFL when Cicely saw an advertisement for the Scottish National Anti-Suffrage League being paraded among those for the WSPU exhibition at which they were appearing. 'Let me frankly admit that this daring attempt to carry the war into the enemy's country took my breath away for the moment,' but, nothing daunted, she discussed it with Edy and they decided to 'beard the Antis in their den'. Unlike the suffrage organisations, the 'Antis' had only a small back office, and when Edy Craig and Cicely asked the lift-attendant to take them there he replied that 'she' had gone out.

> It was too true. At half-past ten in the morning the Scottish National Anti-Suffrage League had locked up her office and departed, telling the lift-man that she had no idea when she would be back. Was she already exhausted by admitting crowds of new members? Or had she been seized with sudden terror at the possible consequences of her boldness in advertising her address – realised that it might bring her callers of the wrong sort, and bolted with the cold sweat running down her back?[25]

They went away but 'we left her lots of messages. I hope she got them, it must be so dull for her all by herself.' The high spirits of the visit and of the letter in which it is described give an idea of the fun as well as the hard work that Cicely found in the suffrage movement.

And hard work there was in plenty, especially when collaborating with Edy. As the momentum of the suffrage campaign increased so did the demand for performances from the AFL. While the League had no difficulty in finding actresses it lacked material for them to perform. It responded to this crisis by establishing a plays department which was run by Inez Bensusan, an Australian actress and writer of short stories and suffrage articles. She had the enormous task of co-ordinating the performances of AFL members and finding suitable material to perform. None of the actresses could afford to work full-time for the AFL, and while well-known actresses might be available to put on a matinée in London, other professional engagements usually made it impossible for them to appear outside the capital. In most cases Inez Bensusan had to recast the plays for every performance and made appeals in the suffrage press for actresses to send her their touring schedules so that she could use them in AFL performance in the provinces.

Difficult though this was, the lack of material was far more of a problem. Although there was a large number of women writers in Edwardian England, very few wrote for the theatre. As Cicely herself had found out, it was very hard for women to get their plays accepted for performance and if they did the critics were inclined to be hostile. Elizabeth Robins was one of the few other AFL women who had had plays performed in the commercial theatre – *Votes for Women* had been produced at the Court Theatre in 1907. Other AFL and WWSL members had written plays but they had been performed by stage societies and experimental groups where being a woman was not the barrier it was to West End managements. The advent of actress-managers, notably Lena Ashwell who had produced *Diana of Dobsons*, had given some opportunity to women writers but women managers were still very few in number and hampered by financial constraints. With the vigour which seems to have characterised all those women most active for 'the Cause', Inez Bensusan decided that if plays did not already exist she would have to persuade anyone she could to write them. As a result, many women writers, and some men, who had never attempted a play before, and actresses who had never written at all began to write pieces for the AFL. They were usually for a small cast and required little in the way of props or sets. Some were serious dramatic representations of women's inequality; perhaps the best of these is Inez Bensusan's own play, *The Apple*,[26] which shows in painful detail the injustice of a system which values sons more than daughters.

Although there were some serious suffrage and women's rights plays, audiences preferred those which were more light-hearted. A popular theme in AFL plays was the weakness of the anti-suffragists' case. The 'Antis' were depicted as brainless, impressionable women who had not thought seriously about the issues involved. A good example is found in *Lady Geraldine's Speech* by Beatrice Harraden, the prolific and much-read novelist. The attraction of this play lies chiefly in its presentation of lively and interesting women. Although the play was rewarding to perform,

Inez Bensusan had considerable difficulties with bookings. The policy of the AFL was to support all other Leagues, whether militant or constitutional, and, particularly at the beginning, a great many of their bookings were for the NUWSS which was opposed to any kind of militant action. Since the characters in *Lady Geraldine's Speech* are all militants, the NUWSS branches never booked the play. In keeping with its neutral policy the AFL did not usually stage plays with a bias towards any particular suffrage group and its greatest successes were those which dealt less specifically with women's rights and the demand for the vote.

Beatrice Harraden was a very popular figure in the movement – 'To know Miss Beatrice Harraden is to love her,' wrote Ethel Hill in the *Vote* of 11 November 1909. In her forties when she wrote her first play, she had had as good an education as was possible for a woman at that time; Cheltenham Ladies' College and Bedford College, London, a benefit which she owed to an enlightened father. She was a prolific novelist, best known for an immensely popular book, *Ships that Pass in the Night*. For Harraden comradeship among women was one of the best features of the suffrage campaign, and she was confident that the 'old-fashioned type of woman – dearly-loved by old-fashioned man – the woman who to please him belittled her own sex, that type of woman will be as extinct as – well the hansom cab.'[27]

The first outstanding hit put on by the AFL was *How the Vote was Won*, by Cicely and Christopher St John. Cicely had written the story to appear as a pamphlet with cartoon illustrations by C. Hedley Charlton, and Chris St John had seen its dramatic potential and turned it into a play. The farcical plot is typical of Cicely's talent for highlighting the absurdity of arguments by taking them to their logical, and for men, extremely discomfiting conclusion. The play opens on the first day of the women's General Strike when women have given up all work, inside and outside the home, and are demanding that they should be supported by their nearest male relative. The argument is that since men still believe that all women are supported by men the suffragettes have decided to show them what it would be like if it were indeed true. The action takes place in the Brixton home of Horace Cole, a clerk, and his sister Agatha puts the argument in a nutshell:

> Now I am going to give up work, until my work is recognised. Either my proper place is the home – the home provided for me

> by some dear father, brother, husband, cousin, or uncle – or I am a self-supporting member of the State, who ought not to be shut out from the rights of citizenship.[28]

This is a point of view familiar from *Marriage as a Trade*; Agatha's next speech recalls both Cicely's own experience and some of her written discussion of the subject:

> Yes I *was* a lady – such a lady that at eighteen I was thrown upon the world, penniless, with no training whatever which fitted me to earn my own living. When women become citizens I believe that daughters will be given the same chance as sons, and such a life as mine will be impossible.[29]

As ever more distant and disreputable female relations descend on him, bearing news that the Prime Minister is making his own bed and that the waitresses at Lyons Corner Houses are being replaced by soldiers of the Coldstream Guards, Horace is rapidly converted to the justice of the women's demands and rushes off with all the other men to demand the vote for women at once.

The play was directed by Edy Craig and performed for the first time at an AFL matinée at the Royalty Theatre on 13 April 1909. The audience loved it and the critics were uncharacteristically generous – they were more often carping and grudging in their reviews of suffrage plays.

> The story is funny enough, but the way in which it is told is funnier still . . . The fact that it is so acutely controversial is not at all against it – is in fact, a virtue rather than a defect, for the Theatre of Ideas is upon us. All that really matters is that it is clever and witty, and that it kept yesterday's audiences brimming with excitement and in roars of laughter. It is, in fact, a long time since we have seen nearly so amusing a one-act play, and if some London manager does not snap it up for his theatre we shall be rather surprised.[30]

But in fact the play never had a London run; it was performed at the Caxton Hall, Westminster, later the same week and given one performance by the Play Actors at the Court on 9 May, with Cicely playing the militant suffragette Winifred Duncan. It reached its largest London audience, however, at the WSPU Women's Exhibition at Prince's Skating Rink in Knightsbridge.

This exuberant event combined fund-raising with propaganda in a most enterprising way. The decor and most of the goods for sale were in the green, purple and white of the WSPU and the decoration of the hall had been designed by Sylvia Pankhurst. It was dominated by murals depicting a woman sowing facing another bearing sheaves of corn with the motto, 'They that sow in tears shall reap in joy.' The exhibition, which lasted for a fortnight, had stalls selling everything from hand-embroidered baby garments to autographed works of members of the WWSL, Cicely's among them. Beatrice Harraden gave two copies of all her books and the manuscript of *Lady Geraldine's Speech* – which was performed frequently during the exhibition – bound in green leather. Other supporters, including H.G. Wells and John Galsworthy, donated books to be sold for the cause and the WWSL stall made a total of £70. Evelyn Sharp, writing in *Votes for Women*, described the impact of the exhibition on the life of London:

> If the Exhibition meant nothing more than just flying the purple, white and green in the heart of Knightsbridge for a whole fortnight it would be worth while. Never before, perhaps, has the daily desultory conversation of the Western highway into town turned upon 'Votes for Women'; never again, certainly, will any driver who plies for hire between Hammersmith and Piccadilly be in doubt as to the meaning of the militant tricolour.[31]

Accounts of the exhibition in the suffrage press give a good indication of its fun and sense of camaraderie; one excitement, hard for the modern enfranchised woman to imagine, was the chance to vote in a real polling booth on a variety of issues from Daylight Saving to censorship in the theatre. A whole range of entertainment was offered to visitors; a suffragette ju-jitsu demonstration, appearances of the Suffragette Band, 'the performers marched through the Exhibition Hall, arousing delighted cries of enthusiasm' and more sedate musical performances of the Aeolian Ladies Orchestra and the Ellen Vannin Quartette. A rather mysterious attraction, advertised throughout the period of the exhibition was 'Miss Cicely Hamilton's Waxworks', which evidently proved very popular. No explanation of this can be found but it seems possible that it was some kind of *tableau vivant*, presumably depicting events or characters connected with the suffrage struggle.

Encouraged by the success of *How the Vote was Won*, Edy Craig realised that the AFL was now ready to undertake a much larger project and she showed an acute awareness of what the League needed when she approached Cicely to write the *Pageant of Great Women*. Up to this point the League had put on small-scale productions which could be staged easily by a few actresses in a church hall but Edy Craig realised that suffragist audiences relished grandeur and spectacle: they wanted something to expand their horizons and make them more aware of women's achievement, as well as works which reflected their own, more limited experience. Involved as she had been with the WSPU, Edy Craig recognised that part of the appeal of the Pankhursts' rallies and demonstrations lay in their theatricality, their largeness. Now the time was ripe for a piece of theatre which celebrated the whole sweep of women's history, revelling in all the roles that women had played in the past and could play again in an enfranchised future. Pageants, usually telling the history of a town or village, had become very popular, since the production of a pageant in Sherborne, Dorset in 1904. Edy Craig went on producing them until 1946, the year before her death, but their heyday was between 1904 and the mid-1920s. She is satirised in her role of pageant producer in Virginia Woolf's novel, *Between the Acts*, where she appears as Miss La Trobe.

The great advantage of the *Pageant of Great Women* as a means of relating women's history was that although a large number of characters were depicted there were only three speaking parts, so it could be performed by amateurs with minimal professional support. At the première of the *Pageant* at the Scala Theatre in November 1909, however, those depicting the fifty-two great women were anything but amateurs. One aim of this performance, since the purpose of the matinée was to raise funds for the AFL and the WWSL, was to include as many well-known actresses as possible in order to attract audiences. Ellen Terry, Adeline Bourne and Lillah McCarthy were in the cast, along with many, well known in their day, who are no longer familiar names.

In the published text of the play Cicely acknowledges as her inspiration for the form of the *Pageant*, a picture by H.W. Margetson which depicts Woman manacled at the feet of Justice, who is blindfold, while Prejudice, who is of course male, tries to tear her away. In the *Pageant* Woman pleads for freedom while Prejudice argues that she is unworthy of it. As he puts forward each argument against Woman's right to freedom she calls up before him a host of women distinguished for their learning, for artistic achievement, for their qualities as rulers, spiritual leaders or warriors. The structure of the *Pageant* was simply a device within which to celebrate women's strength – intellectual, moral, artistic and physical. Some of the examples Cicely chose would have been unfamiliar to the audience while others, such as Joan of Arc, already had their place in the symbolism of the movement. She betrayed her own concerns in making the two largest groups the learned women and the warriors, and, as befitted a Major-General's daughter, she appeared as Christian Davies who fought in Marlborough's army at Blenheim and Ramillies. Incidentally she provided herself and Christopher St John, who played Hannah Snell – a woman who served in both the army and the navy and ended up a Chelsea pensioner – with splendid opportunities to dress up in male costume and swagger. To judge from the surviving photographs they both thoroughly enjoyed themselves and Cicely took the opportunity of other performances and costume events to appear in drag on a number of occasions. Calculated to please everyone in the matinée audience was the slight deviation from the form of the *Pageant* when Ellen Terry appeared as Nance Oldfield – one of the first English actresses. Stepping forward she announced, 'Nance Oldfield does her talking for herself' and ended with the lines,

> The stage would be as dull as now 'tis merry –
> No Oldfield, Woffington, or – Ellen Terry.[32]

Even the formal language in which Woman greets the award of her freedom from Justice cannot disguise the sense of excitement and celebration of the new dawn about to break for women.

> *Woman:* I have no quarrel with you; but, henceforth,
> This you must know. The world is mine as yours,
> The pulsing strength and passion and heart of it;
> The work I set my hand to, woman's work,
> Because I set my hand to it. Henceforth
> For my own deeds myself am answerable
> To my own soul.
> For this in days to come
> You, too, shall thank me. Now you laugh, but I
> Laugh too, a laughter without bitterness;
> Feeling the riot and rush of crowding hopes,

Dreams, longings and vehement powers; and knowing this
'Tis good to be alive when morning dawns![33]

No wonder Ellen Terry described it as 'The finest practical piece of propaganda'. Cicely was clearly pleased with the production and particularly with Lillah McCarthy's portrayal of Woman – even if on this occasion she did not see the *Pageant* under ideal conditions. In an undated letter to Lillah McCarthy she wrote:

Dear Miss McCarthy,

I don't feel I thanked you half enough this afternoon – not only for your performance but for your kindness all through and the trouble you took with a lengthy and I am afraid tiresome part. My only regret was that being for the greater part of the performance crouched under the conductor's stand with my ear against a cello I could see next to nothing of you and hear very little – no reflections on your voice intended. But what I did see and hear was quite enough to earn the sincere thanks of an author who was not I hope too exacting in rehearsals?[34]

The suffrage papers were predictably delighted with the matinée but even *The Times* was moved to observe:

> the unique interest of the performance lay . . . in those separate parts of it which gave the idealistic view of the cause of women's suffrage. Apparently the whole of the large audience were in enthusiastic sympathy with the movement. But even its opponents must have been struck by the intense earnestness and the absolute good taste with which these ideals were presented . . . No one seemed tired by the length of the performance. Even for those who do not believe in the wisdom of the cause it was an afternoon to be remembered.[35]

The *Era* and the *Stage*, the two theatrical trade papers, attacked the matinée for being propagandist – the charge they levelled against nearly all the work of the AFL and WWSL. There is no doubt that these two journals thoroughly disapproved of actresses indulging in political activity, considering that it compromised their art. The *Era* even conducted a poll in 1913 which purported to show that the majority of actresses were indifferent to the issue of enfranchisement. In view of the immense support for the AFL within the profession one wonders whose opinion they asked. In the end the most telling and important response to the *Pageant* came from suffrage groups up and down the country – they wanted to stage it themselves.

Edy Craig was in charge of these productions and brought with her the wardrobe for the entire cast as well as the three actors for the speaking parts with her – Cicely frequently played the part of Woman. Edy Craig had a ruthlessly practical streak when it came to casting the *Pageant*. Everyone, it seemed, wanted to play Joan of Arc and this could cause serious bad feeling when:

> Edy Craig had to deal firmly with some lady of entirely unsuitable appearance who, by sheer determination or the pulling of strings, had got herself cast for the part. There was one such occasion when protest was furious and the would-be representative of the warrior saint not only walked out of the theatre herself but led a small procession of friends and family after her.[36]

Not that this prevented Edy from putting on a successful show: 'she was always at her best in emergencies'.[37]

The AFL took up a great deal of Cicely's time; it held frequent meetings which she sometimes chaired and she was working very closely with Edy Craig and Christopher St John. Edy Craig stayed firmly on the production side but Christopher St John was Cicely's co-author twice; the only occasions Cicely ever worked so closely with another writer. At the same matinée as the *Pageant*, the AFL staged a short one-acter by Cicely and Christopher St John, *The Pot and the Kettle*. A knockabout comedy which pokes fun at anti-suffragists for their inconsistency, it has little intrinsic theatrical merit but the Scala audience were delighted by its rumbustious humour. One of the 'antis' in the play defines suffragettes as 'a lot of female roughs who bite policemen and actually think the word obey should be left out of the marriage service'. When this same young woman is charged with assault and battery for hitting a suffragette who was disrupting an anti-suffrage meeting, she laments, 'Now I am not a womanly woman', but explains her action by saying, 'she had on a fawn coat and a black hat with daisies in it; but she was really a suffragette – though I didn't know it – she looked just like anyone else'. In the end the suffragette withdraws the charge against the 'anti' and invites her to lunch instead. Cicely and Christopher had a great deal of fun at the expense of the 'antis' and their stereotyped notions of womanhood and, with all the advantages of writing for a partisan audience, were able to generate an enthusiastic response. The play is a romp, the sort of thing friends might easily hatch up together out of a series of anecdotes and jokes.

On 11 December 1909 the WFL held a Yuletide festival at the Albert Hall where the *Pageant* was the central event of the evening, this time with Mrs Despard, the WFL president, joining the cast as St Hilda. The *Vote* commented, 'The pageant alone would make the success of any festival.' *How the Vote was Won* and *The Pot and the Kettle* were also performed during the day. These were major attractions and the two plays were crowded out when they were performed in a small auditorium. Like the WSPU Exhibition this festival, dominated by the challenge 'Dare to be Free', was a mixture of stalls selling handicrafts and suffrage literature, serious political debates and entertainment. As Cicely observed much later in the foreword to an edition of the *Pageant of Great Women*, the suffrage campaign was 'the first political agitation to organize the arts in its aid', and the Atelier, together with the Artists' Suffrage League was responsible for much of the decorative and design work of the campaign.

It is no wonder that Cicely gave up so much of her time and energy to the suffrage campaign. She might have had to work hard at other things to pay the bills, but her suffrage speaking and playwriting and acting gave her a sphere where she was appreciated and valued. The unhappy child in Clapham had waited a long time for the kind of warmth and comradeship she experienced now. And this was just the beginning.

Five

Marriage as a Trade

When one contemplates the range and sheer number of Cicely's activities in the years of her greatest suffrage involvement, it is her energy above all which strikes one as remarkable. Unlike many of the women with whom she was working, Cicely was not well off, indeed she was often actually poor, and she earned her living by writing and acting without any family money to fall back on. At this stage in her life she could not afford the cooks and servants who eased the lives of her more fortunate contemporaries; like the independent women who have followed in her footsteps, she had to look after herself. Her sister Evelyn, who lived with her until 1929, may have helped with the domestic chores, but in any event it is hard to imagine Cicely leading a very domesticated existence. Solely on the evidence of her public engagements, she simply would not have had the time.

It is typical of Cicely that thoughout the suffrage campaign she worked with all factions, militant and constitutional. This was possible because her main concern was not with winning the vote but with challenging the view of women as wives-and-mothers and nothing more. Thus while she was a member of the WFL she was perfectly happy to address a meeting of the WSPU or act in a matinée for the NUWSS. Her first allegiance had been to the NUWSS and she revived that connection when, in February 1909, she joined the editorial board of a new journal, the *Englishwoman*. In the preface to its first issue the editorial board declared:

The *Englishwoman* is intended to reach the cultured public, and

> bring before it in a convincing and moderate form, the case for the Enfranchisement of Women. The power which women undoubtedly possess has never gone together with recognized responsibility, and the want of responsibility and seriousness has been the offence and defence of women for centuries. Women would be in a better position, and would even be intellectually improved, if they were recognised and admitted as a responsible part of the social machine.[1]

As constitutionalists, most of the board were far less radical in their view of the relations between the sexes than Cicely was, and editorial policy reflected that view:

> Whenever any question admits of two points of view the woman's view will be taken, but we hold that as the world is made up of men and women, and they work together in real life, nothing much is to be gained by dissociating them violently in literature, and indeed in the conduct of life.[2]

It comes as something of a surprise to find Cicely, whose clear espousal of the 'dissociation' of women and men in *Marriage as a Trade* was to appear later the same year, putting her name to such a statement, even though she would undoubtedly have supported the contention that 'the bulk of women who hold that women should have a vote are neither flighty nor hysterical, but can put forth their reasons plausibly and clearly, and justify their demand by their own personal character and intellect'.[3]

Why then did Cicely choose to become associated editorially with the *Englishwoman*? The high seriousness of its tone contrasts sharply with the humorous and witty approach which distinguishes her work for the AFL and WFL. I believe that her decision shows a characteristic reluctance to become identified too closely with any single point of view and a determination to use her talents in as many areas of the campaign as possible. She may also have been attracted by the serious approach to art, literature and politics which the *Englishwoman* adopted and recognised that any contribution which she made to it would reach a wider audience, one different from that which enjoyed her articles in the suffrage press. Cicely may have been a suffragist but she was also a professional writer and she could not afford to ignore any opportunity to make her work better known and thus advance her career.

Her colleagues on the editorial committee included two of the most redoubtable members of the NUWSS, Lady Balfour and Lady Strachey. Jane Marie Strachey, mother of Lytton and of the suffragists Phillipa and Marjorie, was remembered by Virginia Woolf at the time of her death in 1928 as:

> The type of the Victorian woman at her finest – many-sided, vigorous, adventurous, advanced . . . she seemed to be cast on a larger scale, made of more massive material than the women of today . . . One could easily imagine how, had she been a man, she would have ruled a province or administered a Government department.[4]

In 1909 Lady Strachey was nearly seventy and after many years in India had returned to England, where she supported the cause of women's suffrage with great vigour. The presence of women like her on the editorial board was a powerful argument in constitutionalist terms since she was clearly the equal of any man. But she had already dealt with that point in one of her pamphlets published between 1907 and 1909. Here she refuted the objection to women's enfranchisement that 'There has never been a woman as great as the greatest man.' But, she added, 'Votes are not given as competition prizes . . . It does not seem reasonable to a sweated work-woman to be told that if she wants to be listened to she should have written *King Lear*. To be sure Tom Smith did not write it either and yet he has a vote.'[5]

The range of contributors to the *Englishwoman* was wide. The first issue contained articles by Beatrice and Sidney Webb, the Socialist MP Philip Snowden, Eva Gore-Booth, Millicent Garrett Fawcett and John Masefield. This mixture of the literary and the political continued, in addition to accounts of foreign countries, reviews and articles on industrial issues, until the journal ceased publication for financial reasons in 1921. Cicely had left the editorial board by then; she is listed at the end of 1911 but is no longer a member by 1915. Possibly she resigned at the outbreak of war in 1914. The *Englishwoman* was a woman-orientated version of the many intellectual and literary magazines of the Edwardian period. In common with many of them its readership declined sharply in the period after World War I, and with the vote won much of its *raison-d'être* had disappeared.

In volume 1 (February to April 1909), the magazine published

Cicely's one-act play *Mrs Vance* which had first been performed by the Play Actors in 1907. It is surprising that the *Englishwoman* published the play – perhaps the committee wished to show its new readers how diverse its offerings were to be. Certainly the play's literary merit is very slight and it is not theatrically challenging, as so many of the Play Actors' productions were. It may, however, have been the subject matter rather than the quality of the writing which influenced their decision since the play could certainly be accused of outraging conventional standards of morality.

Undoubtedly the play's outspokenness would have shocked audiences in 1909. Its admission that middle-class women drank to excess and that their husbands could wish them dead so that they could live instead with the governess transgressed all the accepted norms of society; even if such behaviour did exist it was not considered suitable for discussion on the stage. It is not immediately clear why Cicely chose to write a play on this topic, although the playwrights of the 'New Drama', among whom she counted herself, did deliberately deal with subject matter which would challenge, even shock, their audiences. It is also possible that she wanted to show that marriage was not always as easy and idyllic as its propagandists, notably those who wanted to restrict women to the role of wife-and-mother, tended to make out. Like several other of Cicely's one-acters, *Mrs Vance* depicts a single moment with great intensity but it lacks both the theatrical merit and perhaps more importantly, the humanity and understanding, she showed in dealing with controversial subjects in her later plays, *Phyl* and *The Brave and the Fair*.

Cicely's most detailed analysis of marriage, however, was not in the form of a play but in a prose work. In 1909 she published perhaps her most influential book, *Marriage as a Trade*. This was a book that changed women's lives. In her autobiography Lady Rhondda attested to the impact it had made on her thinking about women's role in society and Elizabeth Robins called it 'an original and courageous book'. Emmeline Pethick Lawrence welcomed it for shedding 'the pitiless light that reveals the squalid and ugly facts of women's servile and degraded position in the body politic'.[6]

Feminists had been arguing since the time of Mary Wollstonecraft that women were as capable as men of a full range of work and occupations; that there was nothing inherently 'natural' in their role as wife-and-mother and therefore there was no reason why it should be the only occupation open to them. Cicely took the argument many stages further, insisting that women became wives not from choice but because it was the only means of livelihood open to them and that, 'the trade of marriage tends to produce its own particular type; and my contention is that woman, as we know her, is largely the product of the conditions imposed upon her by her staple industry'.[7] The book examines all aspects of women's lives in the light of the fact that for most women marriage is the only way they have of making a living. This fact, so she argues, has affected every facet of human relations and always in such a way as to put men at an advantage. Society reflects women's economic subjection and the whole human race pays the price for that state of affairs. Cicely goes on to define her terms:

> By a woman, then, I understand an individual human being whose life is her own concern; whose worth in my eyes . . . is in no way advanced or detracted from by the accident of marriage; who does not rise in my estimation by reason of a purely physical capacity for bearing children, nor sink in my estimation through a lack of that capacity.[8]

The emphasis on marriage, the insistence on seeing women only in that role is, Cicely claims, something that men have dreamed up to make themselves important:

> He [man] still clings to the idea that a wife is a creature to be patronised; with kindness of course – patted on the head not thumped – but still patronised. While he is yet unmated his dream of the coming affinity still takes the shape of someone smaller than himself who asks him questions while he strokes her hair.[9]

Men may claim that in return for this dependent role women enjoy male protection and chivalry but this much-vaunted chivalry is 'a form, not of respect for an equal, but of condescension to an inferior'; furthermore, men dictate the terms upon which it applies in relations between the sexes:

> In order to secure this preferential treatment in unimportant matters, you must put no strain upon our courtesy, and you must defer to our wishes in more important things; you must not trespass upon the domain that we have reserved for our own use, you must not infringe the rules which have been laid down for your guidance and whose aim is to secure our own comfort.[10]

Much of the book draws attention to the opportunistic nature of male expectations of women. Thus when, like Cicely herself, a young woman has no one to support her she is expected to go out and make her own living, despite having grown up in the belief that such a course of action was unthinkable. And when she does try to make her own way she receives scant encouragement from anyone else:

> The young man begins his life in an atmosphere of encouragement and help; the young woman in one of discouragement or at best indifference. Her brother's work is recognised as something essentially important; hers despised as something essentially unimportant – even although it brings her in her bread.[11]

Similarly, while the middle-class man expects women to be incapable of physical effort, the peasant expects women to be strong enough to do all kinds of hard domestic and agricultural labour. And why, she asks, disingenuously, is women's work always whatever men do not want to do themselves?

> One wonders why it should be 'natural' in women to do so many disagreeable things. Does the average man really believe that she has an instinctive and unquenchable craving for all the unpleasant and unremunerative jobs? or is that only a polite way of expressing his deeply rooted conviction that when once she has got a husband she ought to be so thoroughly happy that a little dirty work more or less really cannot matter to her.[12]

With innumerable, small, well-chosen examples Cicely undermines all the arguments about women's 'natural' role, pointing out over and over again that for women marriage is an economic arrangement and they therefore conform to the expectations of their 'employers'. And these expectations, in some respects at least, are not very high, with the result that women have been forced to avoid fulfilling their potential as individuals:

> For generation after generation the lives of women of even the slightest intelligence and individuality must have been one long and constant struggle between the forces of nature endeavouring to induce in them that variety which is another word for progress and their own enforced strivings to approximate to a single

> monotonous type – the type and standard set up for them by man, which was the standard and ideal of his own comfort and enjoyment.[13]

For Cicely, 'Of all the wrongs that have been inflicted upon woman there has been none like unto this – the enforced arrest of her mental growth.' No group of women has suffered more from this limitation than those who aspire to be artists:

> It is the systematic concentration of woman's energies upon the acquirement of the particular qualities which are to procure her a means of livelihood by procuring her the favour of a man that has deprived her steadily and systematically of the power of creation and artistic achievement; so much so that the commonly accepted ideals of what is known as a womanly woman are about as compatible with the ideals of an artist as oil is compatible with water.[14]

Thus when women do paint or write the results are unsatisfactory, artificial. Only a woman, Cicely argues, can realise how 'weak, false and insincere is the customary feminine attempt at creative art'. This was a new defence of women against the charge that there had been no women artists as great as Shakespeare or Leonardo. Most women could do no more than produce 'a more or less careful, more or less intelligent copy' of the masculine conception of their emotions in a certain situation. Women writers do not write great love poetry, she argues, because for them love is largely an economic transaction. After all 'no stockbroker, however exultant, has ever burst into lyric rhapsody over a rise in Home Rails, no grocer lifted up a psalm of praise because his till was full'.

Of course, Cicely is somewhat overstating her case, carried away by the exuberance of her own rhetoric, but fundamentally her argument is sound. Luckily for her she was able to work with other women who thought like her and were able to celebrate the reality of women's experience in their novels, drama and graphic art, even in the pageantry of their processions. Nor did they shrink from depicting the darker side of women's lives, the suffering and the limited opportunities. These women, striving to be true to their own vision knew, as Cicely wrote proudly:

> That any woman who has attained even a small measure of

> success in literature or art has done so by discarding, consciously or unconsciously, the traditions in which she was reared, by turning her back upon the conventional ideals of dependence that were held up for her admiration in her youth.[15]

With malicious logic Cicely punctures male self-importance and self-satisfaction and proclaims her belief that once women realise their own potential they can do anything – and the experience, as she evidently knows, is most exhilarating:

> To no man, I think, can the world be quite as wonderful as it is to the woman now alive who has fought free . . . Her sphere – whatever it may prove to be – no one but herself can define for her. Authority is to her a broken reed. Has she not heard and read solemn disquisitions by men of science on the essential limitations of woman's nature and the consequent impossibility of activity in this or that direction? – knowing all the time, that what they swear to her she cannot do she does, is doing, day by day.[16]

She knows, however, that to men, women like her are a threat and that men often meet that threat with brutality:

> the rage of persecution against the witch has so much in common with the customary male policy of suppressing at any cost, all deviations from the type of wife-and-mother-and-nothing-else, that one cannot help the suspicion that it was more or less unconsciously inspired by that policy.[17]

There are modern feminist historians who would go even further and argue that there was nothing unconscious about it.

In one of the angriest sections of the book, written in a style quite devoid of the wit and high spirits found elsewhere, Cicely discusses the effects of male sexuality on women and acknowledges that there are risks in marriage far graver than the loss of independence. Clearly, like so many of her feminist contemporaries, she was appalled by the sexual double standard and the way it enabled men to infect their wives with venereal disease, of whose very existence most women were totally unaware. She discusses the subject unflinchingly, treating it with bitter irony as an occupational hazard of the trade of marriage:

> I have been astonished at the number of women . . . who seem to have hardly more than a vague inkling – and some not even that – of the tangible, physical consequences of loose living . . . I remember the thought which flashed into my mind – we are told we have got to be married, but we are never told that![18]

Cicely's distaste for and anger with patriarchal society's attitude to male sexuality extends to all its manifestations. Men, as she sees it, will exploit women sexually and then blame women for male behaviour as long as society gives them the power to do so. And they will make sure that they do everything possible to retain that power:

> The extreme reluctance of a male electorate to raise what is termed the age of consent in girls is perhaps the most striking example of this tendency of the stronger to shift the responsibility of his misdeeds onto any shoulders but his own – even onto the shoulders of a child.[19]

Here Cicely is referring to the great difficulty experienced by campaigners, led by Josephine Butler and the journalist W.T. Stead, in getting the age of consent raised from twelve to sixteen in the Criminal Law Amendment Act of 1885. They finally made their point when Stead revealed in his newspaper how easily he had procured a twelve-year-old girl for prostitution. Ironically he was prosecuted and sent to prison for this, even though he had had no intention of doing anything other than proving irrefutably how girls were exploited as a result of the low age of consent.

Cicely also considered that male attitudes were responsible for the way birth control was denied to women, forcing them to bear more children than was healthy or financially tolerable. Cicely was deeply committed to the cause of birth control, having seen the appalling consequences to women of too many pregnancies when she travelled the country as a touring actress. If male sexuality was so uncontrollable then women should at least be able to protect themselves from some of its consequences. Most men, she claims, prefer to see women as 'unintelligent breeding machines', a phrase whose callousness expresses her perception of the alienation of men from the reality of women's experience. As usual, men's beliefs about women work to their own advantage and her analysis of male resistance to birth control is savage: 'man has laid it down that woman finds instinctive and unending joy in the involuntary reproduction of her kind. One sees the advantage of such a comfortable belief to a husband disinclined to self-control.'[20]

Cicely's tone is not, however, consistently sombre. Despite the fact that much remained wrong with the institution of marriage and that for many women there was no alternative to it, some progress had been made. Married women would benefit from the changes that spinsters had brought about: '[the spinster] inevitably, by awaking her envy, drags after her the married woman who once despised her and whose eyes she has opened to the disadvantages of her dependent situation'.[21] Cicely leaves her readers in no doubt that she vastly prefers the condition of spinster; she claims that the male writer of a newspaper article had forced her, by his arguments, to consider whether she really felt no envy of married women and she took the research very seriously, consulting both married and unmarried friends:

> The first step, naturally, was to ascertain what were the special privileges which were supposed to arouse in those deprived of them a sense of maddened envy . . . I have ascertained the privileges of the married woman to be, at the outside, three in number . . . They are as follows:
> 1. The right to wear on the third finger of the left hand a gold ring of approved but somewhat monotonous pattern.
> 2. The right to walk into dinner in advance of women unfurnished with a ring of the approved, monotonous pattern.
> 3. The right of the wife and mother to peruse openly and in the drawing-room certain forms of literature – such as French novels of an erotic type – which the ordinary unmarried woman is supposed to read only in the seclusion of her bedroom.
>
> I cannot honestly say that one of these blessings arouses in me a spasm of uncontrollable envy, a mad desire to share in it at any cost . . . I have never yet felt the desire to study French novels of an erotic type; but if I do feel it, I shall have no hesitation in perusing them in public – even on the top of a bus.[22]

One of the charms of *Marriage as a Trade* is the sense it conveys of the excitement and exhilaration of a woman caught up in changing the world and, she hopes, shaping it in her own image. Cicely was by no means the first spinster to write a critique of marriage – a large number had appeared, in both fictional and non-fictional form, in the final decades of the previous century and many of them made points similar to Cicely's, although usually not on such a broad front.[23] The achievement of *Marriage as a Trade* was that it brought together all the arguments and presented them in an entertaining and readable form. Even so it does not pull any punches; women are the way they are because men have forced them to develop along certain lines by depriving them of any option but that of pleasing men in order to ensure a lifetime's career as wife-and-mother. Left to themselves women would be as creative, adventurous and nonconformist as Cicely herself. It is clear that Cicely had little time for men; she pretends not to be criticising them but she makes it apparent that she thinks men are dangerous to women – often physically and always mentally and psychologically. Furthermore they are weak, selfish and dishonest, protecting their advantage with every trick in the book and constantly shifting ground in order to make it harder for women to refute their arguments. Sentimental and limited in their vision, they have, by their monopoly of the means of livelihood open to women, denied women freedom of thought and driven them to pretend a view of the world as limited as men's own. As a result:

> It is not easy for a self-respecting woman to find a mate with whom she can live on terms demanded by her self-respect . . . If we are more or less politely incredulous when we are informed that we are leading an unnatural existence, it is not because we have no passions, but because life to us means a great deal more than one of its possible episodes.[24]

Instead of compromising their integrity, many women were discovering a solidarity with other women, experiencing the pleasure of sharing all aspects of their lives with people who were fighting the same battle. Cicely was in no doubt that such women, working together, could change the world:

> Those women who are proving by their lives that marriage is not a necessity for them, that maternity is not a necessity for them, are preparing a heritage of richer humanity for the daughters of others – who will be daughters of their own in the spirit, if not the flesh.[25]

In August 1909 Cicely wrote to Elizabeth Robins who had written to congratulate her on the book. With charming modesty she tells Robins that she looks forward to seeing her and finding out where Robins thinks the book fails. She goes on:

> I am conscious that it is experimental and may be biased by my own temperament and experience of life. But it represents what 'Votes for Women' means to me – the refusal to be judged only by the standard of 'attractiveness', and therefore, whatever its faults and blindnesses, it has a bit of faith behind it – your letter was so good I don't mind saying this to you.[26]

The last sentence is very revealing; it took a great deal of trust before Cicely was prepared to tell anyone, even such a close colleague as Elizabeth Robins, what she really believed about anything. It is, however, clear from the letter what Cicely saw as the central concern of her book: nothing less than woman's complete autonomy – the right to be judged for herself and not in relation to pre-ordained standards established by men. Many of her fellow campaigners agreed wholeheartedly with her point of view, but when one considers the actual position of women at the time when she was writing, and indeed the norms by which women are judged to this day, the revolutionary nature of her argument becomes apparent.

Equally revolutionary were the terms in which she couched her argument. Her sustained use of the language of commerce and business to describe romantic love and marriage brought what had always been seen as private concerns into the public domain. By her choice of this frame of reference in which to discuss marriage she stripped it of its romantic and emotional trappings and challenged the fundamental division society has always made between the private and the public spheres; the former the province of women and the latter the sole preserve of men. Women, she implied, belonged everywhere and men were no longer to be allowed to claim that their relations with their wives were beyond the scope of analysis and reform. To use a phrase popular with her 'daughters of the spirit' – the feminists of the 1960s – the personal is political, and Cicely was among the first to proclaim it loud and clear.

After World War I Cicely became a much more sober and discreet writer, but in her suffrage writing, and especially in *Marriage as a Trade*, she allowed her imagination to roam free. She played with ideas; approached issues from new angles and all the time wrote with an eye on her comrades in arms. More than any other of her works it gives the modern reader an insight into what it felt like to be part of something as vast and revolutionary as the suffrage movement. All aspects of women's lives, all analyses of human society were available for reappraisal and for a woman so recently set free the challenge was irresistible.

In September 1909 the WFL prepared to launch its own journal, the *Vote*. The WSPU had long had its own paper, *Votes for Women*, and the WFL wanted to have a means of communicating news of the campaign to its members which would reflect its own particular emphasis on events. On the masthead of the preliminary issues Cicely is named as editor together with a woman named Marion Holmes, but when the first issues finally appeared in October the same year, Cicely was not one of the editors and Mrs T.P. O'Connor had joined Marion Holmes. It was probably pressure of work which caused Cicely to withdraw from the editorship since she was already writing a good deal for the movement and still trying to earn her living by a variety of other means. Her break with the *Vote* cannot have been acrimonious since she contributed to it until the outbreak of war.

It is noticeable how much of Cicely's suffrage journalism at this time was written to amuse and entertain her readers. The earliest preliminary issue of the *Vote* mentions another of her pamphlets which she had presumably written as a result of the good response to *How the Vote was Won*. Called *Beware! A Warning to Suffragists* it is a slight but entertaining verse illustrated by a number of women artists including Mary Lowndes and C. Hedley Charlton. It purports to urge women to avoid becoming involved in the suffrage campaign lest they end up in Holloway:

Take warning by
Her awful end
and don't to poli-
tics attend.
Don't earn your living –
If you can,
Have it earned for you
By a man.
Then sit at home
From morn to night
And cook and cook

With all your might.
It may be slow –
But you can say,
'It's just as slow
In Holloway.'

The first two issues of the *Vote* contained 'History of the Votes for Women Movement: concluding chapters', written by Cicely and with an editorial footnote, 'the previous chapters are fortunately lost'. As in *How the Vote was Won*, Cicely's fanciful imagination is allowed full rein as she dreams up extraordinary escapades supposedly engaged in by suffragists to get the vote. The humour of Cicely's contributions may seem full of in-jokes, but it acts as a reminder of the fun that women derived from their involvement with the cause; for the first time they belonged to organisations where in-jokes were possible, where humour as well as hard work was shared.

Cicely's final new venture of 1909 was her involvement in the founding of yet another organisation whose purpose was to harass the government into giving women the vote; the Women's Tax Resistance League. On 22 October Margaret Wynne Nevinson chaired a meeting at the house of Dr Louisa Garrett Anderson at which Cicely moved a resolution, 'that an entirely independent society be formed, quite separate from any existing suffrage society with the object of spreading the principles of tax resistance and that a committee be formed to consider how the movement had best be carried out'.[27] 'No taxation without representation' had been the cry of many groups fighting for political justice and many women decided that if they did not have the vote they should not pay taxes. Obviously this form of protest held the greatest appeal for women who earned their own living and therefore paid income tax but the League's archives contain records of women who protested by refusing to buy dog licences and women who owned property refusing to pay municipal rates and other property taxes. Lena Ashwell withheld the taxes due on the Kingsway Theatre and made a speech on the subject from the stage of the theatre. She also, like Lillah McCarthy and Cicely among many others, refused to pay her income tax. Cicely was elected to the first committee of the League, but she was not good at attending committee meetings; indeed she missed more than she attended. Considering how many other meetings she attended during this period her frequent absences are perhaps not surprising.

The Inland Revenue dealt with those who refused to pay taxes by seizing their property and selling it at auction in order to recover the tax. The tax resisters made great political capital out of these sales and friends and supporters paid large sums of money for the lots, especially for objects which had any kind of symbolic significance. Suffrage insignia in particular always fetched disproportionately high prices. The suffrage press wrote about the sales in some detail and, as with so many suffrage events, they were often turned into impromptu parties. Flora Annie Steel, distinguished and formidable novelist and president of the WWSL, refused to pay either rates or taxes.

> But my refusals were really great fun, and we had quite a festival when they came to sell me up. The village was tremendously interested, sympathetic and excited and there was loud cheering the first time when my publisher, Mr Heinemann, brought in the first lot which was put up, for £10 – more than the whole of my rates. And it was only the first chapter, in manuscript, of *On the Face of the Waters*. [her best known novel][28]

Cicely's situation offered rather less opportunity for drama. After a lengthy correspondence with the tax inspector:

> . . . the collector himself arrived on my doorstep, saying he thought he would like to talk things over with me, as I wrote such very nice letters . . . Strategically I was in a very favourable position – in fact my advantages were very much envied by my fellow resisters. I had practically nothing that could be seized and sold up, no furniture, no valuables of any kind.[29]

Cicely's surprising lack of possessions was partly due to the fact that most of the furniture in the house belonged to her sister who had bought it while Cicely was away on tour, or it was on loan from friends, and partly because of Cicely's relative poverty. In any event the Inland Revenue finally lost its patience and decided to sell her up. Cicely complied by producing a list of her saleable property and wrote to tell them that, 'as far as I could see, I was possessed of some books, a strip of elderly carpet, and a kettle – and I should be interested to see what they fetched'.[30] The Revenue left her in peace for a while and then sent a letter warning that if she ever acquired any other property it would be seized in payment of her debts. Cicely replied that she had managed very well up to that point by borrowing other people's furniture and that she would simply continue to do so.

In her autobiography Cicely speculates on what would have happened if World War I had not interrupted nearly five years of tax resistance, 'My name in due time might have been added to the honourable roll of suffragette prisoners; I might have funked and given in. I really don't know . . .'[31] Cicely certainly does not seem the sort of woman to funk anything so perhaps she would have stuck it out like her friend Evelyn Sharp. Sharp, as a confirmed pacifist, did not, like Cicely and most of the other resisters, settle her tax debts at the outbreak of war. She held out, despite being forced to live without furniture and despite constant harassment by the authorities, until women over the age of thirty won the vote in 1918.

Six

For the Sake of Another Woman

In her writing Cicely stressed her resistance to being judged by standards of charm and attractiveness and the way she dressed was one way of asserting this resistance. At the time she wrote *Marriage as a Trade*, Cicely was in her mid-thirties with large grey-green eyes and what Lady Rhondda described as 'orange-tawny hair' swept softly back from her face. In all her photographs she has a steady and direct gaze and her full, well-chiselled mouth does not betray even the hint of a smile. When one sets her against the great actresses of her time, Lillah McCarthy or Lena Ashwell for instance, one can see why Cicely said that her looks were not of the sort to get her a part on sight. She was a very good-looking woman but without the flamboyant beauty of Ashwell or McCarthy. And this lack of flamboyance was, I believe, intentional, part of her resistance.

In most of the photographs taken during the suffrage period Cicely is wearing a severely cut jacket over a white shirt with a floppy bow tie. In only one, dating from the early days of her involvement with the WFL, is she dressed in a traditionally feminine way, in a dress with a laced bodice, and wearing a necklace. Perhaps it was this kind of outfit that the *Time and Tide* journalist had in mind when she described Cicely as having 'sacrificed her individualism to the extent of adopting the conventionally feminine form of dress'.[1] In any event she abandoned it shortly after becoming active in the WFL. In one photograph, taken at a suffrage march in 1910, she is standing with Edy Craig and Christopher St John who are both wearing carefully trimmed picture hats in which they – Christopher St John in particular – look distinctly ill at ease. Cicely, by contrast, looks resolute but comfortable in a simple panama with a curled brim – no concessions here to the 'feminine note' upon which Mrs Pankhurst placed so much emphasis. Cicely had no time for the elevation to the pinnacle of desirability of what she called the 'silly angel' type of woman:

> Silly angels, may from the male point of view be desirable and even adorable creatures, but one would not entrust them with the building of temples or the writing of great books. (Personally I would not entrust them with the bringing up of children; but that is another matter.)[2]

It is not surprising that Cicely made a very definite attempt to dissociate herself from such a view of 'feminine' women.

Whatever her feelings about the militant tactics of the WSPU, Cicely admired Mrs Pankhurst for her 'forcefulness, her combative energy'; to her these were qualities of which a woman could be proud and she for her part intended to make it clear from her style of dress where her sympathies lay. Clothes and appearance were always an important issue for Cicely – a way of making a statement about herself. In photographs published in newspapers in the late 1920s when Cicely was enjoying the greatest public recognition of her career, there is what looks like an almost studied carelessness in her appearance. Her hair, now cropped, is not carefully combed and the collar of her golfing cardigan crushes that of her blouse. In one photograph, a large one, taken for the *Morning Post* 'Portrait Gallery of Distinguished British Women', she poses half-face wearing a most extraordinary battered felt hat whose curling brim suggests that it is ancient as well as unbecoming. When Lady Rhondda wrote Cicely's obituary, she commented that she was 'often wonderfully carelessly dressed' and that 'one would scarcely have suspected that she was really an actress'. Once she no longer had a professional obligation to look elegant Cicely was happy to dress in a way which reflected her view of the tyranny of marriage over women's lives. Women took pains with their appearance in order to catch a husband; she did not want a husband so she dressed to please herself.

For Cicely one of the great pleasures of the suffrage campaign was the opportunity it gave her to work closely with other women. One of the most striking sections of *Marriage as a Trade* for a modern reader is that in which Cicely explores women's relations with each other. She discusses the way that any independent woman 'has come to rely upon her own sex for the help which she herself is willing enough to render.'[3] Men, she says, cannot understand what women feel for each other:

> He has forgotten that it was a woman, who for the sake, not of a man but of another woman, went out into a strange land, saying 'Whither thou goest I will go; thy people shall be my people and thy God my God.' To him, one imagines, that saying must always have been a dark one; to us there seems nothing strange in it.[4]

Cicely seems here to be writing from her own experience, and if she is then she is surely acknowledging the centrality of women in her emotional life. Certainly in her own sparse accounts and in references to her in other people's writing men seem to have featured in her life hardly at all and when they did it was always in a professional context. If I were writing about a modern woman these facts might lead me to speculate that she was a lesbian and such speculation should not be ruled out just because my subject lived in a different era. Some women have always lived openly as lesbians and there has never been any difficulty in describing them as such but with the growth of lesbian feminism the political dimension of lesbianism has become much more important and that means that it is a matter of some significance whether or not a biographer describes a woman as a lesbian. If women in the past made decisions to live their lives independently of men and with and for other women we, as historians and biographers, owe it to them to draw attention to the political nature of their life style and the only satisfactory way that I know of describing that life style is 'lesbian'. In writing about women like Cicely in this way, I am not at all concerned with what they did in bed but I am very much concerned with all the other choices that they made about other women.

If we are to discuss sexuality we must consider the question of how to decide whether a woman who lived in the past was a lesbian and that leads on to the even more difficult issue of how we define the word 'lesbian' in a historical context. In most of what has been written about lesbians by non-lesbians, and especially in what has been written by men, great emphasis has always been placed on genital contact: unless it can be 'proved' what two women did together in bed we have no right, so we have been told, to claim that they were lesbians. This is an absurd criterion since very few people, homosexual or heterosexual, discuss their sexual activities publicly or leave detailed records for posterity. Some diaries do exist which contain such details but they are very rare and it is very unlikely indeed that women of Cicely's generation, who were very reticent about personal matters of all kinds, would have recorded such things or have preserved the records if they had. Even if genital contact is not the issue historians and biographers who assert that certain women were lesbians are always told that they must produce 'evidence' to prove their point. No one is ever asked to prove that someone was heterosexual – that is always assumed – and many people have been claimed for heterosexuality on far shakier grounds than those which have been deemed inadequate to 'prove' homosexuality. Ironically, absence of evidence to the contrary is often adduced to 'prove' that someone was heterosexual whereas lack of any evidence of heterosexual relationships is not considered enough to 'prove' that a woman was a lesbian.

With the growth of lesbian historical studies, new ways of approaching these issues have become available and there is now a variety of possible models for interpreting women's relationships. Blanche Cook has argued that 'women who love women, who choose women to nurture and support and to create a living environment in which to work independently and creatively are lesbians',[5] whereas Ann Ferguson has rejected this definition on the grounds that it excludes women who worked with men (Virginia Woolf for instance). She insists that women must deliberately take on a lesbian identity in order to qualify as lesbians. Thus by her definition a lesbian is a 'woman who has sexual and erotic-emotional ties primarily with women' or who 'sees herself as centrally involved with a community of such women' and who is a 'self-identified' lesbian.[6] If one uses Ferguson's criteria, women who work with men can be included in the lesbian community provided their primary emotional and erotic energy is woman-centred.

In trying to decide whether Cicely can be described as a lesbian I have reluctantly rejected Cook's definition as too vague – although in her terms Cicely was certainly a lesbian – and turned instead to Ferguson's. We do not know if Cicely had sexual relationships with other women and there is nothing in the surviving material in which she explicitly defines herself as a lesbian but in every other way she fulfils Ferguson's criteria, especially in terms of the community within which she chose to live her life.

Throughout the suffrage campaign Cicely's two closest associates were Edy Craig and Christopher St John. These two women had lived together since 1900 and were joined in 1916 by Clare 'Tony' Atwood; the *ménage à trois* lasted until Edy Craig's death in 1947. Christopher St John destroyed all their letters and papers after Edy Craig's death so there is no documentary evidence for the nature of their relationship but, using the criteria discussed above, it is appropriate to describe them all as lesbians. Other indications of how Christopher St John saw herself come from her autobiographical novel *Hungerheart* in which she desribes her relationship with Edy Craig as well as other relationships, perhaps fictitious, with various female members of the European aristocracy. Aristocrats obviously appealed to Christopher St John; later in life she developed a passion for Vita Sackville-West, who treated her with cavalier indifference, encouraging her devotion but denying her any of the attentions a lover might expect. In November 1932 they met in London and Vita Sackville-West allowed Christopher St John to travel back with her in the direction of her home at Sissinghurst as far as the railway junction at Tonbridge, in which unlikely setting 'She gave me a lover's kiss. In all my dreams of her I never dreamed of that . . . I never knew unalloyed bliss with V except on that November day.'[7] In December the same year they spent a night together but, although Christopher St John remained besotted with Vita Sackville-West the experiment was not repeated. Although she was ruthless to Christopher St John's tenderer emotions, Vita Sackville-West looked after her and Tony Atwood when Edy Craig's death left them bereft and penniless.

One way in which historians can know about lesbians in the past is when women are identified as lesbians by other, known lesbians and such an identification helps to increase our understanding of Edy Craig. After Vita Sackville-West had met Edy for the first time she wrote to a former lover, Evelyn Irons,

> The producer is the most tearing old lesbian – not unlike your friend Radclyffe Hall – but without any charms for me I hasten to add . . . Seeing me trying to sharpen a pencil, she came up, and took it away, 'Here me give that,' she said, 'no woman knows how to sharpen a pencil.' You may imagine Orlando's indignation.[8]

Physically, there was no resemblance with Radclyffe Hall. The similarity must have been in Edy Craig's manner and in the fact that she seems to have seen herself as different from other women. Later, in the 1930s, Radclyffe Hall and her lover Una Troubridge, surely the most famous and public lesbian couple of the twentieth century, became close friends of the Smallhythe trio and the women visited each other a great deal, clearly relishing the freedom to be themselves in each other's company. On one occasion when they dined with Radclyffe Hall and Una Troubridge, Christopher St John wore a black velvet smoking jacket with vast, bell-bottom trousers. At one point Radclyffe Hall and Una Troubridge even contemplated building a house at Smallhythe in order to be as near as possible to their friends. This friendship tends to support Vita Sackville-West's description of Edy Craig as a lesbian and since Christopher St John was besotted with Vita at the time there can be little doubt about where her inclinations lay. Certainly Vita Sackville-West's assessment of Edy Craig must be granted the authority of the recognition of one lesbian by another but one must also ask what she meant by the word 'lesbian'. Given her own life I have no hesitation in saying that by 'lesbian' she meant a woman who loved and had sexual relations with other women as she herself did and as is well documented in the biography of her by Victoria Glendinning.

As well as working with them Cicely spent a great deal of her time with Christopher St John and Edy Craig. Several of her few surviving letters were written from Smallhythe and she often stayed there for as long as a month at a time. At one point, it seems, Christopher St John was not entirely cordial in her feelings towards Cicely. She had always been jealous so perhaps she feared a rival for Edy Craig's affections. 'I am sorry C thinks Cicely H is a humbug,' wrote Ellen Terry to her daughter some time during the suffrage campaign, 'I thought she liked her.'[9] Whatever the reason for the comment the bad feeling did not last, although one does gain the impression that it was Edy Craig who was Cicely's special friend.

The Smallhythe trio were by no means the only women in Cicely's circle who shared their domestic lives with other women while working publicly for women's causes. Lady Rhondda, whose friendship was so important to Cicely that she recorded her gratitude for it in her will, and who, as editor of *Time and Tide*, played an important part in developing Cicely's career in the 1920s, was a case in point. She married but was not well suited to matrimony and became a militant suffragette. She went on hunger strike when sent to prison for setting fire to a pillar box and obtained a divorce as soon as a change in the law in 1923 made it possible – still an unusual course of action for any woman at the time. She lived for many years with Theodora Bosanquet, one time secretary to Henry James and later literary editor of *Time and Tide*. Lady Rhondda's autobiographical writings, like Cicely's, give little away, although Theodora Bosanquet is often mentioned as her travelling companion. All her private papers have been destroyed. The deliberate destruction of material which in the case of such an important public figure might have provided an opportunity for a biographer suggests that Lady Rhondda intended to keep her private life completely private – and her relationship with Theodora Bosanquet is the most likely reason for this. Lady Rhondda was very proud of her achievements as a magazine proprietor and editor so her desire for privacy must have been very strong indeed to override her desire for posthumous recognition.

Another of Cicely's friends and colleagues, Elizabethe Robins, lived with Octavia Wilberforce from 1908 until she returned to America in 1940, supporting Octavia emotionally and financially while she struggled to become a doctor despite lack of education and the opposition of the Wilberforce family. Leonard Woolf, who met the women when Octavia Wilberforce became Virginia Woolf's doctor, described Octavia Wilberforce's relation to Elizabeth Robins as 'that of a devoted daughter', which suggests that the twenty-six-year gap in the women's ages blinded him to other possible interpretations. He did, however, recognise something important about Elizabeth Robins when he wrote of 'that indescribably female charm which made her invincible to all men and most women.'[10] Certainly Elizabeth Robins lived in a network of women all her life. According to Jane Marcus, 'She rejected the demands of the heterosexual life and turned to a network of women writers in Boston for solace and strength and went to Ibsen's Norway with the widow of Ole Bull, the violinist.'[11] And, Marcus adds, 'Much of her life was spent encouraging younger women to careers in medicine and her capacity for intense bonds of friendship and love with other women was extraordinary.'[12] Although as with any relationship we shall never know the exact nature of Elizabeth Robins' connection with Octavia Wilberforce, we do know that they took quite extreme measures to protect their privacy. Their correspondence survives in transcribed form but with the beginnings and ends of the letters – precisely the place where one would expect to find endearments – excised. After the prosecution of *The Well of Loneliness* for obscenity in 1928, women who had happily and proudly lived their lives with and for other women felt that it was necessary to protect themselves from public scrutiny and consequent opprobium if the true nature of their relationships were revealed. Such self-censorship has denied us much material about lesbians who lived earlier this century.

If one draws on the evidence of the way in which Cicely lived her life there can be little difficulty in describing her as a lesbian. She had a large circle of women friends with some of whom she was intimate and among her intimates were women who can definitely, by any criteria, be described as lesbians. She lived her life in a complex network of women, literary, theatrical and political, and men are notable by their absence. Her passionate commitment to the cause of women's rights and the underlying assumption in so much of her writing, both journalistic and literary, that women are morally and in every other way superior to men only serves to underline the fact that the basic and most important allegiance in her life was to women. When she wrote 'she [the woman artist] may waste years in attempting to draw inspiration from *a form of love which it is not in her to feel*' (my emphasis)[13] she may well have been thinking of her own efforts to come to terms with her rejection of heterosexuality; certainly none of her work celebrates relationships between men and women.

Judith Schwarz in her book *Heterodoxy* uses a very simple yardstick to decide whether women in the past were lesbians: 'did they know [that they were lesbians]? and did they act on that self-knowledge? And if they didn't did they still, to all intents and purposes, live their lives as if they had?'[14] Using that yardstick, or indeed any of the others proposed by lesbian-feminist historians, I would have no hesitation in saying that Cicely Hamilton was a lesbian.

Seven

How the Vote was Won

The period from 1910 to 1914 was one of the most hectic of Cicely's life. She was working hard to develop her career as a writer, building upon the success of *Diana of Dobsons*, and at the same time she was putting an immense amount of time and energy into the suffrage campaign. The extent to which she managed to combine the two testifies to her enthusiasm and determination. After the grimness of her childhood and early career she was not going to waste any opportunity to succeed professionally or to enjoy the company and companionship of other women. Between the beginning of 1910 and the outbreak of World War I, Cicely wrote three full-length plays and turned two of them into novels, wrote three one-acters and adapted a novel for stage performance. She also appeared in twelve plays. In some of these her parts – often at matinées – were small but it was a punishing schedule for a woman who was also writing features and articles for newspapers, marching in suffrage processions and appearing on public platforms to make speeches for the cause.

The publication of *Marriage as a Trade* and the enormous popularity of *A Pageant of Great Women* had made Cicely into a celebrity within the suffrage movement and she was much in demand as a speaker. Although she often claimed to be too busy, and with her schedule that seems a reasonable excuse, she was susceptible to persuasion. In the New Year of 1910 she was staying with Edy Craig and Chris St John at Smallhythe when her friend and fellow WWSL member Evelyn Sharp wrote to invite her to address a branch of the WSPU some time in January. Cicely declined on the grounds that she was staying at Smallhythe until the end of the month, recuperating perhaps from all the hectic activity at the end of the previous year, but in asking Evelyn Sharp to invite her 'another time', she added, perhaps surprisingly, 'I am always willing to speak for the WSPU. I spoke for [?our] Chelsea one the other week.' Evelyn took her at her word and Cicely capitulated, not one feels entirely reluctantly, writing to Evelyn: 'you are a persistent devil – I have been making solemn vows not to speak – on your soul will lie heavy the guilt of perjury.'[1] Clearly her commitment to the cause by this time transcended her objections to the tactics of the WSPU. Both the AFL and the WWSL had enshrined in their constitutions the willingness to support any other suffrage society with their productions, so presumably as far as Cicely was concerned this also included public speaking appearances.

Cicely addressed a variety of issues in her speeches. This was essential since, at least in London, her audience probably contained many who had heard her speak before, but certain themes recur. Most important was her conviction that the women's movement was about far more than the vote, that the implications for society of the change in women's attitudes transcended any political changes that might come about, and that men would have to revise their ideas in line with women's new perception of themselves. Speaking in November 1910 Cicely responded to a speech in the House of Commons by F.E. Smith, later Lord Birkenhead. She concentrated on him, she said, because he had realised that: 'there was something more than politics behind it and it was that something more that he endeavoured to oppose'.[2]

In his speech F.E. Smith had claimed that if all the great women in history had never lived: 'the great sum of human happiness to which woman had contributed by her womanly faculties would not have been affected'.[3] Cicely contended that when Smith said 'human' he really meant 'male' and that men were alarmed by the fact that women were beginning to see themselves as human beings with rights and responsibilities and with other purposes than to contribute to male happiness. The growing autonomy of women was what Cicely saw as the greatest gain from the campaign for the vote and she recognised that it was that which men feared most. Working together women had discovered all manner of new qualities:

Some good, some bad – that they were not credited with till

circumstances called them out. Pluck and determination, for instance, and let us admit it – a distinct touch of rowdyism. Very sad no doubt; but we don't lift up our hands in horror every time the human male gets high-spirited and excited; why should we be unduly horrified over similar tendencies in the human female.[4]

Of course, Cicely and probably many of her audience, were delighted at the new rowdiness in women; it was just another aspect of their defiance of the standards men had set for them. Men are going to have to learn, Cicely argued, that they are no longer so important to women: 'that in the future there are many things you [women] will prefer not to have done for you but to do for yourself.'[5] At the end of the speech she softened the emphasis on female autonomy by claiming that until women possessed their own souls and controlled their own destiny they would have nothing to give to any man. There is, however, no mistaking the tone of the speech; rowdy, independent women represented Cicely's vision of ideal womanhood and to her, despite the nod in their direction, men are of little significance. The title of the speech shows that Cicely understood very well what most men felt about the suffrage campaign – it is called 'The Disillusionment of Man.'

Cicely ended this speech with the statement that while it was more blessed to give than to receive that was not at all the same thing as having it taken from you and she returned to that argument in what was perhaps her most impressive speaking engagement – a public debate with G.K. Chesterton. This was organised by the International Suffrage Shop and held at the Queen's Hall in March 1911. Chesterton was a formidable adversary and it is an indication of Cicely's stature within the movement and her skill as a speaker that it was she who took him on. Chesterton belonged to that tribe of Edwardian men of letters, which also included Wells, Shaw and Hilaire Belloc, who had opinions on everything and produced streams of pamphlets, journalism, novels and plays on the issues of the day. He was Catholic, conservative and as determined an eccentric as Cicely herself, appearing in great all-enveloping cloaks and large black fedoras. What is remarkable about the whole encounter is the underlying belief that something useful could be achieved by this kind of debate. At best it provided a forum for the exchange of ideas but it is very unlikely to have changed anyone's mind.

Cicely opened the debate by claiming there were a vast difference between how she saw women and how Chesterton did and then went on to emphasise yet again that men were no longer the centre of a woman's world, that women had revolted against the insistence that they should above all be attractive to men.

> No doubt there are women in this room who have felt like myself, that the attraction of men was not the only thing that would bring us happiness in this world. For me that day was the beginning of my life . . .[6]

She went on to exult in the fact that women were experimenting with their own lives, and to emphasise that a woman's first duty was to herself, and that she was quite capable of achieving things without male intervention.

Chesterton's response was predictably patronising, heaping lavish praise on Cicely's eloquence. After expressing surprise at her contention that women had been torpid and lacked drive until that time, he went on to say that there was no class division between the sexes and correspondingly no class loyalty among women. That was the heart of his argument, and that of many others who opposed suffrage – when they were not foretelling the dire consequences which would befall society if women stepped outside their accepted role they were claiming that women did not have a shared consciousness or a shared commitment to change and that they were far better off relying on men to take care of them. Chesterton denied absolutely that any aspect of women's role had been imposed on them by men and claimed that any differences that might exist were ones that women themselves had chosen or had at least agreed to. Chesterton's romantic notions of history became apparent with his argument that democracy was not worth much anyway and that women were better off not 'mixing in the excitement of the market-place', as he put it.

Cicely's retort to all this, vigorous though it was, must have sounded very familiar to many of her audience. She argued once more that while women for men was a voluntary institution, for women it was a business, and that the only qualities men valued in women were those which were valuable in a wife. Chesterton then went on to plead stupidity: that as an ordinary man he could not understand Cicely's arguments. But he also continued to hammer away at the notion that: 'it is a normal thing if you are a man to be a husband and it is a normal thing if you are a woman to be a wife'[7] and to reiterate that men had always respected women. It seems that, by emphasising the idea of the normality of marriage and by stressing the importance of sex attraction, Chesterton was trying to impute abnormality and unnaturalness to Cicely and those who agreed with her. Certainly one of the commonest and most vicious caricatures of suffragettes was to present them as men in skirts, as harpies and unwomanly women. Chesterton did it with great subtlety but the gibe is still there. Perhaps this antagonism was evident to Cicely during the debate; in any event the one element uncharacteristically absent from her speech on this occasion is humour. Apart from one side-swipe at the 'Antis' it seems to have been delivered completely straight. Her speech also lacked the energy and animation which is usually so much in evidence. Surely so experienced a trouper was not overawed by either her surroundings or her adversary?

It may be that Cicely was more comfortable addressing fellow campaigners, certainly her speeches to such groups have more of the energy and dynamism that one thinks of as her hallmark as a speaker. In June 1910 the WFL entertained the WWSL 'and a large number of these gifted and useful ladies accepted our invitation', so it was appropriate that Cicely's speech on that occasion should be on 'Women and Art'. The sentiments of the speech echo those of the relevant part of *Marriage as a Trade*: that women failed to produce great art, not because they were innately incapable of doing so but because they had never known what they wanted from life and were thus unable to produce sincere work representative of their own experience. Conventional expectations stunted women as artists: 'but it was necessary to live spiritually, intellectually and physically to the utmost, to produce great things'.[8] While women worked to please others rather than themselves they would never produce great art, but every opportunity was now ahead of them: 'They were now at the beginning, and the earth was open to them. It was only when they knew their heritage that they could perfectly understand.'[9]

Cicely had celebrated the excitement of being a woman artist at a time of great change in other speeches too and did so again in an address to the Central London Branch of the WFL in January 1911. The main purpose of this speech, entitled 'The Spirit of the Movement', was to urge toleration and understanding between different groups of suffragists. She pointed out:

> We must learn to encourage in other people, and learn to tolerate in other people – in other women especially, because they are not used to the process – the thinking for themselves. Think of the years, the generations, that women have been told they must not think! What wonder that they make some mistakes when they begin to use the rusty instrument.[10]

Women, Cicely argued, were enjoying a unique opportunity:

> It sometimes seems to me that when once women have felt their feet and are able to look round clearly and say what they think, the women who write or paint will have an enormous pull for a generation or two over the men who write or paint, for the men will have only the old ideas to work on but they will every one of them be new to us.[11]

The arguments she was putting forward in this speech were clearly ones she felt strongly about, namely that suffragists could not be expected to agree and that 'Because there are divisions there need not necessarily be quarrels.' As she had done elsewhere Cicely stressed her belief that 'The right of freedom of speech is worth everything.' Throughout her life this was one of the cornerstones of Cicely's world view and she could not bear to think that women, newly freed to think for themselves, should deny the right to each other. This concern for tolerance among her fellow suffragists sprang from her conviction that the suffrage movement was not just a political campaign. To her it was:

> One of those movements which occur every now and then in the history of the world, as if people suddenly revolted from the materialism with which perhaps they had been contented for generations, and as if they had been stirred by a wave of what I call the Spirit and they have tried to get a little nearer to what they felt things ought to be.[12]

Such conviction, which has an almost religious tinge to it, helps to explain the passionate commitment that Cicely and so many of her comrades-in-arms felt to the cause; to them it represented nothing less than the chance of total revolution. Cicely was realistic enough to acknowledge that: 'Very often the result is entirely inadequate to the hopes that stirred it up, but there has to be that spirit, or nothing happens – nothing that is real and true; things happen but not facts, not the real thing.'[13]

One of Cicely's most interesting suffrage articles during this period was published in the *English Review* in April 1912. Called simply 'Man', it contains some of her most outspoken writing on the subject. It is a mark of her growing confidence that she should publish such an attack on men, not in a suffrage journal or periodical with a largely female readership but in a mainstream magazine, and it is a sign of her new-found eminence that they published it. There is a great confidence about this piece; it has a dash and bravura that earlier writing lacked and it was clearly intended to stir up vigorous argument – which it did. The gist of the article is that up to this point in the suffrage campaign men have been exempt from criticism by women, mainly because women have been too busy establishing their own identity to bother much with men. This, she warns, will change when women gain equality with men and so she intends to view the subject from the position of an equal. Cicely is ironic about the 'tenderness' with which Man is treated at suffrage meetings: 'Let him take note of . . . the almost holy indignation with which the average speaker will repel the unthinkable suggestion that the Cause is 'anti-man'; and mark the unfailing applause that follows her heated outburst.'[14]

Women react like this, she suggests, because they have not got over their habit of reverence for men – an affliction Cicely herself certainly does not share. Throughout the article she concentrates on aspects of the relationship between men and women, about which suffragists and others had tended to be very reticent. Men, she says, want to emphasise the differences between themselves and women as a means of asserting their superiority. This is why they place such stress on motherhood, one area where women can shine without presenting any competition to men, while, 'In every other capacity [women's] inferiority is not only taken for granted but encouraged and most strongly recommended.'[15] When Cicely comments that the dislike of the average man for a woman who in any way resembles him, 'in manner, in habits, in taste or appearance', is founded on a fear of 'losing caste', she appears to be attempting to explain the reaction she herself elicited from men and suggests that independent, possibly lesbian, women were perceived as a threat then as much as they are now.

The article is quite ruthless in its attack on male behaviour and attitudes, and hits the mark hard despite its humorous tone. It is interesting that the reply to this article, published in July the same year, came not from a man, but from a fellow member of the WWSL – May Sinclair. May Sinclair's riposte, 'A Defence of Men', accuses Cicely of stripping men bare and of omitting much that is good about them. Her reply totally lacks the humour and irony of Cicely's original article and its feminism is much more moderate than Cicely's radical pronouncements. It is as though May Sinclair felt that Cicely had gone too far and that her arguments would damage the cause: Cicely seems almost to have reached the point where she did not care what the opposition thought.

Cicely's suffrage activities other than writing continued to be many and various. In June 1910 she again marched, this time in a joint procession of the WSPU and the WFL organised in support of the government's Conciliation Bill which had passed its first reading on 14 June. The WFL contingent, of which Cicely was part, had been designed and organised by Edy Craig and gave the League a chance to show that it was just as good at this sort of thing as the WSPU. The march was held the day after public mourning for Edward VII came to an end and this greatly increased the impact on the public of the women in white with the colours of their leagues and bearing their elaborate and colourful banners. Between ten and fifteen thousand women took part in the procession which stretched for two miles. This was Cicely's fourth march; she had walked in 'the first nervously, the rest joyously' and this time she carried the WWSL banner. Her impression was that the crowd was friendlier than it had been two years before, 'words of encouragement were plentiful and not only from women'. In spite of that she had one regret: 'We would give much many of us to see such a march go by, but that is a thing forbidden; our duty is not to admire but to march.'[16]

In 1911 Cicely collaborated with Dame Ethel Smyth to provide the words for a march which Dame Ethel had composed for the WSPU. This was originally intended for the Pageant of the Leagues in December 1911, an event for which she wrote all the music. Ethel Smyth was a passionate and fiery supporter of the Union and deeply attached to Emmeline Pankhurst. Formidably pugnacious and the most loyal of friends, she was always quarrelling with those who did not share her politics or her own high opinion of her talent; on the other hand she was famous for never holding a grudge. She was prone to falling violently in love with other women, some of whom were not attracted to her. Late in life she conceived a passion for

Virginia Woolf and bombarded her with letters, messages and presents, especially flowers; Virginia Woolf described the experience as akin to being seized by a 'giant crab' and though somewhat flattered did not reciprocate. Cicely admired Ethel Smyth's energy and wholeheartedness and was elated to be her collaborator – even though she had not been Ethel Smyth's first choice and had a justifiably poor opinion of the verses she eventually wrote: they are fervent but otherwise undistinguished. In the same year Cicely and Edy Craig were delegates at the sixth annual conference of the Women's Freedom League; evidently Cicely was now prepared to be more involved in the bureaucratic and administrative aspects of the campaign than she had been up to this point.

A great deal of her work for the cause, however, continued to be done through the AFL and the WWSL. The *Pageant of Great Women* was still tremendously popular with suffrage societies up and down the country and Cicely often played the role of Woman herself. In 1910 she appeared in Swansea, Beckenham, Middlesborough, Sunderland and Ipswich. In November the same year her one-act play *The Homecoming* was performed at an AFL/WWSL matinée at the Aldwych Theatre. This play, which was performed later as *After Twenty Years*, deals with the reunion of Mrs Daly and her daughter on the latter's return after twenty years in America. She reveals that she had lied to her mother about her life there and that she had in fact been living with a man to whom she was not married and who finally left her for a younger woman whom he had married. Her mother accepts her back without reproach. The play is rather sentimental for modern taste but Cicely's contemporaries liked it very much. The *Stage* considered it 'strong and affecting',[17] while the *Era*, which commended the acting very highly, called it 'pathetic and intense'.[18] *Votes for Women* commented that: 'It has the note of sincerity which sounds through all Miss Hamilton's work',[19] the *Vote* wrote about the play at some length, describing it as, 'a tense moment from a woman's life' and commending it as 'Beautifully written, beautifully acted, it was a little bit of life flashed on a tiny canvas, but strangely sincere.'[20] Cicely's skill as a dramatist was developing all the time and she caught the tone of the reunion and of the mother's loving acceptance of her daughter with great accuracy. As the reviews show she also had the knack of appealing to public taste, even though she declined to use this facility when she was writing full-length plays – there she always tackled more demanding subjects. *The Homecoming* is the only one of Cicely's plays to deal with the mother–daughter relationship and there are no others which deal in any way with parents and children. Many of her main characters are orphans and it is possible that her early loss of her own parents made her reluctant to deal with the topic. Certainly the mother in *The Homecoming* is an idealised version of motherhood, refraining completely from making any comment on her daughter's past behaviour. The idealisation may well reflect Cicely's regret at having been denied the opportunity to enjoy an adult relationship with her own mother.

Cicely was not alone among her friends in being busy at this time; not content with her time-consuming commitment to the suffrage campaign, Edy Craig founded an *ad hoc* theatrical company, the Pioneer Players, in 1911. The Pioneers was a subscription society which put on single performances of plays which would never receive a run in the commercial theatre. The company was feminist rather than suffragist, providing a showcase for women as actors, writers, designers and directors, and also employing women in traditionally male preserves: doing the accounts and the lighting, building scenery, and stage-managing. The company's policy was to 'produce plays dealing with all kinds of movements of contemporary interest' and 'to assist societies which have been formed all over the country in support of such movements, by helping them to organise dramatic performances'. Cicely sat on the committee which Edy had chosen to help her fulfil these objectives, and she had also been persuaded to write a play for the inaugural performance. This was at the Kingsway Theatre, still run by Lena Ashwell, who appeared in one of the other plays on the programme, Chris St John's *The First Actress*. Given the people involved in this project it is not surprising that the audience was chiefly composed of women. According to the critic from the journal *Stageland*:

> I looked at the packed house, at the rows and rows of women and gloried in them. Such bright, happy women, full of strong life and joyous optimism. Such clever, beautiful women. Pioneers indeed they are, and I wondered what our grandmammas would have thought of them.[21]

This was the kind of audience that Edy and Cicely loved to play to and Cicely's play, which she also directed, *Jack and Jill and a Friend* was clearly written for just such a partisan public. Light and 'modern' in tone, it deals with the difficulties of being a woman writer – and of making men behave sensibly. The play is essentially a comedy and as such does not set out to offer a detailed political analysis of the problems of a woman who wants to be taken seriously as an artist – or by extension as a career woman of any sort – by her prospective husband. Even liberal men, the play suggests, find it hard to accept true female equality when it affects them personally. The play is light-hearted, but it is convincing in its depiction of life as a struggling writer and here it obviously draws on Cicely's own experience.

Christopher St John's play dealt with the struggle of Margaret Hughes, the 'first actress' of the title, to play women's parts on the stage and the third play performed was Margaret Nevinson's *In the Workhouse* which, as we have seen, appalled most critics. Many of the reviewers agreed with *The Times* in feeling that they wanted no part of the Pioneer Players. Needless to say their objection was political: 'We had walked in so innocently imagining that the Pioneering of the Pioneer Players was to be dramatic, not (if we may be pardoned the ugly word) feminist.'[22] Later, when the company had become more established, the *New Statesman* could write that they were: 'A real contribution to the liveableness of life in London. In their choice of plays the Pioneers have been enterprising and judicious. The acting has been excellent.'[23] Cicely's involvement lasted until, like so much else, the Pioneers disappeared at the outbreak of World War I.

This was a busy and demanding time for suffrage activists and at times it seemed as though success was near. The records show that both the AFL and the WWSL continued to hold meetings, 'At Homes' and debates very frequently. Cicely went on producing material and appearing in performances. She wrote the prologue for an AFL matinée at the Lyceum on 29 November 1912 and before that, in February of the same year, had been on the organising committee for a WWSL matinée held at the Princes Theatre. The performance concluded with another of those tableaux so beloved of the WWSL and the AFL as showcases for famous and popular actresses who supported the cause. In it the heroines of his plays appear to Shakespeare in a dream, each speaking a few words appropriate to her character:

> When Miss Cicely Hamilton, a right queenly Lady Macbeth, cried scornfully, 'We fail! But screw your courage to the sticking place and we'll not fail' . . . audience and performers alike were

as one in feeling the aptness of each brief quotation in varying phases of their common object.[24]

Life in the suffragist theatre was not always totally harmonious, however. In February 1912 Cicely wrote to complain to the Society of Authors that one of her plays had been given a pirate performance in Liverpool although she did not mention which one. In the letter she adds, 'Between ourselves some suffragists are the most unscrupulous thieves and they [? misuse] my property all over the place.'[25] It must have been galling for Cicely who gave so much to the movement to be taken advantage of in this way.

1913 brought one of the greatest disappointments of the suffrage campaign. An attempt was made to add an amendment to a bill granting full adult male suffrage which would widen its scope to include women but the Speaker ruled that if such an amendment were passed it would alter the nature of the bill so fundamentally that it would have to be withdrawn. In May the same year the government supported a Private Member's bill which would have given women the vote but it was defeated by forty-eight votes. It was in this political climate that *Votes for Women* published a brief article by Cicely called 'A Moral Revolution'. Evidently intended to console campaigners for the imminent defeat of the government's Franchise Bill, the article draws attention to the gains which have been made in the course of the campaign. Most notably, Cicely claims, women, even women opposed to the vote, have discovered that they have a role to play in public life and are prepared to demonstrate, make speeches, and even in some cases smash windows. As Cicely put it, 'The boundaries had widened for her and for all of us – the moral and physical boundaries.' Above all women had gained freedom:

> Freedom, be it remembered is responsibility, the power of making a choice – of making a wrong or silly choice as well as a right and noble one. Persons who have no power of making a choice – who do the right thing, not on their own responsibility, not on their own initiative, but because they are under the impression that they can't do anything else – may be comfortable, orderly decent souls but they certainly are not free.[26]

In learning to take responsibility for their own decisions and their own actions, women had gained a major victory even if they did not win the vote – they had won nothing less than their 'most human identity'. No article shows more clearly what Cicely considered to be the really important gains of the suffrage campaign.

Careers cannot be made simply by campaigning, no matter how important the cause, and alongside her suffrage work Cicely was busy writing and acting. Much of what she wrote was journalism but she continued to produce work for the theatre and also acted in one long run in the West End as well as appearing in a number of plays for short runs or single matinées.

In November 1910 *Just to Get Married* opened at the Little Theatre where it ran for thirty-one performances until the beginning of December. It was then revived for a further thirty performances in January and February the following year. In 1912 it was given twenty-four performances at Maxine Elliot's theatre in New York.

The Little Theatre was very new when *Just to Get Married* opened, and like the Kingsway was run by a woman; in this case Gertrude Kingston who combined the role of actress and manager and quite often directed as well – she directed this play for example. The theatre in John Street, later John Adam Street Adelphi, was destroyed in 1941 but in its day was famous for its tasteful décor – a Wedgwood blue auditorium with attendants also dressed in Wedgwood blue. Gertrude Kingston was an ardent feminist and suffragette and in designing her theatre took great thought for the comfort of her female customers:

> It is the intention of the manageress to cater for the play-going public, particularly ladies, who require comfortable surroundings while enjoying a theatrical performance, and to that end there will not be any pit or gallery, the auditorium being entirely devoted to stalls and seven boxes.[27]

It was not only the auditorium which was revolutionary in design: 'The stage has been freed from conventional stage cloths, exteriors being represented by a system of "horizon" lighting introduced with much success by Herr Reinhardt on the German stage.'[28] Women actor-managers like Gertrude Kingston and Lena Ashwell were making very determined efforts to change the nature of the theatre and make it a place where women, both as audience and as writers, could feel more at home. Gertrude Kingston's policy was to put on a new play every month but the name of the author was not released until the Monday before the play opened and the critics had written their reviews. The reason for this seems to have been that she was anxious for women authors to have their work presented and evaluated without prejudice. While this was a good idea in theory it does not always seem to have worked in practice. The reviewer in the *Vote* described the secret identity of the author of *Just to Get Married* as: 'The pleasantest sort of secret, the secret which everyone knows.'

The plot of *Just to Get Married* explores in practice the issues discussed theoretically in *Marriage as a Trade*. Georgina Vicary, an unmarried woman of twenty-nine, is introduced by her scheming aunt, Lady Catherine, to a gauche Canadian named Adam Lankester whom she wants her niece to marry. Georgina, terrified by her impending thirtieth birthday and the impossibility of facing spinsterhood, colludes with her aunt and accepts his offer of marriage. Georgina has great qualms about agreeing to marry Adam but, unlike her friend Frances who has chosen to remain single and make her own living, however meagre, by working as an illustrator, she has not been educated to look after herself. As she says, rather desperately, to Adam at one point, 'What is a perfectly useless woman to do but marry?' Urged on by everyone except Frances, Georgina keeps up the charade of loving Adam until on the day before her wedding she tells him she cannot marry him after all. She is disgusted by her own behaviour and because she has some feeling for him wants to protect him from a loveless marriage. Georgina decides to run away to her friend Frances and when she arrives to catch the train to London, Adam is in the waiting-room. As they talk over what has happened she realises what a fine man he is and that she loves him and she finally asks him to marry her provided it is not out of pity. They go off to London together to marry quietly.

The ending obviously aroused some controversy since Majorie Strachey, in her long and detailed critique of the play in the *Englishwoman* of December 1910 felt the need to defend Cicely: 'Having decided to make the play a comedy, it was inevitable that she should have that terribly abused happy ending.' It reads as though Cicely knew she had to end the play like this but that all her instincts told her that Georgina would have been better off setting up house with Frances.

Despite its – justifiable – reservations about the third act *The Times* was largely enthusiastic about the play:

> The first two acts were so good, so shrewd in observation of personal details, so true in their picture of the well-to-do family, so deadly in their indictment, so adroit in their mixture of witty comedy with dead earnest tragedy – for it was indeed almost that – that a feeble third act could not destroy their merit.[29]

Just to Get Married is an excellent example, possibly even better than *Diana*, of Cicely's consummate skill in walking the line between polemic and entertainment. Her great strength as a playwright probably lies in her combination of interesting, often challenging ideas with attractive, skilfully written dialogue. Praise for the play was universal – in spite of reservations about the third act – and that, given its overtly feminist point of view, was most surprising. In fact the play's presentation of the issues gave most trouble to those who already shared Cicely's viewpoint. Constance Tite in the *Vote* commented of the audience reaction on the first night:

> At the end of the second act the enthusiasm was tremendous – the heroine had repented of her unscrupulous hoodwinking of an honest man, and parted in wrath from her scheming aunt – but the third act was evidently harder to accept.[30]

Like most successful shows of the period *Just to Get Married* went on a national tour as soon as it closed in the West End.

Cicely's next full-length play was altogether less successful with both audiences and critics. It was first produced at the Royalty Theatre, Glasgow, as *The Cutting of the Knot* in March 1911 but it was February 1913 before it was seen in London – in only two performances at the Little Theatre by the Pioneer Players and produced by Edy Craig. It was published as a novel in 1916. At its London performance and as a novel it was known as *A Matter of Money*. The theme of the play is the difficulty of ending unhappy marriages when those involved have no money of their own and also the complexity of human relationships – the idea that passions are rarely clear-cut. Lucia Coventry is married to a wealthy man whom she no longer loves but on whom she is dependent financially. She is in love with Dr Channing, a married GP with a child. When their affair becomes publicly known, Dr Channing realises that divorce from his wife will mean professional and thus financial ruin for himself which in turn will mean destitution for both Lucia and his wife and child. Lucia's only solution is to commit suicide on the railway line.

Critical response was mixed but the reviewers all agreed with *The Times'* critic that it:

> was never in danger of becoming a mere thesis play . . . the question constantly arose – Is it really a matter of money? Is it not rather a question of love? which showed that the play . . . is not a thesis play, but a play of human hearts and sufferings.[31]

The reviewer in *Votes for Women* also felt that the play transcended the mere exposition of an argument.

> . . . the poignancy of the tragedy depends, not on the close connection between economics and morality but on the human suffering involved when human passions clash with expediency and with codes of morality . . . and [the play], incidentally demonstrated the injustice of allowing morality or happiness or both to depend upon a settled income.[32]

Cicely's concern for the injustice and unhappiness brought about by the financial basis of marriage shine through, but the very nature of the subject and the way it is treated prevent her from drawing on her greatest strengths as a dramatist. The delineation of character is excellent but the play lacks the verve and wit which make other of her plays so delightful. The *Stage* commented:

> This is, we suppose, what Cicely Hamilton had been driving at in the composition of a painfully depressing and, in parts only, technically clever piece. Her design probably was to show how mean, base, selfish, cowardly and generally despicable men are, and how loving, devoted and trusting their women folk are.[33]

One wonders if he saw the same play as the critic from *The Times*. Certainly the men in the play are not particularly sympathetic characters and Cicely does stress their egotism and self-obsession but they are not caricatures and neither are the women ciphers. Lucia's suicide does seem a little far-fetched but it is made clear throughout the play that she is a woman of strong passions, unlikely to be able to accept compromise or defeat. There is an ordinariness about Mrs Channing and Lucia's rather gruff sister-in-law which makes them very convincing. With characteristic directness Cicely had written a real 'problem play' which addressed an important issue of the day – there had recently been a Royal Commission on divorce – rather than a play like those of Henry Arthur Jones for example who often invented a trivial moral problem in order to solve it satisfactorily in the course of the action. Whatever its technical limitations it is an honest and courageous play – but its subject ensured that it never enjoyed a London run.

In April 1911 Cicely had achieved a lifelong ambition – but one that had ceased to have any real meaning for her. She appeared in a long-running West End play – George Bernard Shaw's *Fanny's First Play*. Cicely no longer thought of herself chiefly as an actress, so when she was asked to call at the Little Theatre she did not imagine she was about to be offered a part. She had directed Lillah McCarthy in the *Pageant of Great Women* and Lillah McCarthy had been instrumental in persuading her husband, Harley Granville Barker, who was directing *Fanny*, to offer Cicely a part.

The plot of the play is largely insignificant – chiefly an attack on the stuffiness of the English middle classes – but the main interest lies in the play within a play written by a young woman called Fanny. The audience of this play is made up of theatre critics whom Shaw attacks for their inability to pronounce on a play unless they can fall back on preconceived ideas about the author. Cicely's part is in the play within a play; she portrays the mother of the heroine, Margaret Knox. The pious Mrs Knox is an appealing character since for much of the time she is the mouthpiece of tolerance and good sense. Reviewers dismissed the play as 'very harmless, good-humoured, middle-aged fun', but *The Times* praised Cicely's performance very warmly. Despite its lukewarm reception from the critics the play was a great popular success: it transferred to the Kingsway in December 1911 and ran until just before Christmas 1912.

The play brought Cicely more work as an actress in the commercial theatre, again in association with Lillah McCarthy, who was by then running the Little Theatre. She instituted a series of Tuesday and Thursday matinées and inaugurated the scheme with a triple bill: George Meredith's *The Sentimentalists*, Harley Granville Barker's *Rococo* and J.M. Barrie's *The Twelve-Pound Look*. Cicely's part as Virginia in *The Sentimentalists* was not reviewed but her portrayal of Lady Sims, a downtrodden second wife in *The Twelve-Pound Look* was well received. *The Daily Telegraph* thought she played the part to perfection and *Sporting Life* considered that she gave 'a clever picture' of Lady Sims. When the play transferred to the Duke of York's Theatre for thirty-five performances in 1913, Cicely again played Lady Sims.

Cicely's success as Mrs Knox had quite an effect on her career for a while and led to her being cast as Mrs Barfield in a dramatisation of George Moore's *Esther Waters*, performed by the Stage Society. In her autobiography Cicely observed: 'There was a time . . . when a London manager whose play contained the part of a religious woman would usually think of me as the actress to play it . . .'[4]

In the play when Esther becomes pregnant out of wedlock, Mrs Barfield, unlike many employers of the time, supports and helps her, and the play contained a daring *coup de théâtre*, as the *Pall Mall Gazette* recorded:

> There is a notable movement in the first act, in which Esther's God-fearing and pitiful mistress kneels with her on the kitchen floor and the two women pray to Heaven . . . It is one of the most daring things we have seen in a modern play, violently out of harmony with the chatter of others that precedes and follows it.[35]

Cicely attributed her success in such parts to having once heard what she described as a perfect prayer at a prayer meeting she had walked into by chance. The woman who was praying spoke briefly and quietly but:

> There was love in her voice and also great need – you knew she called on God because she had to. This I remember, I held my breath and was afraid to stir, and I believe it was the same with all who heard – the beauty of the prayer had power on us.[36]

That experience helped her, when as Mrs Barfield she had to kneel down and pray on stage. It was a very difficult thing to do but she held the audience from beginning to end of the prayer. The author George Moore was deeply moved and said it was the finest acting he had ever seen and the *Star* commented: 'The dignity and fervour which Miss Hamilton lends to her work is well known.'[37]

Cicely's output as a writer is remarkable and so is the way in which she managed to combine writing with acting. In April 1912 Lena Ashwell directed Cicely's one-acter *The Constant Husband* at a special matinée at the Palladium in aid of the Babies' Home and

Day Nursery at Hoxton. The title page calls the work a 'sketch' and it is really little more than that although it does manage to make one or two telling points about the relationship between the sexes. The twist in the plot – that women can prefer a successful career to marriage – which undercuts the play's conventional opening is neatly written and wittily handled but the play can hardly be considered a major work.

Neither can Cicely's next full-length play, *Lady Noggs*, adapted from a story by Edgar Jepson. The critic of the *Stage* asked rather tetchily: 'What is Miss Cicely Hamilton doing in this gully? From *Diana of Dobsons* onwards has she not set adventurous ships on the dramatic waters?'[38] and for once one is tempted to agree. Since there is nothing political or ideological about the play the only reasonable conclusion is that Cicely wrote it for the money, the *Stage* wondered if she did so because in the play the Prime Minister is made to look extremely silly, but that explanation is rather far-fetched. The critic was probably reminding his readers of Cicely's suffrage allegiances. *The Times* described the play very succinctly as follows:

> Lady Noggs is a pretty, if slightly bread and buttery fairy tale all about a shrewd little fairy who, by the exercise of her own little wits, got 1) rabbit for the sick old woman of the village, 2) a curate-husband for her deserving governess, and 3) by foiling an attempt to steal a treaty, salvation for Europe.[39]

The Lady Noggs of the title is, it should be pointed out, an extremely precocious little girl, the sort of child who appealed to at least some Edwardian taste. The only redeeming feature of the play was the acting; none the less it ran for fifty performances at the Comedy Theatre.

In the same week as it reviewed *Lady Noggs, The Times* reported:

> Mr Iden Payne proposed to produce at Oxford next week a new play entitled *Phyl* by Miss Cicely Hamilton, but after the play had been submitted to the Vice-Chancellor he vetoed its production. *Phyl* has not at present been given elsewhere but it is stated that it will shortly be produced, probably at a provincial theatre.[40]

Phyl had been submitted to the Lord Chamberlain's department and licensed for performance at the Royalty Theatre, London, in 1911 although it had never been produced. Oxford was the only town with an independent censorship system, a system in which the Vice-Chancellor of the University sat in judgment on the plays to be performed in the town's theatres. His criteria were usually harsher than those of the Lord Chamberlain, presumably because he felt he had a responsibility for the morals of the university's undergraduates. He tended to ban anything which dealt with difficult moral issues, as *Phyl* does, but licensed revues and other more light-hearted entertainments.

In the end *Phyl* was first seen at Brighton West Pier Theatre in March 1913 and then at the Gaiety Theatre in Manchester in 1918 but it was never produced in London and its early difficulties probably prevented it from doing as well as it deserved. The play is yet another variation on the theme of marriage as a trade but is much less grim than *A Matter of Money*. Phyllis Chester, governess to the Ponsonby children, is trapped by the dreariness of her life. She has been brought up by her sister Cathy who is worthy but dull, and sees no way out of her current situation. The children are unpleasant to her and she is at a low ebb when Jack Elliott arrives. He is a totally conventional hero – rich, charming and kind – and he and Phyl begin to spend time together. Because of this Mrs Ponsonby sacks Phyl with no references but Jack continues to be interested in her and they go away together. The next act opens in Mentone where Phyl and Jack are staying at the same smart hotel as the Ponsonbys. Phyl is very happy and makes no secret of the fact that she and Jack are not married. Cathy arrives to take Phyl back home but she resists, with great charm, and when Cathy refers to her conscience she replies: 'The wages of virtue were twenty pounds a year and my keep – and the wages of sin are this.'

Cathy replies that she will take her back whenever she wants to return. In Act III Jack's friend Westmacott reveals that Jack's solicitor has spent all Jack's money speculating and that he is therefore broke. Jack decides to go to Queensland and also decides that he must give up his friendship with Phyl. He feels he has ruined her life but she, who originally believed that she only went away with him for the excitement, realises how much she cares for him. Jack asks her to marry him but she refuses, saying: 'Do you think I am asking to be paid in that way?' She says that she does not care if she is respectable, but she knows her sister will be pleased so she accepts Jack's proposal.

The play is in many ways a conventional romantic comedy but its great innovation – and presumably what affronted the Vice-Chancellor of Oxford – is in the portrayal of Phyl herself. She is an intelligent, charming and attractive woman unable to bear the terminal boredom of her situation. She is neither wicked, vulgar nor a gold-digger and her decent, virtuous sister remains loyal and does not denounce her as a hussy. She is indifferent to marriage and agrees to it in spite of herself. By the lights of the conventional morality of the time she should have been harshly punished for her behaviour but instead finds love with a good man and sets off to start a new and probably happy life in Australia. Again Cicely suggests that all women do not want marriage and that a preference for an independent life does not make them reprobates.

Cicely had been busy and successful during these years but this does not mean that she experienced no setbacks. In March 1912 she suffered an attack of appendicitis and was still convalescing in the country in May of that year. A persistent problem for playwrights at this time was that of copyright; in order to establish copyright a play had to be performed at a special copyright performance – publication was not enough. In 1909 *Diana* was published in serial form in the *San Francisco Examiner* attributed to someone called O'Brien, and Cicely had to fight hard to establish her right to the play. There were no reciprocal copyright agreements in those days and the editor of the newspaper claimed that the fact the play had been printed in England and contained no statement of copyright invalidated her claim to ownership of the copyright. Eventually she received £50 in compensation and donated £5 of it to the Society of Authors' pension fund. Piracy was also a problem in 1913 when the Society of Authors helped her to sort out whether or not a performance of *Just to Get Married* in Manchester had been authorised. Cicely always fought very hard for her rights as an author; later in 1913 she again asked the Society of Authors for help, this time with a contract for a proposed publication with Chatto and Windus. Cicely was unhappy about the amount of royalties they proposed and announced firmly: 'I always intend to receive an advance even if only a small one.'[41] Chatto and Windus do not seem to have met her requirements; she never published anything with them.

On 29 June 1914 the AFL and the WWSL staged their last spectacular before the outbreak of war. To judge from the account published in *Votes for Women* it easily measured up to the standard of earlier presentations, perhaps unsurprisingly since this 'Pageant of Great Men and Women' was staged by Edy Craig. Cicely, as usual, played a major part in the proceedings:

> There was Cicely Hamilton who combined the beautiful austerity of George Eliot with a sort of decorative Futurist, added at the last moment with the aid of paint and feathers when she obligingly turned showman to do the 'patter' for the march past of the puppets before a crowded assembly of the ordinary suffrage public.[42]

It was all flamboyant, theatrical fun, but those who took part:

> . . . were all brought together by one of the strongest instincts that can unite or sever human hearts and human relationships, the passionate desire for freedom. Woman suffrage has had many battlefields. Its Field of the Cloth of Gold, an interlude in the fight, was certainly the Pageant of last Monday evening.[43]

As events turned out it was not an interlude, more a final grandiloquent gesture.

For Cicely this was nearly the end of the happiest, most exciting period of her life. War was declared on 4 August 1914 and for her Philip Larkin's lines from 'MCMXIV' have a terrible truth: 'Never such innocence, Never before or since, . . . Never such innocence again.'[44] Everything she was to write, everything she was to think from now on would be coloured by her experience of war.

Eight

Never Such Innocence Again

It has become a commonplace that World War I marked a watershed in world history and that Europe was never the same again but, commonplace or not, for Cicely it was literally true. At the end of July 1914 Cicely and a friend spent a few days away from London staying in the Weald of Kent. In those unimaginable days before the arrival of the wireless, their failure to see a morning newspaper meant that they were totally cut off from news of what was happening in the world. In the evening they reached London: 'Where the word "Ultimatum" flared from a newsagent's shop . . . That was the beginning – the word "Ultimatum"; the sign that the world we knew from our childhood was passing.'[1]

Like so many other writers Cicely found herself unable to continue with her work – it seemed that all that mattered at that moment was the news. She was offered the chance to join a theatrical tour to the United States and knew that it would be a splendid opportunity for her, well paid and giving guaranteed work for a number of months. She turned it down, unable to bear the thought of leaving an England newly at war. Instead she joined Edy Craig and Christopher St John hop-picking near Smallhythe and worried about what was happening in France. Hop-picking was very hard physical work, especially in the hot weather of September 1914, but it could not distract Cicely from her pessimistic conviction that the German army would reach Paris. She had, after all, been educated with the daughters of German officers at her school in Bad Homburg and still believed what they had told her about the invincibility of the Kaiser's army. When the Germans were stopped at the Battle of the Marne, she regarded it as little short of a miracle.

Cicely was not one to sit on the sidelines for long and so she followed the suggestion of her friend, the journalist Vera Collum and wrote to Dr Elsie Inglis, founder of the Scottish Women's Hospitals, offering her services and citing as qualifications her ability to keep accounts, speak tolerable French and write adequately in that language. She was offered a job as a clerk at a salary of 10s a week.

At the outbreak of war many women doctors looked for ways in which they could put their hard-won medical skills at the service of their country. Within the first month a number of schemes were started by individuals and organisations for the formation of hospital units officered by women. All medical provision for the armed services was the responsibility of the army and there was, of course, no place for women doctors in the army of 1914, so they had to organise themselves independently. The Women's Imperial Service League established one hospital staffed by women and sent it to Antwerp and Dr Louisa Garrett Anderson and Dr Flora Murray organised and maintained by public subscription a military hospital of a hundred beds at Claridges Hotel in Paris. Dr Inglis' enterprise was on a far larger scale and one of its fundamental principles was that every job in every hospital should be filled by a woman. With the assistance of the Scottish Federation of Women's Suffrage Societies, Dr Inglis brought together a number of women prepared to serve in her hospitals and went to offer them to the War Office. The War Office turned them down. With the lack of vision, even of common sense, which characterised much of the conduct of the war, the army doctors and bureaucrats saw no place for women in medical units at the Front. Convinced that women would be unable to exert the necessary military discipline, they dismissed the whole idea out of hand. Undaunted, Dr Inglis arranged funding for her project from the suffrage societies, from public subscription and from the Cambridge women's colleges of Newnham and Girton, and, under the auspices of the Red Cross offered her units instead to Britain's allies. Neither France nor Serbia had a nursing profession so they were in great need of skilled women. There were three units in France, two in Serbia, one of which was led by Dr Inglis herself and one in pre-revolutionary Russia. The units in Serbia suffered terrible hardship, dealing with a typhus epidemic as well as the casualties of war, and were interned by the Germans, eventually returning to Britain in 1917. The Scottish Women's Hospitals, the only all-women organisations so near the Front, eventually won the approval and esteem of the Allied authorities. They were never given the opportunity to care for the British soldiers.

In November 1914 Cicely was among the advance guard which crossed the Channel in a severe gale and was sent to turn the Abbaye de Royaumont from an abandoned Cistercian abbey into an efficient military hospital. The Abbey was 25 miles north-east of Paris and 12 miles from the casualty clearing station at Creil. It was on the edge of the forest of Chantilly and, at the time they moved into it, about 30 miles from the trenches, although the line moved away from it during the course of the war. The Germans had briefly occupied it during the advance on Paris in the autumn of 1914 and 'the salons on the ground floor were littered with straw in which the German Uhlans had bedded their horses'.[2]

Apart from the brief German occupation the Abbey had been uninhabited for about ten years and 'the dust of centuries lay all over' when the group of 'specially selected, robust' members of the hospital staff under the command of the medical director Miss Frances Ivens arrived to begin their task. Frances Ivens was a surgeon from Liverpool with a considerable reputation for professional skill and for refusal to be defeated by circumstance. She remained in charge at Royaumont throughout the war and was much decorated by the French for her services. In a long letter, written on Christmas Eve 1914, Cicely gave a vivid account of the early days of the hospital for the benefit of the management committee back in Edinburgh:

> The abbey in all its magnificence, was ours; but during those first few days it did not offer us very much beyond magnificence and shelter. It had not been lived in for years, and its water supply had been cut off when the nuns left for Belgium. Hence we carried water up imposing staircases and along equally imposing corridors.[3]

The advance party spent two weeks scrubbing the place clean, their only source of water a single tap in a distant kitchen. Despite the dirt the icy conditions discouraged the women from washing more than their hands and faces and Cicely records that she washed as infrequently as possible. Their baggage had not arrived from Paris and they slept rolled up in blankets and overcoats on mattresses stuffed with straw from a local farm. All the craftsmen needed to put the place to rights had been conscripted into the army and it was some time before they could find anyone to attend to the plumbing, mend broken doors or repair the many shattered windows. Slowly the men they needed materialised, so repairs could begin. Equally slow was the arrival of equipment from England; they had to manage as best they could:

> We borrowed teacups from the village ironmonger and passed the one knife round at meals for everyone to take a chop with it. We were as short of lamps as we were of knives – shorter; and we wandered around our majestic pile with candle ends stuck in bottles, little twinkling candle-ends that struggled with the shadows under the groined roofs.[4]

But like many of her fellow workers Cicely had some lingering regrets when modern amenities arrived: 'We are getting electric light in now and already I find it in my heart to regret those bottled candles with their Rembrandtesque effects.'[5] It is easy to imagine that Cicely not only enjoyed the beauty and oddness of her surroundings but also the challenge of creating an efficient organisation out of nothing and against heavy odds. She probably enjoyed it the more because once again she was working alongside the sort of dynamic, forceful women with whom she had always found common cause.

By just before Christmas 1914 the hospital had its full complement of doctors, nurses, orderlies and chauffeurs with a Frenchman in charge of certain aspects of military administration such as soldiers' pay and military decorations. He had no jurisdiction over the hospital staff, but was known as M. le Directeur. At this point Frances Ivens decided that the hospital was ready to admit patients and applied to the French military authorities for permission to do so. The date of the inspection was not announced in advance and the staff waited on tenterhooks for the officials to arrive. When they finally did so the electrical work was not yet completed and they objected to the fact that one of the wards had been sited in a former dormitory on the second floor when there were unused rooms at ground level. The inspectors refused the hospital permission to receive patients until these and other defects had been put right. The staff was very dispirited by this and some of them harboured suspicions that the French authorities were unwilling to send their men to a hospital run entirely by women. There was no longer the pressing need that there had been for hospital accommodation since there was a lull in the fighting in France and the abbey was so close to Paris that it was competing with the well-equipped hospitals of the capital. Later, when the pressure was on, they were only too glad to use Royaumont.

In order to relieve the gloom engendered by the unsatisfactory inspection Frances Ivens ordered that Christmas dinner should be a fancy-dress party followed by tableaux and the staff devoted great energy and ingenuity to devising costumes out of the scanty materials that they had to hand. Cicely was called upon to make the after-dinner speech and rose magnificently to the occasion:

> Suffice it to say that her words included not only a humorous survey of the staff's weeks of heroic (and condemned) endeavours, but a deserved appreciation of the efforts of the two *cordon bleus* who had succeeded in providing a real old-fashioned Christmas dinner of turkey and plum pudding.[6]

Cicely was in her element as the director of these revels and organised the tableaux which followed dinner:

> They were given in the Blanche ward, and represented the history of the building of the Abbey and the dramatic phases of its transformation into a military hospital. To this pictorial representation Miss Hamilton contributed a running commentary of humorous inspirations which convulsed the audience with continuous and reparative laughter. Even M. le Directeur, in all his world-wanderings, had never before experienced so unique an evening's entertainment.[7]

The enthusiasm and energy which the staff put into entertainments and recreation is just one of the aspects of life at Royaumont which seems to have made it special. The experience of working there made a deep impression on many of the women and the unit had a very strong sense of identity. Some attributed this to the influence of Saint Louis, the king of France who had been responsible for the building of the Abbey: 'The soul of Royaumont is a curious, almost a tangible thing . . . It is a thing mystic and forceful that will leave us, each one of us, different from that which we were before it touched us.'[8]

Another explanation is that for most of the women at Royaumont this was their first experience of living and working with other women, women with whom they shared a supremely important task. Almost all who worked at the hospital came from middle-class families and many had never worked before. The French were particularly struck by the fact that the orderlies were women who had never had to undertake domestic work themselves and yet were prepared to scrub and clean and carry heavy stretchers up six or seven flights of stairs. The cooking was done, at least at the beginning, by two women who had taught fancy cookery at an establishment for young ladies in Edinburgh and the driving by young women sufficiently privileged to have driven their own cars before the war. These women learnt to become mechanics too and were often among the most hard-pressed of the staff. During the busiest times they frequently worked a 21-hour day ferrying casualties to the hospital. Only the doctors and nurses were professionals and as such were paid for their work. The women who served at Royaumont kept in touch long after the war had ended and continued to produce a newsletter until 1976. The Abbey itself was extremely beautiful despite having suffered much damage during the French Revolution.

> The cloisters [were] surrounded by the original walls, the Tower high above, a formal French garden with privet and box hedges, and roses and wisteria smothering the pillars, terraced gardens on top and a fountain in the middle. An artist's paradise and on moonlight nights of breathtaking beauty.[9]

In between surges of activity there was a great deal of waiting for something to happen and during the lulls the staff spent much time outdoors enjoying the countryside. The Forest of Lys was a favourite place for walks and Cicely found comfort in the cultivated as well as the natural landscape:

> And there were other compensations, whereof one of the greatest was the country round, the Forest of Chantilly and its borders . . . in those days our neighbouring villages were still country villages, and the road to Paris in springtime was lovely with the foam of orchards.[10]

Staff accommodation was in the east wing of the Abbey where, during the first winter, the walls ran with moisture. Coal had to be brought from England and so the rooms were heated by wood fires. Logs were stacked in a great heap in the entrance hall and every time anyone went upstairs she carried a log, to reduce the pile in the hall. Even with the fires, living conditions were basic:

> Our bedrooms . . . were monks' cells with stone walls and mullioned windows. There was a mattress on the floor, a packing case for bureau, basin and water jug and a rubber bath, as there were no staff bathrooms. Bats frequently flew around the room at night as monastic windows could not be screened and nightingales sang outside.[11]

Gradually living conditions improved and the staff did at least have proper beds. As they prepared the ground-floor rooms to become wards they found a great deal of furniture, much of which was put to use, and in January 1915 they were given permission to receive their first casualties. The first batch numbered only six and it was some time before the authorities at the casualty clearing station had real confidence in the work the women were doing. The Abbey's reputation for efficiency and a high standard of nursing care grew steadily but in the great rushes of work which followed 'pushes' at the Front it was enough simply that the hospital was there. They were under greatest pressure in May, August and September 1915 and in July 1916 during the Battle of the Somme: 'During that first week in July three hours consecutive sleep was an inconceivable luxury, yet no one regarded her share in such a time as other than a privilege.'[12] During the Battle of the Somme the pressure on beds became so great that the refectory was turned into 'Canada' ward and they admitted 300 patients in three days. The ward was opened on behalf of the Canadian Red Cross by Elizabeth Montizambert, who was later to become a close friend of Cicely. The injuries they treated were mostly shell, grenade and bullet wounds, with many of the most dreadful being caused by shrapnel. A particular scourge during World War I was gas gangrene caused by a bacillus which entered wounds from the soil and caused the wound to swell up with gas. The stench from these wounds was appalling and the gangrene often necessitated amputation of limbs. Careful nursing was the most effective treatment since the wound had to be bathed continuously in order to relieve infection; Royaumont had a particularly good rate of recovery from gas gangrene.

Even though most of the women at Royaumont were middle-class the distinctions between doctors and nurses and between nurses and orderlies were rigidly observed and they ate at different tables in the beautiful Gothic refectory. The doctors also had a separate sitting-room and in her capacity as senior administrator Cicely shared this and their table at meals. Only a few of the doctors were able to work at Royaumont throughout the war, most notably Frances Ivens and Agnes Savill, a radiologist who cheered both staff and patients with the pianola she had transported all the way from England. Other doctors, some very distinguished, came to work as locums. Among these were Louisa Martindale who was there in August 1915 and the Dean of the Royal Free Medical School, Louisa Aldrich-Blake. Louisa Aldrich-Blake made two visits to the hospital, in the summers of 1915 and 1916 and was such a formidable presence that the patients christened her Madame la Générale.

Cicely found her encounters with a group of women so unlike those of her own literary and theatrical circles very instructive although she felt that their experience of human beings at their most frail and vulnerable led them to 'underestimate their normal strength and intelligence'.[13] Cicely herself was a source of puzzlement to some of the other workers at the hospital, especially in her determined resistance to regulation and regimentation. She could not bear institutional life and her first instinct when confronted with a rule was to bend it as far as she could. The bicycle on which she rode round the neighbouring villages, visiting the local people with whom she had become friendly, was forbidden for private use but this did not stop her from making expeditions, partly to drink *un petit verre* with her friends and partly to escape from the restrictions of hospital life. It was not that she was unsociable, quite the contrary, it was simply that she preferred not to have sociability thrust upon her. The uniform of the Scottish Women's Hospitals was grey, with Gordon tartan facings and hatband – very suitable in Cicely's case since her father had been in the Gordon Highlanders. But sentimental attachment did nothing to reconcile Cicely to wearing a uniform and when she could she wore a French workman's blouse instead. In the early days of the hospital she did many odd jobs about the place and on one occasion an elderly Scotswoman who had joined the staff as matron stopped her as she returned to the hospital dressed in her blouse, wearing muddy boots and with a large bundle of firewood over her shoulders. Matron asked her if it was true that she had been an actress and when Cicely replied that it was she asked bluntly, 'Then what has brought you to this?'

> I cannot remember exactly what I said in answer to this astonishing query; but if she had not been so kindly, so serious and so Scotch, I should certainly have told her: 'The drink'.[14]

Other members of the staff also thought Cicely worthy of comment. In a letter dated 26 December 1914 Dorothy Harvey Littlejohn wrote home:

> . . . there is also a Miss Cicely Hamilton, a thorough Bohemian. She writes books, perhaps you have read some of them. I don't remember any of their names at present. She is the 'clerk' and a most understanding person and fortunately sees the funny parts.[15]

Cicely was by no means the only unconventional woman at the Abbey. Marjorie Starr wrote, in a letter of 13 December 1915, 'Three rather peculiar girls are sitting round the fire . . . One is smoking a pipe so you can imagine the style. I suppose they are suffragettes.'[16] The women were probably chauffeurs, many of whom conformed to the stereotype of 'mannish' women still associated with suffragettes, and there were probably others for whom Cicely had some fellow feeling. She makes no mention of friends during her time at Royaumont but since she writes so little about her friends anyway this is not surprising. She does however mention that there was an orderly, identified only as D, who filled her hot-water bottle every night. It was with just such small personal services that girls at boarding school showed their devotion to older girls upon whom they had crushes and given the affection that Cicely inspired in other women it is tempting to see D's behaviour as an example of such behaviour.[17]

Dorothy Littlejohn may have found Cicely understanding but it was well known at the hospital that she could also fly into rages. And the remark most likely to produce such a rage was the apparently harmless 'I hope I get a medal.' Surprisingly for the daughter of a much-decorated army officer, Cicely had a deep-rooted hatred of what she considered to be cheaply earned medals and she dated her prejudice to an event she witnessed in Beauvais while waiting for one of the permits without which travel in wartime France was impossible. As she watched a parade of men receiving military honours, she noticed that one of the men waiting was an elderly civilian, receiving the *croix de guerre* on behalf of his dead son.

> When the ribbon was pinned on the workman's coat, a woman beside me stirred and drew a breath – a young woman dressed all in black; and then, the ceremony over, she went forward to meet the old man. I remember a thin fine rain was falling, and they said not a word as they met; but the woman took out a square of white handkerchief, unfolded it, spread it on her hands, and stood waiting. The father unfastened the cross from his coat and laid it on the linen, and they stood in the rain and looked down on it . . . all they had received in exchange for the life of a man! Then, slowly, they walked away together; she was carrying the medal as a priest might carry the Host.[18]

To Cicely the abiding memory of that scene, a symbol of the appalling waste of human life going on all around them, justified her rages.

But life was not all grim. In her capacity as administrator Cicely travelled all over the war zone delivering food and clothes to refugees, collecting truck-loads of supplies from the Channel ports and sometimes making endless slow journeys on trains that stopped at every halt and every siding. Whatever she was doing Cicely found time to observe the people around her and how war affected them; to notice how random suffering could be so that while one village might have been totally destroyed its neighbour remained intact and the inhabitants could make a good living supplying the needs of the troops. One of her tasks was to deal with officialdom, with the endless problems of passes and permits which made life so difficult, often unnecessarily so. Cicely was harsh on the pencil-pushers, 'Good honest patriots, all busily engaged in hindering other people at their work', and despised the many soldiers who had a 'good war' safely behind the lines.

In fact Cicely was herself a pencil-pusher with a substantial workload. It was, in the main, dull work:

> No one who has ever seen military papers could possibly belittle the courage and perseverance necessary to cope with the clerical

> needs of a large hospital. Every day copious notes are recorded concerning every man in hospital, arrival or *evacué*. The details are more military than medical and offer no interest to the compiler.[19]

The part of her clerical duties which gave Cicely the greatest pleasure was book-keeping. One reason for this was the fact that she had to take the books to Paris to be audited by the Ritz Hotel's chief accountant. When the audit was complete the accountant gave her an excellent tea and kept her up to date with all the latest gossip about the war. All this made a break from the frequent monotony of life at the hospital, but she also enjoyed the book-keeping for itself:

> Once I had grasped the common sense of my figures and begun to think of them not as rows of francs and centimes, but as symbols for food, fuel, medical necessities, furniture – once I had begun to do that, they were a fascinating game.[20]

Cicely's capacity for relishing new experiences was inexhaustible, even in the middle of a war. Much less pleasant than her excursions to Paris was her attendance at the funerals of men who had died at Royaumont, a duty she found very distressing and never became hardened to. Almost as bad was dealing with the bereaved relatives who had managed to attend despite the difficulties of travel. The atmosphere at Royaumont was intensely friendly, care was given on a very personal level and relationships between patients and staff often became close; it must have felt as though she was endlessly attending the funerals of friends.

Life in a military hospital was very erratic, busier than anyone could manage for days, sometimes weeks, on end while one of the 'pushes' was on at the Front and then very quiet with nothing much happening at all. During these lulls the hospital offered medical help to local civilians but there was still time for the staff to play hockey, very popular at Royaumont, and dragoon the reluctant French soldiers into various kinds of impromptu sporting activities. More popular with the men were concerts, some of which they arranged themselves, tableaux, dances and fêtes of various sorts. Cicely was naturally often called upon to organise these entertainments. In December 1915 she produced the opening scene of *Diana of Dobsons* and played the part of Diana herself; the staff agreed that she was 'splendid' in the role. Her past as a public speaker meant that:

> The Chief Clerk is also called upon to make extempore speeches in French at concerts or at the presentation of military decorations, and never has Miss Hamilton failed to delight her audiences, French and English, by her resourcefulness on these occasions.[21]

French theatrical parties came out to Royaumont since the hospital was so near to Paris and when a party came from the Comédie Française Cicely was deputed to make the speech of thanks. The leading lady was so delighted by what Cicely said that she leapt on to the platform and clasped her in a 'vehement embrace'. Disguising any surprise she might have felt, Cicely 'returned the embrace with interest – to the applause of the assembled hospital'.[22] The poor matron who had been so confused by Cicely's past career was equally taken aback by this outbreak of Gallic emotion – and by an Englishwoman who knew how to respond to it.

Other visitors, even more distinguished, came to visit the hospital and heap praise and medals on *les écossaises*. In September 1916 the President of France himself, M. Poincaré, was at Rayaumont and Cicely and Frances Ivens turned this into a grand and formal occasion. But in spite of all the compensations Cicely was becoming restless at Royaumont. The initial challenge was over and the satisfaction of helping to run an efficient hospital in such good company was no longer enough. Before she left in May 1917 she wrote to the committee in Edinburgh; her letter makes it clear that she was not leaving in any unfriendly spirit:

> I should like to say this, those of you whose work lies at home can hardly realise its indirect effect for good upon the men and women with whom we have come into contact. I do not judge by official compliments which are always flowery – or the polite remarks of visitors; I judge by all the little things I have seen and heard, the interested and often puzzled questions of my French friends and acquaintances. So far as my observation goes, the work of our countrywomen in France stands high in public estimation; we are still accounted curious, we are occasionally a jest, but it is always a kindly jest; if we are not always understood we can say with truth we are trusted. It is something to have

> served for two years and a half with those who have proved themselves worthy of trust and for that alone I shall always remember Royaumont.[23]

Wherever she was and whatever else she was doing, Cicely was always a writer, and furthermore a writer who tried constantly to explain and make sense of what she saw. Her book *Senlis*, published in 1917, was in its way a contribution to the war effort, a reminder of the ruthlessness of the Germans and of the appalling suffering this war was inflicting on civilians as well as soldiers. Cicely liked France and felt empathy with the French people, an empathy strengthened by living and working among them for two and a half years. In *Senlis* she gives an account of the fate of the town and its inhabitants based on a visit she made there in December 1914 when atrocities still had the power to shock. The fate of the town and its inhabitants had become famous and so Cicely had gone to see it for herself, horrified at the barbaric behaviour that this war was calling forth in combatants.

As the Germans advanced towards Paris in September 1914, the French army, driven before the invading forces, reached Senlis. Many of the inhabitants had fled at the approach of the German army but others remained behind even when the bombardment of the town began. When the Germans marched into the town, believing they had driven out the French soldiers, they were surprised to encounter pockets of resistance. They met the challenge in a dreadful way. Wherever they encountered enemy fire they sent groups of French civilians taken at random from among the population ahead of them as they advanced towards the French guns. In some cases the French soldiers realised in time what was happening and held their fire but in others the civilians were shot by their fellow countrymen.

For Cicely this use of civilians was significant because it showed the totality of modern warfare; warfare in which soldiers could cold-bloodedly use civilians, including women and children, as stalking-horses; warfare in which there were no longer any rules. It was important too because it showed that the Germans had failed to recognise that certain behaviour would inevitably stir up profound loathing and hatred; that even in total war there were limits to what could be tolerated:

> It was because of the horror inspired by such sins that they

counted in a military sense. They stirred the loathing even of the unimaginative; they disposed once for all of the pacifist argument, 'What if the Germans did come; we should not be any worse off'. They made it impossible to suffer the victory of a nation that countenanced such sins.

The story of Senlis helped to harden the heart of France – and for that reason alone is worth remembering.[24]

Cicely had grown up in a military family and much of her early childhood had been spent in army barracks, a fact she regarded as a source of pride. A journalist on *Time and Tide* (26 January 1928) reported her as saying, 'It is not everyone who has the privilege of being born in a barracks' and it is tempting to see some of her abhorrence of World War I and the military tactics it threw up as the response of a woman who had grown up believing that wars were fought according to rules and that when such rules were obeyed war was no more than a necessary evil. War as she saw it in France broke all these rules and she had to acknowledge its true horror for the first time.

The Germans occupied Senlis for a week and claimed that civilians as well as soldiers had fought against them. In reprisal they summarily executed the mayor and systematically burned the town, street by street, quarter by quarter. Whole areas were razed to the ground, but others remained virtually unscathed. As Cicely sat at a window in the town four months later she wondered whether 'the sight of a banner of wanton, vainglorious flame – whether the echo of a thunder that betokened my countrymen's retreat would not have wakened even in me a most parching thirst for revenge.'[25]

Cicely is very much present in the book, exploring her own response to events, wondering how the English would have behaved in similar situations and meditating upon the nature of modern warfare. Looking down from the ramparts of Senlis she contemplated the destruction of French towns rooted in the landscape and lamented that they will be replaced by: '. . . Featureless little cities that have not grown, measured out by the block and the yard; with sham-Gothic sheds for churches, and barns built of corrugated iron in the place of good grey stone.'[26]

Her accounts of the war give a useful indication of the impact events made on thinking observers as they came to understand the many ways in which their world was being changed for ever.

When Cicely went to Royaumont she went as a pioneer; after two and a half years of war she was looking for a new challenge. In May 1917 she applied to join the Women's Auxiliary Army Corps (the WAAC). Women were not, of course, expected to fight; as its name suggests the WAAC came into being in order to provide the back-up services needed by the army and thus free men to fill the gaps in the fighting units caused by the appalling loss of life sustained in two and a half years of slaughter. Much of the work done by the WAAC was clerical and Cicely's experience at Royaumont, especially her experience of book-keeping, stood her in good stead. She was accepted into the WAAC and sent back to France in charge of a postal unit. There was, however, one problem – the army was completely unable to tell Cicely how much they would pay her as a WAAC officer; and for her this was an insurmountable difficulty.

Money was always a problem for Cicely; throughout her life she struggled to make ends meet. Unlike many women of her class she had no source of income other than what she earned herself and although her own needs were small she supported other members of her family. She never says who these people are but it was probably her beloved aunts Lucy and Amy and perhaps her sister Evelyn with whom she shared a home until 1929. Thus while other middle-class women could afford to do their patriotic duty without worrying about a salary this was not a luxury available to Cicely. She had already served with one of the most respected women's units, she was not shirking what she saw as her moral obligation but neither could she ignore her domestic responsibilities. In the end she withdrew from the arrangement she had made with the army and joined Lena Ashwell's organisation Concerts at the Front. Unexpectedly she was back in the familiar world of theatre and suffrage campaigners.

At the outbreak of war all suffrage campaigning had been suspended and with the release of the eleven suffragettes still in prison in August 1914 many of the most militant elements in the movement were prepared to co-operate with the government and use their influence with the women of Britain to mobilise them for war work. A great many women with the suffrage movement were deeply opposed to the war and later became involved in pacifist organisations campaigning to bring it to a rapid conclusion. Lena Ashwell, however, was not one of these and she saw the war as an opportunity to show what women could do – an attitude shared by Emmeline Pankhurst who, in 1915, led a government-sponsored campaign to encourage women to sign up for war work at home in Britain. Lena Ashwell had been involved in the formation of the Women's Emergency Corps, made up of the AFL, the WFL and the Women's Tax Resistance League, which established a register of women who were qualified and willing to help with the war effort. When she proposed that they should be trained to work on the land she was told that such preparation was quite unnecessary since the war would be over by Christmas. With the determination which had always characterised her, she proposed an alternative use of the actresses' talents: to entertain the troops waiting in camps all over England to be sent to fight in France. The AFL organised travelling companies to play three nights in rotation at each of the fifty army bases and by November 1914 they were performing at Aldershot and Colchester, and the following spring at Grantham, Purfleet, Newhaven and Dover.

Once most of the troops had left England Lena Ashwell offered to organise concert parties which would perform at the Front but she met considerable resistance from the military authorities. Prejudices about the immorality of actors, and especially of actresses, meant that the army was very reluctant to encourage their presence in France and Lena Ashwell had to give all manner of undertakings about the high moral tone of the material that would be performed. The Young Men's Christian Association (YMCA) was responsible for providing recreational facilities for the troops and when Lena Ashwell put her organisation under their auspices the army was prepared to agree to concert parties travelling to France. Many within the YMCA itself had grave doubts about this rather unlikely partnership but they gradually became reconciled, especially when they saw what a good effect the concerts had on the men's morale. Lena Ashwell felt that acceptance of her organisation was an important recognition of the respectability and importance of the acting profession. The first concert party went to France in February 1915 and gave thirty-nine concerts in fifteen days. The performers were paid fees of between one guinea and £7 10s a week to meet their expenses at home. To begin with the groups were concert parties, musicians and singers with one member who did recitations or told jokes. The troops loved them.

By the time Cicely joined the organisation in May 1917 Concerts at the Front had expanded its scope to take in straight acting as well as music and recitation. Gertrude Jennings, an old ally from AFL days, had run an acting company and Lena Ashwell herself had appeared in some of their productions; the enthusiastic reaction this company had received made her believe there was scope for a repertory company operating from the important base camp at Abbeville. In this town on the Somme, which was also a major railway junction, were based all the administrative and support services essential to an army and here too were the headquarters of Cicely's rep company. Like the other groups they performed under the auspices of the YMCA:

> The huts run by the YMCA were the usual scene of entertainment for the troops. There were several of these huts, six or eight at the least in Abbeville itself and its immediate surroundings, besides others scattered more distantly about the area. The 'camp-followers' of the YMCA were quartered for the most part in hostels – houses leased for the purpose from their French owners – and we of the entertainment business had a good-sized hostel to ourselves . . . Conveyance of the parties to the various destinations was by car, usually of the lorry type, into which was packed a party, its properties and makeshift effects. Make-up and dressing, as far as was possible, would be got through before starting, since dressing accommodation at huts and hangars was not always extensive or convenient.[27]

In the summer of 1917 the main focus of fighting on the Western Front had been in Flanders, around Ypres and Passchendaele, some of the grimmest, most pointless fighting of the war, with the opposing armies for much of the time helplessly bogged down in mud. By November that year activity had died down and Cicely wrote, exactly one year before the Armistice: 'Decent amusement does make an enormous difference to the men out here. One of the characteristics of life in "Somewhere in France" – a characteristic not insisted upon by the newspapers is its daily dullness.'[28]

Her comment does seem surprising, although it was presumably truer of life at a base camp than of units stationed near to the front line. Dull it may have been, but that did not mean it was easy to establish a company. In a base camp such as Abbeville plenty of actors were available from among the troops stationed there. Some were amateurs and others professionals but as they were not part of her company Cicely could not depend on them.

> At present I am struggling to establish a small repertory theatre

> for the troops in one of the army areas; the difficulties are enormous of course as one's arrangements are liable to be upset at any moment – one of my best actors has just been snatched away as a minor consequence of the German advance into Italy. All the same we get along somehow and Miss Ashwell (under whom I am working) is increasing my company as far as women are concerned.[29]

One-act plays were the mainstay of the company, although they also performed scenes from longer plays. Among the latter were *School for Scandal* by Sheridan, J.M. Barrie's *Quality Street* and *Just to Get Married*. Among the one-acters were Barrie's *Twelve-Pound Look* in which Cicely had appeared before the war and her own *Mrs Armstong's Admirer*. Cicely may well have written this play especially for the company since there is no record of its performance before this. As one might expect of a play written for performance to troops in wartime, *Mrs Armstrong's Admirer* is entertainment pure and simple. It is one of the few plays of Cicely's later career that is totally devoid of any political content; it is cleverly written but little more.

At Christmas 1917 Cicely's nativity play, *The Child in Flanders*, was performed in collaboration with the WAACs based at Abbeville and later at GHQ. It must have been very affecting for those who had spent much of the previous year amid the mud and shell-holes of the Flanders plain. In the play five tableaux of the nativity with appropriate Christmas music are flanked by two scenes set in the cottage of a French peasant. Three soldiers, an Englishman, an Australian and an Indian, seek refuge there for the night of Christmas eve on their way to Arras. When they find that the peasant's wife has just given birth to a son they give him whatever gifts they have; a mouth-organ, a muffler and a coloured handkerchief. When they wake in the morning they have dreamt of the nativity and as they leave the sound of guns changes to an angelic chorus of 'Alleluia', followed by the wartime tune 'The trail that leads to home'. The use of music in the play is very important and calls on the resources of both a choir and an orchestra; some of the musical forces may have been provided by the WAACs.

The production of *The Child in Flanders* was unusually lavish but even so did not require much in the way of scenery or props. Writing to ask the general secretary of the Society of Authors, Mr Thring, to suggest plays which might be suitable for the company to put on, Cicely reminded him of the restrictions: 'They must of course not be too exacting in the matter of scenery and though we hope to accumulate a wardrobe by degrees, dressing is still a difficulty; the men especially – as they naturally have nothing but khaki.'[30]

Cicely also asked if Mr Thring would negotiate with some of her fellow playwrights over the waiving of fees for plays which were performed to the troops, performances at which no money was taken. Mr Thring replied that out of respect for Cicely herself and because they knew she had the best interest of the profession at heart they were prepared to agree to her request.

Cicely's rep company went out into the forward areas entertaining the troops at the.Front but it also expanded its operations in the town. In December 1917 it took over the local theatre and staged productions on a commercial basis, charging admission and paying professional actors a proper fee. Playwrights whose work was used were also paid and Cicely made a point of notifying the Society of Authors. As a professional writer herself she was punctilious about payment to other writers, war or no war. Any profits from these performances went to finance the company's work. Calling itself the YMCA Dramatic Company, the company put on three one-act plays directed by Cicely, who also appeared in one of them, and later staged a more ambitious production – *The Taming of the Shrew*.

In March and April 1918 the Germans launched a major offensive on a front stretching from Ypres in the north to Rheims and the River Marne in the south. As they pressed forward the Paris–Calais railway line was cut at Amiens and German planes began to bomb targets in France for the first time in the course of the war. Abbeville was an obvious target for air-raids because of its military importance and even more because its railway junction had now become a very busy point on the line between Paris and the Channel ports. As the Germans again advanced towards the Marne as they had done in 1914, and as they bombarded the capital with the vast gun known as 'Big Bertha', the civilian population began to evacuate areas they no longer considered safe. But the entertainers stuck to their posts. In a letter of 3 April 1918 Cicely wrote:

> We are carrying on as usual – in fact we have been giving rather more performances than usual during these last few days of stress. Most of these shows, of course, are given in the YMCA

> huts and no money is taken. Some of the natives, I am afraid, are rather puzzled by this 'business as usual' attitude when they are either removing themselves further or considering doing so; all the same, though they may not admit it, I think it gives them a certain amount of confidence and I am sure that it is good for the men in the camps to have something beside war rumours to talk about.[31]

When one considers what was happening at the time she wrote that letter, the extent to which Cicely was able to maintain a stiff upper lip seems quite remarkable and yet, beneath the carefully cultivated nonchalance she was undergoing, at the age of forty-five, the most fundamental change of her life. With the bombardment of Abbeville her way of looking at the world changed for ever. The bombs that fell on the town did more than destroy buildings, they turned a witty woman in love with life into a grim recorder of human frailty – for a time at least.

Cicely had been in France since the early months of the war and had seen much that was shocking and distressing, but after those months in Abbeville, months when she was doggedly carrying on with her job under appallingly difficult conditions, she was never the same again. On the night of the first air-raid there was a concert and as the pianist Jean Buchanan played a programme of Chopin and César Franck the bombs began to fall. With considerable coolness she finished the piece and the audience did not move until it was over. When Cicely stepped outside at the end of the raid one of the drivers, a young man whom she subsequently discovered to be a 'nerve case', told her that her office had been hit and everyone in it killed. Despite the direct hit the occupants emerged unhurt from the very solid cellar in which they had taken refuge and a similar cellar saved the lives of many people when the entertainments hostel was hit a few days later. The living quarters were undamaged but the concert hall was destroyed. In the face of such frequent and dangerous attacks, which always took place at night, the authorities decided that no one except essential military personnel should sleep in the town. Every night the entire population moved out into neighbouring villages or camped out on the edge of the Forest of Crécy. The actors were taken out of the town after their performance and returned every day to rehearse and prepare their programme. Despite the difficult conditions they never failed to turn up or to carry out their programme. One actress reacted to the stress with typical British eccentricity; despite the fact that she was camping out she insisted that she could not sleep without her pink flannelette nightgown.

One night on a hillside outside Abbeville Cicely had a profound insight into the changes that had come upon civilisation, changes that could not help but destroy humanity itself:

> On one of these nights, the worst that I remember, the invaders scored a direct hit on an ammunition dump in the Somme valley; and it was while I lay and watched the glare in the sky that the world was changed for me.[32]

Writing much nearer the event she pondered the irony of modern warfare:

> In the old wars men sheltered behind walls and found safety in numbers; our states and social systems are what they are because safety was in numbers and in walls. But in our wars, the wars of the air and the laboratory, the wall like enough is a trap that you fly from to the open and there is danger, not safety in numbers – the crowd is a target to the terror that strikes from above . . . what we saw was but a promise of terror to come, a foreshadowing of full-grown achievement. Lying on the hillside one glimpsed something, at least, of the chaos of full-grown achievement. The chaos of a people, an industrial people, driven out of its towns and kept out of them; not returning as we did in the comparative safety of daylight but – by gas or continuous raiding – kept out of them. And not only kept out of them, but kept on the run; driven hither and thither, reduced to starvation and savagery.[33]

From that night on, so she claimed, Cicely ceased to believe in progress and came to think of civilisation as temporary, insubstantial, doomed to inevitable, man-made destruction. Increasingly she fitted together in her mind the implications of scientific warfare, the effect upon human morality of machines and the destruction of the individual conscience by blind obedience to the herd instinct, to produce a world view of appalling grimness; a conviction that humanity was set on an inevitable course towards barbarism and savagery. Modern society, she believed, would not be able to withstand the onslaught of the monster it had itself created – the monster of science in the service of war.

All wars involve civilians but the difference in World War I was in the scale of the involvement and in the number of former civilians who were there to witness it. Any army of volunteers and conscripts backed up by organisations consisting very largely of women was very different from the armies that had gone off to fight the wars of Queen Victoria's Empire. The only other major war in living memory, the Boer War, had been fought by professional soldiers and volunteers on another continent, and although the British had interned civilians in concentration camps, there had not been the massive disruption of population which had happened in France and Belgium, nor the deliberate attacks on civilians and the wholesale destruction of their towns and cities. The attitude which made civilians into legitimate military targets was new and shocking. As Cicely herself put it in *Senlis*:

> Modern warfare is so monstrous, all-engrossing and complex, that there is a sense, and a very real sense, in which hardly a civilian stands outside it; where the strife is to the death with an equal opponent the non-combatant ceases to exist. No modern nation could fight for its life with its men in uniform only; it must mobilize, nominally or not, every class of its population for a struggle too great and too deadly for the combatant to carry alone.[34]

There were certainly many other people at the time whose experience of this war made them share Cicely's view, but few can have formulated such complex theories on the basis of their experiences. Characteristically she wanted to understand the implications of what had happened and, not content with recording events and her response to them, she tried to fit them into a philosophical system. Both the Christian religion and earlier mythology made sense for her in a new way. Finally, she said, she understood the prohibition placed by God on eating the fruit of the Tree of Knowledge, since:

> If and when our civilization comes to its ruin, the destructive agent will be Science; man's knowledge of Science, applied to warfare, meaning slaughter not only of human bodies, but of human institutions, of all we have created through the centuries.[35]

On that 'red, evil night' as she called it, Cicely began to be convinced that if science destroys civilisations it will not be for the first time. The myths of Icarus and Prometheus, she argued, showed that other civilisations had been destroyed before and, in order to prevent further destruction, wove stories which would illustrate the dangers of scientific knowledge and explain 'the malignant power of the chemist and the engineer'.[36] Taking these ideas a stage further, Cicely postulated that the tales of dragons, demi-gods and flying carpets were legends that peoples reduced to what she called 'barbarism' used to explain the locomotives, engineering feats and aeroplanes of previous scientific civilisations: 'if our civilization destroys itself utterly, its successors, barbarian and disinherited, will inevitably look back to an age of magician and demi-god'.[37]

Cicely was not alone in her attempts to make sense of the horror of the preceding four years nor in her determination that it should never happen again. What is striking about her response is that it does not differentiate in any way between the behaviour of men and that of women. Many of her former comrades in the suffrage movement believed that women should work for peace separately from men since the world in which wars happened was a male-dominated one, reflecting the natural warlike propensities of men and men only. Women, they argued, were naturally peace-loving and co-operative and could use these qualities to bring about a more harmonious world. Cicely rejected this point of view as wishful thinking, both before the war and during it; it was not until the 1920s and 1930s that she began to make some slight distinction between male and female attitudes to war. Later she was to explore her ideas in detail in her novel *Theodore Savage*, but for the time being, 'stunned and purposeless' after her experiences at Abbeville, she went on with her life as best she could.

Nine

A Red Evil Night

Battered by her experiences in Abbeville Cicely returned home on leave in the late summer of 1918, but Lena Ashwell needed her services back in England, so instead of relaxing in London she went to join Lena Ashwell's theatre company in Winchester. In 1917 Lena Ashwell had taken the Palace Theatre, Winchester, as a base for her work in England. There were a number of military hospitals in the area as well as camps for American soldiers on their way to France and as part of the fleet was based at Southampton 20 miles away it was a convenient location. Concerts at the Front put on entertainments for all these groups as well as for returning prisoners of war. It was here that Cicely spent the remainder of the war, preoccupied by her fears of the end of civilisation and unable to concentrate on her work.

Before going to Winchester she had finished the first of her war novels, *William, an Englishman*, which won the Femina Vie Heureuse Prize in 1919. Although the book does not express so apocalyptic a vision as the later *Theodore Savage*, it makes bleak reading. Set in the war that was still being fought as Cicely wrote it, the book is mainly concerned with the moral education of William Tully but in the course of charting William's development Cicely paints a grim picture of the effect of mass movements on the moral judgment of individual citizens and a very vivid and painful picture of Europe at war. The book begins in a somewhat satirical vein with Cicely describing her two main characters with considerable irony. William Tully is a clerk who, when his mother dies unexpectedly, becomes involved in socialist and pacifist organisations. The dislike of extremism which Cicely has acquired in her suffrage days is apparent and it extends to William's girlfriend Griselda Watkins:

> A piece of blank-minded, suburban young-womanhood caught into the militant suffrage movement and enjoying herself therein . . . Like William she had found peace of mind and perennial interest in the hearty denunciation of those who did not agree with her.[1]

Cicely's tone makes clear that she considers William and Griselda's position on peace and feminism unacceptably extreme but she none the less credits them with genuine commitment to their various causes. The problem, as she sees it, is that their commitment comes from a position of almost complete, and at times wilful, ignorance and that their opinions are based on totally inadequate information:

> They had never been to Germany and knew nothing of her history and politics; but they had heard of the Germans as intelligent people addicted to spectacles, beer and sonatas and established on the banks of the Rhine. And – the Rhine being some way off – they liked them.[2]

As a result of associating only with people who share their opinions they are unaware of the wider political and moral context of their ideas. Their pacifism, for instance, amounts to the belief that:

> One should take arms against tyranny and in a righteous cause – and so [they would] have found themselves in entire agreement not only with their adversary but with the Tory Party, the German Emperor, the professional soldier and poor humanity in general.[3]

William and Griselda marry in 1914 and spend their honeymoon in a remote valley in the Belgian Ardennes where they create an atmosphere of 'truly advanced suburbia' in the cottage where they are staying. William goes on writing a tract and Griselda reads the radical books belonging to the cottage's owner. Despite a continuing ironic tone in much of this section of the novel, Cicely does depict the tenderness of their relationship well.

Since they do not speak French they remain totally isolated from the life of the village and so fail to realise that war has broken out. It is only when they decide to cut short their honeymoon because they miss the excitement of their lives in England that they meet drunken German soldiers and find out about the war. Even then they do not realise the true gravity of the situation because, 'they had come to look on the strife of nations as a glorified scuffle on the lines of a Pankhurst demonstration'.[4]

William and Griselda are taken prisoner and at this point the tone of the book changes. As Cicely explores William's response to the horrifying events which overtake him the writing takes on a new immediacy in the account of the shooting of two civilian hostages by the Germans:

> [One of the hostages] tried to speak to [his wife] again, but she silenced him by drawing down his head to her breast; she held it to her breast and pressed it there; she rocked and swayed a little from side to side, fondling the grizzled hair and kissing it to a stream of broken endearment. Her grief was animal, alike in its unrestraint and its terrible power of expression; convention fell away from her, in her tidy dress and with her dowdy hat slipping to one shoulder she was primitive woman crooning over her dying mate.[5]

Griselda is taken away from William and as he goes to search for her he becomes a credible character for the first time, caught up in his own fear and despair but also prepared to try and help an injured German soldier who had earlier been kind to him. When he eventually finds Griselda she backs away from him, terrified, and he realises that she has been raped by the Germans. They fall in with a party of refugees who help them. Cicely emphasises the generosity of the other refugees to William and Griselda and the difficulty William has in recognising what is happening to him.

To be a refugee is to be dehumanised, totally at the mercy of forces over which one has no control. All Cicely's abhorrence of what she had seen during her time in France is channelled into her compassionate account of human suffering.

Despite William's devoted and desperate attempts to take care of her, Griselda dies of the wounds inflicted at the time of her rape and William is befriended by Edith, a competent, cosmopolitan Englishwoman. When he arrives in Paris on his way home to England he experiences a most disconcerting dislocation. For days he has been travelling in filthy, overcrowded cattle trucks on a railway system over which no one has any control and suddenly he arrives in a clean, orderly city where there are trams in the street and plenty of food in the restaurants.

> There, in the open space before the Gare du Nord, he stepped back suddenly from the world of nightmare into the world as he had always known it . . . The change from horrible to normal surroundings – from brutality and foulness to the order of a great town was so sudden and complete that it took away his breath like a sudden plunge into cold water . . . for a crazy moment it seemed to him that the last few days were impossible. Their fantastic cruelty was something that could not have been . . . and he almost looked round for Griselda.[6]

This strange juxtaposition was something Cicely had herself experienced frequently as she moved about the country and she was always disturbed by the arbitrariness of war and its effects.

Back in England William now wants to fight, not because his ideas have changed as a result of intelligent consideration, but in order to take revenge for Griselda. Initially he is rejected by the army because he is too short and he is wild with anger. At the height of his rage he attends a meeting of the International Brotherhood, the pacifist organisation to which he belonged before the war. William rages that they do not know what they are talking about, 'I've seen a man with his legs like red jelly,' he says, and tells them how meaningless their work is; 'Resolutions in minute books against wrongs like Griselda's and his own!'[8] Eventually William is sent to France as a clerk.

Depressed and disillusioned he works drearily on. In this section of the novel Cicely attacks wartime bureaucrats and depicts the weariness of all those caught up in the machinery of war. While sheltering from an air-raid William talks to a cockney sailor who has been crippled. The cockney points out to William how limited his view of life was before the war: 'If you're a fool or a coward you herd with a lot of other fools and cowards and you all back each other up. So you never come face to face with yourself.'[9] As they shelter in the cellar the two men reflect upon the irony of the excitement everyone had felt at Blériot's first flight across the Channel. As the sailor remarks, 'We thought we was all going to flap about like birds and instead the most of us go scuttling into holes like beetles what the cook's trying to stamp on. That's flying – for them as don't fly.'[10]

In the end both William and the sailor are injured in an air-raid and William dies friendless in France. His experiences have not made him a hero; he never had the opportunity to put any of the lessons he had learned into practice. His is a small-scale tragedy, but a real one.

The early part of the book is to some extent marred by Cicely's ironic attitude towards William and Griselda. The transition to their role as sympathetic characters comes rather abruptly but from that point onwards the novel comes alive. Griselda is never very fully explored, although the depth of her suffering after the rape is well portrayed, but William, rendered incapable of independent thought, by his education and upbringing, tries to make sense of events and of his own response to them.

Cicely's contemporaries thought very highly of the book; the reviewer in the *Englishwoman* is representative:

> Miss Hamilton's inspiration never fails. From first page to last this is a masterpiece, and its rigid restraint adds a thousandfold to its value. It was written, we think, out of a great pity, a great love, a deep indignation and a white-hot righteous anger.[11]

Apart from the intrinsic value of the book there is some biographical interest in observing the way Cicely attempts to work out, for the first time in her fiction, the moral dilemmas with which the war had presented her. She had never been a heedless militant nor a pacifist, but in depicting William's struggle to come to terms with the inadequacy of pacifism as a response to tyranny and his reluctant acceptance that there are campaigns more compelling than the fight for women's suffrage she offers some insight into the concerns which preoccupied her at this time and which contributed to her own anguish of spirit.

Working with Lena Ashwell's company was no longer a pleasant experience for Cicely; she was still haunted by her vision of the collapse of civilisation and was unable to concentrate on anything else. She wrote a few articles but nothing sustained. Nowadays she would probably be described as having a nervous breakdown and be offered some form of medical help, but in the aftermath of World War I England was full of men, and to a lesser extent women, who had been severely traumatised by their experience of active service and only the worst cases were given treatment. It is most unlikely that Cicely sought any help; it would have been in character for her to have kept her problems to herself and coped as best she could.

In September 1918 Cicely received news that the younger of her two brothers, Raymond, had been killed at Hargicourt. He died on his birthday, 18 September: he was thirty-nine years old and serving in the New South Wales contingent of the Australian Imperial Force. He had lived in Australia since he was sixteen and Cicely had not seen him again until 1916 when he was in England recovering from a wound received on the Somme. She also saw him the next time she returned to England on leave but their relationship, while affectionate, was not close. They had had no chance to bridge the gap caused by Raymond's removal abroad when he was still little more than a child.

After Denzil Hamilton's death Raymond had been looked after by his aunts Lucy and Amy and his death was a particular blow to them. In the spring of 1919, when Cicely was again working for Concerts at the Front in France, she visited Raymond's grave in Hesbecourt in the Devastated Area, that part of France which had been rendered uninhabitable by the battles of the previous four years. She sent her aunts a cutting from a bush near Raymond's grave and they responded by sending a box of forget-me-not plants which they asked her to plant on his grave. Cicely realised that with the difficulties of communication in the area she might not be able to go to Hesbecourt again and she was thinking about this:

> And I said to myself – not as a matter of form but because I believed it – 'Whether I plant them or not, it won't make any difference to poor old Raymond; he won't know anything about it'. And on that thought Raymond came.[12]

She did not see Raymond but knew for certain that it was his presence which she was experiencing so intensely. The importance of this event for Cicely lay not in what she saw but in what she felt and she always insisted that words were totally inadequate to express it:

> I know that I was in an atmosphere I had never breathed before; I know that it throbbed so swiftly and strongly that it was impossibe to breathe in it; I suppose I should have died if the ecstacy – for ecstacy it was – had continued . . . . The fact remains that his

apparition – call it what you will – has left me with a conception of love that is beyond the human, of love that it is impossible for me, in the flesh, to attain.[13]

The spiritual dimension of Cicely's life was one that, with characteristic reticence, she kept very private and yet it was crucial to her. She was a Christian in the fullest sense of the word and believed strongly in the survival of the soul after death. After her experience with Raymond she felt that 'the dead no longer seemed very far off',[14] and so it came as no great surprise that three years later when Cicely was praying by the side of her Aunt Lucy's bed as the old woman lay dying, she felt a hand touch her forehead. Instead of following any expected course the hand then 'was drawn slowly *through* my head – right through it; and that happened twice, with a minute or two in between'. Not only did the hand pass through her head but, 'as it passed, each time – and this I will swear to – I felt my hair prickle and rise'.[15] Far from being alarmed Cicely found great comfort in these two experiences since they convinced her of the transcendent nature of love and of its existence beyond the grave.

This conviction inevitably affected the way she lived her life, for as she wrote in her autobiography: 'A life that is complete with beginning and ending will be planned and arranged on different lines from the life that is merely an episode.'[16] Her awareness that her life was only an episode, with another, better, reality at its end did not in any way diminish her determination to change human life as it was lived on earth, but it perhaps provided the strength to sustain her through a lifetime of campaigning and struggle.

It seems somewhat out of character that a woman who was in many ways so sceptical should believe so firmly in supernatural phenomena. During and immediately after World War I many people turned to spiritualism for comfort, as a way of dealing with the appalling scale of loss, and the authors of many books claimed to have made contact, usually with a dead son or husband, 'on the other side'. While Cicely did not herself consult a medium she was very much in favour of them, In addition to Raymond's manifestation and her experience at her aunt's death-bed, Cicely had two encounters with ghosts while she was at Royaumont, and other women who worked in the hospital also commented on their presence there. Cicely observed that one was more likely to see ghosts when one was in a debilitated condition and in November 1916, when these incidents occurred, the whole staff was weary from dealing with casualties from the Somme. One evening at dusk, cycling back to the hospital from visiting a friend in a nearby village, she saw a woman in dark clothes walking rapidly along the road. As Cicely drew near, the woman crossed in front of her:

> I saw we must collide, shouted something – I forget what, but probably the equivalent of 'Look out you fool' – took my foot off the pedal in readiness for the ground and put my brake hard on. And then – nothing happened. The blackness of her dress was against my front wheel – but the wheel went on without impact.[17]

At about the same time Cicely had been troubled by a poltergeist which knocked violently on the door of her room or, if she left the door open in order to thwart it, banged around inside her room. On one occasion she was already in bed when a friend brought her a hot-water bottle and then stayed to chat. As they were talking the door rattled violently and the friend got up to open it. There was no one there and Cicely tried rather lamely to explain it away. As her friend sat down again the poltergeist returned: 'Judging by the sound, a man, and a heavy man, was hurling himself against that door which (this I will swear to) actually cracked on its hinges.'[18] Again there was no one there and with almost incredible reticence the two women apparently did not discuss what had happened. The most extraordinary part of the story is that the women who slept in the next room, separated from Cicely's by a partition so flimsy that she could hear them turning over in bed, heard nothing. Cicely does not seem to have been frightened by these manifestations, merely curious about their meaning and receptive to them as another dimension of human experience.

Although the Armistice was marred for Cicely by Raymond's death so shortly before, she welcomed it as a chance to settle down again in London and resume a more ordered way of life. But the delay in demobilising troops meant that Concerts at the Front still had an important job to do and so, with a much smaller company – there were only six of them altogether – Cicely returned to France in January 1919. The company, which put on one-act plays, was based at Amiens, a town still half empty and in a fairly ruinous condition. From Amiens they travelled out to camps in the neighbourhood where soldiers were engaged in a variety of tasks which were necessary before France could return to normality. Dismantling gun emplacements and barbed-wire barricades, collecting unexploded mines and shells, salvaging stores and dealing with the vast number of unburied bodies were among the jobs being carried out by a disgruntled peacetime army. The Allies were using German prisoners of war to do some of the work and there were a number of POW camps in the area where Cicely's company provided entertainment for the guards but not officially for the prisoners. Some, however, did manage to slip in at the back of the hall and the authorities were prepared to turn a blind eye to their presence.

Cicely recovered some of her enthusiasm for life while she was based at Amiens; as a result of her background, she always felt comfortable with military men and, despite her dislike of regimentation, seems to have enjoyed her dealings with the army. In one photograph she stands, wearing a battledress jacket, among the officers while the rest of the company, male and female, sits in front. It was not only the officers for whom she had fellow feeling; she had a great deal of sympathy for the private soldiers, German as well as British, whom she met through her work. Many were very young and very homesick and on more than one occasion Cicely provided both German prisoner and British guard with a shoulder to cry on.

The landscape of the Devastated Area lived up to all Cicely's worst fears about the effects of modern warfare. During the battles along the River Somme, in an area stretching north and west from Amiens, there had been total destruction; in many places roads and railways no longer existed and: 'To say there was no whole house left in Lens is to say nothing. There was not a whole brick, stone girder, joist or floor board from one end of the town to the other.'[19] The great battles for places like Vimy Ridge and Ypres had rendered the countryside around them totally uninhabitable. Lena Ashwell was deeply distressed by what she saw:

> But as the train passed through the blackened, tortured fields, the horrible stagnant water, the poisoned earth, the ghastly remains of distorted trees, the skeletons of houses, the disused factories, the great over-lapping holes of bombarded corners haunted with black fear, one was filled with a nausea quite indescribable.[20]

Cicely's response was rather different. She was finding her work much more difficult than it had been during the war. Transport was not always easy to organise and many of those with whom she had to work were experiencing the relaxation from tension brought about by the Armistice. Strangely, this brought with it a lack of co-operation and a tendency towards extreme bad temper which was hard to deal with. Even so in the midst of her practical problems Cicely felt a curious sense of tranquillity among all the devastation. It was intensely quiet, without even the usual farmyard noises of the countryside. Cicely felt as though at last 'the land had rest':

> The extremity of its torment had brought about its rest; because it had been made brutal use of, broken and disfigured, it was unfit for humanity to live in, and there was nothing to be done for the time being but let it sleep out its exhaustion. Its torment was over – like that of its innumerable dead . . . and nowhere has spring seemed so miraculous as in those waste, disfigured places of the earth.[21]

Cicely was also very moved by the attitude of the French peasants to the shattered earth and by their determination to reclaim it and cultivate it. She had noticed this close identification with the land earlier when the plumber at Royaumont had wept as he told her of the destruction of orchards on the Somme in 1917. He had said, 'They are ruining our land; it is as if they had wounded our mother.'[22] She must have remembered that conversation as she watched a couple on the outskirts of Péronne building a shelter from debris left behind by the armies and tilling the soil of what had been their smallholding amid the wreckage of war. Throughout 1919 Cicely seems to have been even more receptive than usual to people and events around her as she tried to make some sense of the most appalling slaughter in human history.

The work of Cicely's company was much what it had been before the Armistice, although now they lived and performed under much more trying conditions. Concerts at the Front travelled all over northern France and at Douai were billeted in a chateau:

> There was hardly any glass in the windows and the linen and paper which had taken its place did not keep out the wind. There was no water except what was painfully pumped up, and no light except candles, stuck up without candlesticks on tables and mirrors.[23]

Performing in evening dress in unheated huts, often with shell holes in them, rather diminished the pleasure to be found in their work, but it was greatly appreciated by their audiences. Even army chaplains, notorious for their suspicion of actors, acknowledged how much their presence helped the soldiers' morale.

In May 1919 they moved on again, this time to Cologne, which was occupied by half a million British troops. Here living conditions were very different as they were billeted on German families and drew rations from the army canteens which were well stocked with everything an army of occupation might want – at a time when the German people were suffering from shortages of almost all basic necessities. Cicely had an advantage over most of her companions since she spoke fluent German but even so, perhaps because she understood the German character so well, she found that being billeted on the local population could be difficult. In one instance the woman of the house bullied the orderly who looked after Cicely and her companions unmercifully and generally terrorised her unwelcome lodgers. Cicely called in the billeting officer to remonstrate and since he was young and rather timid he suggested that she should do the talking: 'While I, with a firmness born of apprehension insisted that he was the man!'[24] The German woman must have been alarming indeed to drive Cicely to take refuge in womanly weakness.

While the company was based at Cologne they put on performances at the Deutsches Theater but the pleasure of acting in a proper theatre after years of Nissen huts and tents was marred by the attitude of the theatre's technical staff. They refused to work for their erstwhile enemies and the company came near to calling in the army to force them to co-operate – at gunpoint. Fortunately such extreme action was not necessary.

The company presented much the same repertoire of plays, yet again to satisfied audiences. In the course of their work they met many old friends from France and generally seem to have fitted comfortably into the life of the army of occupation. The soldiers, however, were very different from those in France – very young men called up just before the end of the war who had never seen a shot fired in anger. The roads in the Rhineland were very strictly patrolled and on numerous occasions the company, returning after a performance, was halted by one of the road patrols. Once the driver stopped so suddenly that Cicely nearly pitched through the windscreen. He apologised and explained that the raw recruits did not use their discretion and obeyed orders to the letter; this meant that if they ordered a vehicle to stop they might very well shoot without giving it time to pull up, and he did not want to take that risk.

Despite such hazards life was much pleasanter in the beautiful countryside of the Rhineland than it had been in the Devastated Area of France. Cicely was still haunted by the aftermath of her experiences at Abbeville. When she looked at the Hohenzollern Bridge in Cologne she found it impossible to see it as solid and real; to her it seemed insubstantial – a phantasm. Even so, in a city like Cologne there were compensations, pleasures which Cicely had missed during her years of service in France. Most notable of these was the opera and she went to as many performances as she could, enjoying not only the music but its unifying effect on the audience, which was made up of both German and British people.

> All our values shifted with the raising of the baton; till the curtain fell they were values of art, not politics. I believe it was almost as much for this Peace of the Music (as I used to think of it) as for the music itself that I looked forward to my nights at the opera. A genuine peace to which both sides submitted in willing agreement, and a genuine internationalism, spontaneous and unconscious, born of a common enjoyment.[25]

For a woman like Cicely who had been educated in a world in which Germany and German culture was central to ideas of western civilisation, the estrangement from that country and its music and art caused by the war must have been both strange and painful. In Britain during World War I everything German was denounced as abominable and the music of German composers, even Mozart and Beethoven, was not played. The behaviour of the audience in the Cologne opera house represented a tentative return to an appreciation of the culture which the two countries had shared for centuries.

It was not possible to overcome the gap so easily in daily life; in the main the British and Germans were living side by side but not really mixing. Cicely got on well enough with some of the families on whom she was billeted but she was always aware of the sense of separateness. Until the Treaty of Versailles was signed in 1919 fraternisation was forbidden but some people still managed to make friends across the barrier. Cicely was particularly struck by what she saw one Sunday in July as she picnicked in the woods above

Godesberg. Walking along the same path came a German family also setting out on a picnic and bringing up the rear of the party was the British soldier who was billeted on the family, with the two youngest children hanging on to him, one on either side:

> One thought of the endless graves in France – of men who had died that the road to the Rhine should be opened. And here was one who had lived to reach the Rhine – and picnic on Sundays with those who were yesterday the enemy.[26]

Unlike many, Cicely felt no bitterness about this state of affairs.

Cicely finally returned home in August 1919, somewhat out of joint with the times and aware that the national habit of hatred was hard to shake off and that instead of being turned outward it was now being turned inward to national political strife. Like so many others, eager that World War I should indeed be the war to end war, Cicely joined the League of Nations Union, but she rapidly became disillusioned with the organisation, largely because she found its members unrealistic about the causes of war. Cicely believed that all mankind was naturally aggressive, not just politicians and older people, as some pacifist organisations were arguing at the time. She believed that as a result of human nature war was inevitable – that it could be curbed for a while but that sooner or later it was bound to break out again. This point of view was quite unacceptable to those who believed that if nationalism were abolished countries would no longer find it necessary to fight. She did not agree either that imperialism was a major cause of war and thus set herself even further beyond the pacifist pale. Peace could, of course, be brought about by a total refusal to fight but Cicely questioned whether the results of such action would really be desirable.

> Peace, like most other good things in the world would have to be paid for, and the price might sometimes be heavy. We might, I said, have to see wrong done and make no move; we might be forced to condone oppression of the weak by the strong – since to take our stand by the side of the oppressed, and help him, as decent impulse prompted, would mean war against the oppressor.[27]

Since Cicely did not believe that war could be prevented she was later to turn her attention to ways in which its effects could be minimised.

Her views on war set her apart from many of those with whom she worked quite comfortably for other causes and her abiding distrust of collective rather than individual morality distanced her from the more radical socialists of her aquaintance. She had been attracted to socialism by its 'theoretical justice' but as she grew older and more politically active she began to have reservations. 'For a time I struggled against my disillusion – but then came the war, and my disillusion was complete.'[28] Her experience of collective life during the war combined with what she had seen during the suffrage campaign convinced her that the kind of society advocated by socialists could not work satisfactorily because it ignored the necessary incentives of 'private gain and private conscience'. In the light of such opinions it is not surprising that the writer H.G. Wells, a friend of long standing, said that, when the Revolution came, he would, very regretfully, have to have her put up against a wall and shot.

Her long absence from England had broken, at least temporarily, many of Cicely's ties at home. Both her private and professional life had to be rebuilt, and it was with her writing that she had the greatest difficulty. Everyone in publishing and in the theatre was convinced that the public was no longer interested in the war and therefore wanted no plays, articles or books on the subject. But at this point in her life the war was all that Cicely wanted to write about. In order to make a living she wrote what she was led to believe the public wanted, but her heart was not in it. In the end she simply had to explore her complex ideas about the nature of war and its effect on civilisation; the result was her fourth novel, *Theodore Savage*. Although not published until 1922 it represents the culmination of her wartime experiences.

Theodore Savage is by far the grimmest of Cicely's novels; Lady Rhondda said of it: 'It seemed grossly exaggerated at the time but it would be almost too haunting for our reading if it were to be republished today [1952]'.[29] For the modern reader, aware of the appalling possibility of nuclear war, it has a particular resonance – the future Cicely postulates could in many ways be a post-nuclear one. She lived long enough to know of the dropping of the atom bombs on Hiroshima and Nagasaki; one wonders if she felt then that her dreadful pessimism about science in the service of war had been vindicated at last.

The opening of the novel immediately captures the reader's attention with hints of some strange transformation in the life of the hero, Theodore Savage: 'In his youth the product of a public school, Wadham and the Civil Service: in maturity and age a toiler with his hands in the company of men who lived brutishly.'[30] The action is set in a rather vague present not unlike the period in which Cicely was writing, with the hero, whose name suggests the duality of man's nature – 'Theodore' meaning 'gift of God' and 'Savage' referring to his lower, human, self – working as a clerk in the Civil Service. He becomes engaged to Phillida Rathbone, the daughter of his superior in the distribution office. Cicely emphasises the civilised and cultured life they enjoy, full of the pleasures of music, paintings, antiques and conservation. It is Phillida's daintiness which particularly delights Theodore: 'she was a porcelain girl'[31]. In the excitement of their engagement they are only vaguely aware of a developing international crisis caused by the refusal of two distant and unimportant countries to accept the attempt at arbitration of 'the League'. In her depiction of the beginnings of this war Cicely is very much concerned to show that international organisations such as the League of Nations are powerless in the face of determined national aggression. It is significant too that the countries are so remote: the world is now a smaller place which offers greater opportunity for war as well as peace. In the same way as Britain was drawn into World War I, by the need to honour a treaty, the country enters hostilities even though it has no quarrel with either combatant. The politicians, Cicely suggests, have allowed Britain to become embroiled because they have given in to mass emotion.

At first the people are excited and united 'in the new comradeship born of common hatred and common passion for self-sacrifice'.[32] Theodore is distressed to see that even Phillida shares in the general elation. For a long time the fighting does not reach England but Theodore and Phillida are separated as he is sent to York and she remains behind to do hospital work. Once the war begins in earnest it is unlike any war that has gone before. Civilian populations are the main target:

> War, once a matter of armies in the field, had resolved itself into an open and thorough-going effort to ruin enemy industry by setting the people on the run; to destroy enemy agriculture not only by incendiary devices – the so-called poison-fire – but by the secondary and even more potent agency of starving millions

> driven out to forage as they could . . . displacement of population, not victory in the field became the real military objective.[33]

For Cicely this is war at its most unjustifiable; a war fought not against tyranny but in response to the workings of supra-national organisations and a war in which civilians are in the front line. It is a war in which all the developments of modern science are used for the destruction of other human beings. Before hostilities have even begun a friend of Theodore called Markham, who is himself a scientist, says 'If the human animal must fight – and nothing seems to stop it – it should kill off its scientific men.'[34] Even if Cicely did not advocate quite such extreme measures she did believe that some restraint was necessary and she uses this novel to dramatise what she imagined might be the results of a failure to impose such restraint. After some weeks of systematic attack from the air the government loses control of the population and the civilians panic and begin to move randomly about the countryside, 'a horde of human rats driven out of their holes by terror, by fire and by gas'.[35] Food supplies are rapidly depleted or destroyed and Theodore finds himself guarding a depot which stores food for the army. Civilians storm the depot:

> Inhuman creatures, with eyes distended and wide, yelling mouths, went down with their fingers at each other's throats, their nails in each other's flesh . . . Theodore clubbed a length of burnt wood and struck out . . . saw a man with a broken, bloody face and a woman back from his shrieking.[36]

With the destruction of the camp Theodore wanders across the ravaged face of the countryside seeking food and shelter. Survivors are concerned only with finding enough to eat and are wary of each other. Humanity is reduced to scavenging and even, in extreme cases, to cannibalism. All ideas of society and co-operation have disappeared along with the rest of civilisation.

For most of the time he is alone. On one occasion he meets a dying writer who says that events prove that religion was right and that mankind is basically evil:

> We never faced our own possibilities of evil and beastliness . . . took no precautions against them. We thought our habits – we called them virtues – were as real and natural and ingrained as our instincts; now what is left of our habits?[37]

Eventually Theodore is joined by a young working-class woman, Ada. Cicely makes much of their class difference and of Ada's dependence and passivity. She is the product of urban, industrial society, quite devoid of inner resources:

> Having lived all her days as a member of a crowd, she was a creature incomplete and undeveloped: she had schooled with a crowd and worked with it; shared its noise and its ready-made pleasures . . . She was a buxom, useless and noisy young woman – good-natured, with the brain of a hen; incapable alike of boiling a potato or feeling an interest in any subject that did not concern her directly.[38]

Cicely's depiction of Ada depends rather on stereotypes – she always speaks in stage cockney for instance – and, although this helps to make a point about the demoralising effect of industrial society, it is rather a barrier to a modern reader's ability to become involved with Ada as a character. On the other hand, Cicely has considerable sympathy with Theodore and makes the point that although privation initially drives from his mind every thought except that of how to survive, once his baser needs have been met his educated intellect provides him with material for speculation and the means to pursue these speculations.

Theodore and Ada live alone together in the woods for several years and during that time their relationship becomes a sexual one. During the same period others who have survived have begun to cultivate the land a little and become skilled hunter-gatherers and, most importantly, once food is more abundant have begun to band together in communities. Eventually Theodore and Ada begin to look beyond their immediate environment. Theodore always hopes that somewhere there will be people with whom he can talk and who share his memories of life before the Ruin, as he calls it, and Ada continues to believe that somewhere there is still a world of shops and picture-palaces. When she becomes pregnant Theodore is driven by her fear of giving birth alone in the wilderness to seek other human beings.

While searching, he is taken prisoner by a group living in a crude settlement. Before Theodore and Ada are allowed to join the group he first has to satisfy the tribe's leader than he knows no science – that he is 'a plain man like us and without devil's knowledge'.[39] At first he does not understand why this is so important but comes to realise that ignorance is a virtue in this community. For generations people have revered education but: 'Now they were seeking to live as the beasts live, and not only the world material had died to them, but the world of human aspiration.'[40] The evolution of this society follows the pattern of earlier human history. Their religion centres on a wrathful, Old-Testament God to whom blood sacrifices are made in atonement for sin. Women are subservient and, 'To a fanaticism dominated by the masculine element the pains of child-birth were once more an ordinance of God.'[41] When their children are born Theodore has to swear that they will not be taught 'the forbidden lore of the intellect'. He has begun to think in mythic terms and wonders then if the story of Lucifer may be merely the story of a scientist who brought ruin on his civilisation. He also makes the connection between the insistence on ignorance and the biblical prohibition, 'Thou shalt not eat of the fruit of the Tree of Knowledge! Thou shalt not eat . . . lest ye die.'[42]

He then comes to see that science and warfare are a literally fatal combination and that the only way to avoid destruction again is to forbid the growth of scientific knowledge.

> So, in times past, had arisen – and might again arise – a scientific priesthood whose initiates, to the vulgar, were magicians; a caste that guarded science as a mystery and confined the knowledge which is power of destruction to those who had been trained not to use it.[43]

Here he is expounding the view that myths prove that scientific civilisations have existed in the past and that they have destroyed themselves just as modern society is poised to do. Surrounded by ignorance and fear, Theodore is one of the few remaining guardians of western culture:

> With him and his like would pass not only Leonardo, Caesar and the sun of Messidor, but Rosalind, d'Artagnan and Faust; the heroes, the merrymen, the women loved and loving who, created of dreams, had shared the dead world with their fellows created of dust . . . Once deemed immortal, they had been slain by science as surely as their fellows of dust.[44]

Because people are violent and cruel the deities they worship are cruel warriors who keep them in thrall through fear but: 'The heaven of the future would find room for gods who were gracious and friendly; for white Baldurs and Olympians who walk with men and instruct them . . . The rise, the long, upward struggle of the soul of man was as destined and inevitable as its fall.[45]

Theodore lives to a great age and even before his death is viewed as a wizard because he not only remembers the Ruin but understands its causes. After his death he becomes a mythic figure – an amalgam of Adam, Merlin and Frankenstein.

Much of the impact of the early part of *Theodore Savage* derives from its depiction of suffering. The emphasis is on hunger and the horror felt at the distortion of the familiar. Cicely skilfully chooses details which will make the terror convincing: 'At the entrance of the village half-a-dozen skeletons lay sprawled in the grass-grown road, and a robin sang jauntily from his perch on the breast-bone of a man.'[46] Always in the background is the world of light and music, the world of Theodore's youth. The end of the novel loses all narrative impetus and becomes an exploration of Cicely's ideas about the nature of history and human society and the place of science in a truly civilised society. Cicely's insistence that human beings must find a way of using science only for peaceful purposes, gives the book considerable power. To read it now, when even the peaceful applications of science are in danger of destroying the earth, is to recognise how far in advance of her time Cicely was. While many flinched at the grimness of her vision, others recognised the truth of what she was saying. The reviewer in *Time and Tide* suggested that politicians were among those who should be forced to read the book in order to understand 'the nightmare that threatens us if we cannot stop the mad process on which we are now engaged'.[47]

Theodore Savage was the major working out of Cicely's ideas about the effect of science on civilisation and, although it was a theme to which she was to return in the future, she was now able to lay it aside for a while and concentrate on other matters. Even before the novel was published she had immersed herself in a variety of new activities and causes.

Ten

Equality First

In the 1920s Cicely became famous; she was interviewed, profiled, photographed and asked for her opinion. She had enjoyed some fame at the time of the first production of *Diana of Dobsons* and within the suffrage movement, but she was by no means as well known then as she became in the 1920s. Throughout the decade Cicely worked mainly as a freelance journalist, writing for newspapers including the *Daily Mail*, the *Daily Sketch*, the *Daily Mirror*, the *Daily Express* and the *Yorkshire Post*. She also contributed to numerous magazines and journals and spoke a good deal in public. As ever, she had opinions on all the important issues of the day and now had little difficulty in finding a forum for her ideas in the press. Her provocative, lively articles seem to have appealed to editors and readers alike and success bred success. In 1922 Cicely was fifty and at the stage of her career when she could expect to reap some professional reward for all the years of hard work. Her reputation as a journalist was high; she was often described as 'the brilliant journalist Miss Cicely Hamilton'. She wrote on a very wide range of social and political issues but, not surprisingly, was particularly in demand as a writer on women's issues. In her autobiography she plays down her continuing involvement in feminist politics but in fact she went on campaigning on feminist issues, in many cases until the end of her life.

Feminist activity in the twenties is a topic about which many misconceptions exist, largely because it has been very incompletely researched. Because much of the writing about feminism in the earlier part of the century has tended to concentrate on the struggle for the vote and because women over thirty were granted the vote in 1918, the less glamorous campaigns of the 1920s have been somewhat overlooked. It is true that the militancy of the pre-war period was over for good and that many suffragettes (notably Christabel Pankhurst and Annie Besant) diverted their energies into other pursuits, but there were still a great many women campaigning on a great many issues.[1]

The multiplicity of single-issue campaigns is one reason why the impact of 1920s feminism has seemed slight to later generations, but in fact many women, Cicely among them, were still campaigning, as they had always done, for one thing – complete equality with men. It is perhaps not surprising that Cicely was prepared to continue the struggle with real commitment – unlike many others she had never seen the vote as a panacea for all the social ills which beset womankind. She had always believed that the suffrage campaign was a way of questioning society's attitudes to women and winning one battle did not mean that they had won the war. The kind of campaigning needed now was less dramatic, less eye-catching. Sitting on committees working in detail on proposed legislation, drafting proposals and lobbying members of Parliament lacked the glamour of processions, plays and hunger strikes, but it was part of the reality of citizenship.

There were some public campaigns, notably on equal pay, but feminists were working now as pressure groups dealing with those in power rather than mobilising public opinion or trying to shame the government into granting their demands by flamboyant demonstrations. In the course of the decade Cicely was to make some odd alliances but at heart she remained what she had always been, an 'equality' feminist. There was much talk at the time of 'new' feminism, campaigns like that for 'endowments for mothers' – effectively family allowances – which emphasised women's difference from men and argued that instead of campaigning for equal pay women should be paid to stay at home and look after their families. Cicely's position was well expressed by her close friend Elizabeth Abbott writing in the *Women's Leader* in 1927.

> The issue is not between 'old' feminism and 'new' feminism. (There is no such thing as 'new' feminism, just as there is no such thing as 'new' freedom. There is freedom and there is tyranny.) The issue is between feminism – equalitarianism – and that which is *not* feminism.[2]

Cicely started the decade in Geneva, as press secretary for the first pre-war meeting of the International Woman Suffrage Alliance. The Alliance had been founded in Berlin in 1904 largely at the instigation of the American suffragist leader Carrie Chapman Catt, who was still its president at the time of the Geneva Conference. The Alliance existed to bring together women from suffrage organisations all over the world to co-operate on women's issues of international concern. It placed particular emphasis on campaigns about working conditions and provision for the needs of working women but was also much concerned with using women's solidarity to fight against nationalism and for peace. It published the journal *Jus Suffragii* as a means of linking the various national branches between conferences and Elizabeth Abbott later became its editor.

At this time Elizabeth Abbott, who was secretary at headquarters, had the task of asking Cicely whether she would take on the job of press secretary. Some thirty-three years later she recalled their first meeting. The committee felt that issuing communiqués from a gathering at which French and German women would meet for the first time since the end of hostilities would be a delicate task but:

> All felt that it could safely be entrusted to Cicely, who could see the small joke as well as the large issue and put both in a form acceptable to the Press. That first interview lies very plain in my memory . . . Quiet, still, almost mono-syllabic, with now and again a questioning or assessing look from those wonderful grey blue eyes . . . So to Geneva she came: and as a result no Conference had a better kind of publicity, for in addition to being actress, playwright and author, she had a flair for the best kind of journalism.[3]

Praise for the work of the press gallery at the conference was universal – clearly Cicely ran a tight ship – but Elizabeth Abbott's account suggests that they managed to enjoy themselves as well. At times nothing significant happened and they had no need to make press statements while at others working overtime meant a good excuse to cut attendance at formal dinners and receptions and dine al fresco on bread, cheese and wine.

Cicely's own experiences during the war made her particularly sensitive to the significance of this meeting.

> Yet, for all the daily smoothness and ease of the proceedings, to one spectator at least it was curiously moving to see on one and the same platform women who had sent their sons and brothers to tear the heart from each other's countries, and to remember what these quiet and businesslike women had been thinking, longing and praying in the years since they last met together.[4]

Many of the delegates to the conference came from countries where women had had the vote since 1913, the date of the previous conference, but there were others, including the host nation Switzerland, where women were not yet enfranchised. Even so, much of the discussion concerned topics other than the vote. The conference passed a resolution on peace and laid out a programme of women's rights political, personal, domestic, educational and economic, and moral. It also passed a resolution calling for an annual International Women's Conference under the auspices of the newly formed League of Nations to deal with women's issues internationally. Cicely, still preoccupied with ways of preventing future wars, considered this resolution quite inadequate because it reflected an attitude 'that is to say, of desire, more or less vague and more or less ardent, for a method of preventing warfare – and but little definite plan or idea of how to attain the end desired.'[5]

Cicely regretted that no one had really addressed the issues she considered important: the fundamental causes of bloodshed. She believed that the delegates had failed to consider adequately the part women could play in preventing future wars because they did not accept the premise that mankind was naturally combative, nor did they realise the magnitude of the threat the world lay under. Women, she conceded, might be able to act as 'a drag and a counter-weight' to the fighting spirit of men, but she doubted whether that would be enough. The deliberations of the conference on the subject of world peace lacked, she felt, the necessary sense of urgency:

> Even admitting that the philanthropic motive is the finer and higher, there can be no doubt that the motive of self-preservation has far more vehemence and drive behind it; humanity conscious that its life was at stake, that it could not continue to make war and exist, would – if the present League of Nations be found impossible – insist on discovering an alternative. Would insist through failure after failure – trying one expedient and another.

> The dread of disaster – man being what he is – is a mightier force than benevolence; and it may be the salvation of the race depends not on education directed to 'a greater and truer understanding of all the peoples of the world' but on fear that is frankly selfish – and enlightenment born of that fear.[6]

In the account of the conference it is possible to see the beginnings of the split between 'equality' feminism and the so-called 'new' feminism. The delegates agreed to divide the Alliance into two sections, for the enfranchised and the unenfranchised countries, and in so doing recognised the far greater possibility of the development of women's rights once the vote had been won. It was within discussions concerning the enfranchised countries that the split became apparent; over 'Endowment of Motherhood' and protective legislation in particular. For the time being the conference did not include demands for any payment other than that of widows' pensions in the Charter and agreed that 'no special regulations for women's work, different from the regulations for men, should be imposed contrary to the wishes of the women themselves'. Equality' feminists, Cicely and Elizabeth Abbott amongst them, were resolutely opposed to any attempt to restrict women's opportunity to work in any occupation or under any conditions. The move in the direction of special legislation for women, even if women themselves agreed to such legislation, was seen by the 'equality' feminists as a dangerous move in the direction of protective legislation which could be used to restrict women's opportunities for employment.

Cicely's involvement in the suffrage conference reconnected her with feminist campaigns and campaigners after the gap enforced by the war. Although she had not abandoned her concern with educating the rest of the population about the real causes of war, despite the profound disagreements of some of her closest friends – Elizabeth Abbott for instance – she had relaxed enough to concern herself once more with a wide range of social and political issues.

When the conference ended Cicely took advantage of her lack of ties at home and set off for Austria to look at the work being done by the Save the Children Fund to relieve the suffering caused by widespread famine both during and after the war. The Austrian currency had become virtually worthless and so many who had formerly been prosperous were reduced to standing in line at soup-kitchens. In the aftermath of war a neglected agriculture and crippled industry were unable either to generate wealth or to feed the population. As Cicely travelled around the country and became aware of the suffering of the Austrian people she began to feel guilty about the artificial wealth granted to her by the rate of exchange, and the food this wealth enabled her to buy:

> I don't say I ever went hungry during those weeks in Austria, but I know that my meals were fewer than usual, for the simple reason that my usual enjoyment of the pleasures of the table was absent; the memory of people who stood in queues for soup was apt to give a bitter taste to one's own more varied meals.[7]

Her experience in Austria made Cicely aware that food shortage leads to tribalism: a hungry community trying to keep what little food it has for itself. This insight became one of the underlying themes in *Theodore Savage*.

Scrupulous as ever, Cicely handed some of her expenses back to the Save the Children Fund and gratefully crossed the border into Switzerland where she ate a large breakfast in celebration of the fact that once more she could 'eat to enjoy', without any of the guilt which had accompanied her meals in Austria.

On her return to England Cicely became involved in several different organisations and wrote for a great variety of journals, but perhaps the most important focus for her at this time was the weekly journal founded by Lady Rhondda, *Time and Tide*, which first appeared in May 1920. A pioneering publication in every way, it was owned, managed and written entirely by women and was totally independent of any political party. Its purpose was to inform and entertain its readers, whether male or female, but its policy reflected the concerns of the women who had newly won the vote and it was committed to keeping them well informed about the political topics of the day so they could make responsible use of their rights of citizenship. By meticulously documenting the activities of the government of the day and by recording how MPs voted on issues of concern to women, *Time and Tide* helped women to identify the areas in which they could act as an effective pressure group; they could be effective because they were informed.[8]

In addition to political coverage there were articles on the arts, books, theatre, music and (later) cinema reviews and short fiction. There were some regular columnists and other journalists who contributed very frequently – Cicely was in the latter category although during the 1930s she did write regular book reviews. She was also, briefly, *Time and Tide*'s drama critic, although this role was more often filled by her friend Christopher St John, who had also, early in the journal's history, written a regular column on music. Cicely's fellow contributors were a distinguished collection of women. Some, like Elizabeth Robins, were old friends; other like Winifred Holtby became friends because of *Time and Tide*. The journal was important as a means of bringing women's writing to a wide public, but the women whose work it published were by no means unknown and most of them were already professional writers. Virginia Woolf contributed occasional articles and short stories, and writers as disparate as Rose Macaulay, Rebecca West, E.M. Delafield and Naomi Mitchison appeared in its pages.[9]

Lady Rhondda believed passionately in the importance of *Time and Tide* and made her regular contributors and especially the directors feel special: they were women who were actively changing public opinion, in the vanguard of the post-war women's movement. One way in which she did this was to entertain the Board formally and when Winifred Holtby became a member of the Board in 1926 she was very impressed by these occasions, as Vera Brittain recorded:

> Her eager youthful delight in attending the regular Board dinners at Lady Rhondda's flat was quite unconcealed; everybody wore their best clothes, and she brought one or two new evening dresses in which to enjoy the still awe-inspiring society of Cicely Hamilton, E.M. Delafield, Professor Winifred Cullis and Rebecca West.[10]

Cicely's contributions to *Time and Tide* were many and varied, sometimes appearing once a week, at other times, presumably when she had other work on hand, no more than a few times a year. Lady Rhondda's editorial hand was light and she allowed her friend considerable latitude; Cicely's articles often stirred up controversy but even today, when some of the issues they address are long forgotten, they are never dull. Cicely saw herself as something of a gadfly, provoking controversy, refusing to mouth accepted orthodoxies on any issue and relishing a good argument:

> I wrote for the paper even in its infancy and, for several years now, have been one of its directors – often in complete and happy

disagreement with the views of other, more progressive members of the board. (I cannot imagine myself living or working quite happily with people who always see things as I do.)[11]

By the 1920s Cicely had developed very decided and personal views on such issues as democracy, collectivism and individualism, and the causes of war. In some respects her views may seem reactionary to a modern reader and they have to be seen in the context both of Cicely's own experience during World War I and of the intellectual and political debates of the time. There was one area where she did not modify her views: women's rights. She remained an implacable 'equality' feminist, committed to a woman's right to choose or reject marriage and/or motherhood. Her articles in the earlier 1920s tend to be largely on political and feminist topics but later in the decade and in the 1930s her articles become more wide-ranging and more often have at least some touch of humour in them.

In 1921 Cicely wrote a series of articles under the general title 'The Commonsense Citizen' in which she examined such topics as the 'meaning of Government' and 'the destructive principle'. In much of her writing on political topics Cicely explored the shortcomings of existing systems and doctrines, and attempted to show what aspects of human nature made such shortcomings inevitable. In Cicely's view:

> The political and constitutional history of the human race is the history of an unending conflict between the will to live and the will to self-direction, between the inborn craving for security and the impulse towards self-government, personal, tribal, constitutional.[12]

Thus the first function of a government is to provide security while at the same time allowing a great deal of self-determination. Cicely never makes entirely clear how this is to be achieved. Communism is, for Cicely, quite unsuitable since 'The idea of Communism runs counter to human experience by demanding complete, not partial, service to the group.'[13] By failing to recognise people's need for solitary and independent opportunity to 'take to the wilderness apart' communism is denying its adherents an essential opportunity:

> But, whatever form it takes, the wilderness is necessary to the

> development of the group as well as the development of the man; if human experience counts for anything the group owes most, if not all, of its progress to those who can stand outside its influence and give it only partial service.[14]

Thus, Cicely argues, collectivism seriously limits human potential which in turn restricts all aspects of human development, both personal and political. Furthermore, she says, collectives do not create, they destroy:

> I sometimes wonder how far the average Labour leader understands what is the real obstacle to many of his publicised aims and aspirations: the fact, I mean, that he is endeavouring to create new systems and institutions with an instrument that can only destroy? Has experience yet taught him that the creative or constructive impulse is a product of the individual mind – which works apart, often slowly and not to order? Or does he still believe that collective action – a number of men acting all together, thinking all together – can be used for any purpose that is not destructive?[15]

Reading this article one is forced to ask what it was that made Cicely so dismissive of her own political experience. She had been a leading member of one of the great collective actions of the century – the campaign for the vote – and yet she was prepared to dismiss all collective action as negative or destructive. True, she had expressed her reservations at the time, as for example when she witnessed the Albert Hall riot, but this wholesale condemnation is hard to accept. Sometimes it seems, she was provocative simply for the sake of stirring up a good old row, but her experience of the war, a supreme example of the collective spirit in action, and the development of socialist states and socialist governments in its wake drove her to oversimplify the issues. If she was to issue a warning against the dangers of collectivism, especially to intellectuals, she could not be half-hearted; the dangers had to be thrown into high relief and any mitigating circumstances ignored. There remains the irony that, while arguing so vehemently that all creative impulses came from individuals, she was herself prepared to give a great deal of time to working with organisations committed to bring about change. True, there was room within these organisations for dissent and disagreement but by the very fact of belonging to them she was surely acknowledging that in some circumstances groups are more effective than individuals. Whatever group Cicely belonged to, however, she did so in response to the promptings of her own conscience and it was to her conscience that she owed her first allegiance. She knew that collective action could be effective but she was only prepared to condone it if members of the group took individual responsibility for their actions; no cause was important enough to justify the reduction of human beings to mere unthinking cogs in a great machine. Indeed she went so far as to argue that the cause was itself invalidated if collective rather than individual responsibility took over since there was no such thing as a collective conscience. Some of her objections to socialism sprang perhaps from her own very strong sense of duty; she found it hard to accept a system which placed more stress on rights than responsibilities. Whether or not one agrees with Cicely's position on all these issues, it is important to recognise and value her commitment to political education and to making the world a place in which the events of 1914–18 could not be repeated.

In her writing about war and its prevention Cicely starts from the position that man is naturally combative and that up until now communities have been held together by the threat of attack from outside and that when the threat vanishes the sense of community also vanishes. Mankind should, she argues, be addressing the vitally important issue of how to 'Discover a method of combining men into communities, brotherhoods, and fellowships that does not involve antagonism and an appeal to the combative instinct . . . And on the solution of that problem depends, it may be, the future of civilisation.'[16]

In the same article she also speculates on whether democracy is an innately inefficient sort of government or whether 'the inefficiency that has hitherto characterised [it] is merely the result of a clumsy working and arises from the multitude's lack of political experience'.[17] Both these discussions lead up to what is probably for her the most important part of the article: the question of whether scientific knowledge, with all the power for destruction that it entails, should be freely available or whether, given man's combative nature and the inefficiency of democratic institutions, it should be restricted in some ways to those who have been trained to use it safely:

> . . . it is the achievements of science that, by bringing the ends of

> the earth together, have raised up new enemies and made possible the slaughter of the human race on a scale undreamed of by our fathers. We are not yet at the end of the achievements of science; and it remains to be seen what measure of personal and political freedom is compatible with our growing knowledge of the secrets and mysteries of nature.[18]

As so often, Cicely was ahead of her time in identifying an important issue. The late twentieth century has seen much erosion of personal and political liberty as a result of the desire of those in power to preserve the secrecy surrounding a wide range of military and peaceful operations. The nuclear industry is only the most obvious of many examples. Cicely's ideas must often have seemed alarmist at the time but in many cases her warnings have proved well founded.

Her ideas and the forcefulness with which she expresses them spring from a passionate desire to make people think about what she sees as the central issues – before it is too late. In an interesting article, 'The Peacemaker as Firebrand', published on 15 September 1922, she discusses the paradox that although women are usually the peace-loving half of humanity, there have been a disproportionate number of women political extremists. Although only one regiment of women fought in all the campaigns of World War I, women like Countess Markievicz had been prominent in national independence struggles. She attributes this to the emotionalism prevalent among political extremists of both sexes and the consequent willingness of male extremists to accept female comrades in arms while conventional politicians prefer to do without women's assistance. Interestingly Cicely does not consider that women's pacifist tendencies have any claim to moral superiority – they are simply essential for the survival of the race.

> the real test of women, as citizens and politicians, will be the extent of their power of inducing the other half of humanity to adopt their own non-fighting habits. These, be it noted, are not necessarily more admirable or virtuous than the habits of the combative or masculine half of humanity. Their claim to preference is simply this: they are the only human habits compatible with the continued existence of a world bent on progress in science and mechanics, with civilisation as we know it.[19]

True to her origins Cicely could not bring herself to condemn militarism out of hand, but she did have sharp words for the male politicians who resisted the presence of 'ordinary' non-extremist women in politics.

> Remembering the need of the world for quiet days, there is something of irony in the reflection that the tendency, so far, has been to exclude from political influence the 'normal' type of woman whose instinct and method is non-combative; and to make the path straight for the feet of the exception – whose creed is intolerance and whose method is unreasoning emotion.[20]

Her assertion that women, unlike men, were not warlike was Cicely's one concession to any fundamental difference between the sexes. At least as far as political and economic issues were concerned they were, she argued, the same; it was only the treatment they received which was different and these differences could and should be eradicated.

In the 1920s feminists, both veterans of the suffrage campaign and younger women, were concerned that they were not making as much progress as they should do now that they had the vote. Cicely's explanation for this was simple: women had been granted the vote at a time when voting was not uppermost in anyone's mind:

> it is safe to say that at the moment the measure enfranchising women became the law of the land a large proportion of those concerned would have been stirred to far greater emotion by the news that Big Bertha had exploded or that bacon had gone down threepence. And this lack of immediate enthusiasm or protest, so far from being reprehensible, showed a praiseworthy sense of proportion; food and the destruction of enemy armaments were of far more importance at the moment than the status of women and the ballot box.[21]

Cicely did not see this as necessarily a cause for concern; 'hence (in view of the recent and very real advance) there is no need for despondency over the present slump in women's movements and achievements'.[22] Such a great advance was bound to be followed by a check and the issues were no longer so clear-cut: 'Unenfranchised, we had our common grievance of exclusion whereon, whatever our views or interests, it was easy to concentrate and hammer; enfranchised, we must needs be class and sectional, divided by our varying needs.'[23]

The problem now facing women was how to make the best use of their citizenship, since 'Political enfranchisement counts for little beside the economic independence which, in some form or other, is the ultimate aim of feminism.'[24] But, she argues, women's quest for this economic independence must not drive them to seek only safe occupations – the Civil Service, for instance – since if they do their independence and thought will be stifled. Working in such organisations did not entail taking risks – which Cicely considered an essential part of a productive life – and she saw such employment as dangerous to the future of women: 'Hence there is probably no more excellent way of ensuring the political subjection of women than by directing their best and most promising brains to a form of employment which covers up failure and eliminates personal risk.'[25]

Cicely was committed to making sure that women got the greatest possible benefit from their new status and she appointed herself a kind of watch-dog, alerting her sisters to the dangers that lay all around them, often masquerading as opportunities. She also pointed out how men managed to subvert systems set up for the benefit of women and to assert male superiority whenever it was possible, for example,

> in such divers spheres as a House of Lords reading its own convenient meaning into an Act intended to equalise the status of the sexes; as a body of men teachers opposing like pay for like work; and an International Labour Authority striving to 'protect' the woman worker out of profitable forms of wage-earning.[26]

This article was prompted by a demonstration for equal political rights and Cicely reminded her readers:

> The old Suffrage motto, 'On the same terms as men,' still needs to be restated at intervals; because now, as ever – in work, reward or enfranchisement – the objection is to these terms. Votes – yes; but not on the same qualification as men! Work – yes; but not under the same conditions as men! Wages – yes; but not at the same rates![27]

Not all Cicely's warnings were quite so serious; in 1927 she wrote an article called 'The Return to Femininity'. In it she argues that in times of war men are happy to have strong womenfolk: 'It was the sturdy Black-Agnes-of-Dunbar types of woman whose presence on the battlements inspired the reasonable hope of finding the keep as he had left it',[28] but in time of peace man's unfulfilled 'desire to subjugate someone or something' may lead him to force women back into complete femininity. This subjection often takes the form of very feminine dress. Cicely urges 'the crop-haired young women of the present day' not to abandon the freedom granted them by current fashion:

> The danger of reaction lies with the young . . . who ignorantly and for the sake of change – will be inveigled into the lengthening of their garments, little inch by inch, little flounce by flounce; until, lo and behold, ere they know what they are doing, they will have lost the precious right to shew their legs! And woman, once more, will be a legless animal – and reduced to the shape of dependence implied by her unfortunate deformity![29]

Cicely did not confine her feminist activities to writing articles even though these were important; she was also an active member of two organisations which campaigned for complete equality for women – the Six Point Group and the Open Door Council. The Six Point Group, founded in 1921, was a political pressure group, which came into being in order to work for women's rights in six specific areas where it was felt that reform was long overdue. They intended to campaign for legislation to be passed through Parliament on the following points:

1. Satisfactory legislation on child assault
2. Satisfactory legislation for the widowed mother
3. Satisfactory legislation for the unmarried mother and her child
4. Equal guardianship
5. Equality of pay for men and women teachers
6. Equality of pay and opportunity for men and women in the Civil Service.

The group felt that these goals were attainable and that they were attainable by the same means; Elizabeth Robins expressed it thus:

> The short way to protect the child is the short way to effect each of the other five reforms: By giving woman the opportunity – real instead of spurious – to take her place as citizen. In other words to make an honest Act out of the Sex Disqualification (Removal)

> Act – that measure which by a sorry paradox has brought woman more closely acquainted with her 'sex-disability'.[30]

The Sex Disqualification (Removal) Act of 1919 would, women had believed, at last give them equal rights with men, enabling them to enter the professions and the universities, serve on juries and as magistrates and, most importantly, work and be paid in any occupation on equal terms with men. As time passed it became clear that although the Act had given women some of the rights they expected, authorities of all kinds found ways around it or simply ignored its provisions. Thus women teachers were still dismissed on marriage although men were not, women civil servants were paid at different rates from men and, most anomalous of all, only women over thirty and with certain property qualifications were given the vote. Thus the Act which women believed would tidy up all the loose ends and make them completely free and equal did no such thing and they had to mobilise their forces to fight all over again. They did hold one procession and mass meeting in July 1922 which followed the route of the old suffrage marches from the Embankment to Hyde Park but most of their energy went, as with the Six Point Group, into lobbying on specific issues.

One of the odder side issues which emerged from the debate over the Sex Disqualification (Removal) Act was the question of the right of peeresses in their own right to take their seats in the House of Lords. While this only affected twenty women it became important because it tested, in open court, the provision of the Act: 'A person shall not be disqualified by sex or marriage for the exercise of any public function.' Lady Rhondda brought the case and initially the court found in her favour but despite the court's judgment members of the House of Lords opposed to women taking their seats managed to prevent the ruling being implemented in the House. In the course of the debate much of the deep-seated misogyny of the men in power became apparent; they were defending what they saw as one of the last bastions of male privilege, and defending it as ferociously as they could. The issue was not settled until the Life Peerage Act of 1958, and animosity continued. In July 1926 Cicely was moved to write a letter to *The Times* drawing attention to the unpleasantness of Lord Birkenhead's attack on peeresses in their own right. She commented:

> . . . his description of a peeress in her own right as 'an accidental

> conduit pipe established in the hope of making permanent male succession' was bound to attract attention, if only because the sentiments of the pot house sound oddly on the lips of a Secretary of State.[31]

Cicely expressed shock that the Lords were willing to tolerate such an attack on 'women of their own order'.

The Six Point Group, in its early days at least, contained many of the women who wrote for *Time and Tide*, and Lady Rhondda was a vital force in both. Elizabeth Robins, Rebecca West, Winifred Holtby and Cicely herself wrote the Six Point Group supplements which *Time and Tide* published periodically. Cicely's contribution was to the supplement 'The Child of Unmarried Parents' – an unusual emphasis for the time, drawing attention to the man's equal responsibility for the child. Cicely argues that current attitudes ignored completely the role of the man in the situation and that the readiness to lay all blame at the woman's door was simply taking the line of least resistance.

She argues that the last person to suffer from the circumstances of its birth should be the child, yet in law and in public opinion it was indeed the child who suffered most. She also suggests that some men may actually care about the fate of their illegitimate children and that such a possibility should be taken into account. Her article sets the tone of the supplement – that men should take more responsibility for their actions and that women and children should not be left to cope alone, stigmatised by society and penalised by the law. Although the argument is much the same as in her suffrage days the tone is more mellow and she is less dismissive of men. The temper of the times had undoubtedly affected her, implacable though she remained on the important issues.

The position of the Six Point Group seems to have shifted somewhat in the 1930s. By the 1940s it was still campaigning strongly for equality between men and women on six main points, but these points had become wider in scope and were defined as political, occupational, moral, social, economic and legal. Because the papers for the 1920s and early 1930s have been lost it is not possible to know when Cicely ceased to be actively involved with the Group but in the issue of *Time and Tide* for 7 November 1931 Dorothy Evans, then secretary of the Group, attacked Cicely for expressing an 'I have had to suffer, you should suffer too' attitude in one of her articles, 'The Cost of the Citizen'. In it Cicely had criticised teachers and postal workers for their resistance to cuts in salary demanded by management because of the weak state of the economy. Dorothy Evans goes on to claim that Cicely has her facts wrong on the question of women's pensions. It seems unlikely, to judge from the tone of the attack, that Cicely could still have been a member of the Group and since Dorothy Evans' position smacks somewhat of 'new' feminism, it is possible that the Group had moved in that direction and that Cicely had, as a result, removed her support.

Despite her insistence that her 'aim, as far as possible [is] to avoid the status of membership in any society',[32] Cicely did join organisations when she was fully committed to their aims. The organisation she belonged to longest – until her death, in fact – was the Open Door Council. Again a lack of records makes it difficult to be sure when she first became involved in the Council's work but she attended a party to celebrate its silver jubilee only a few months before her death. The Council defined its object thus:

> To secure that a woman shall be free to work and be protected as a worker on the same terms as a man, and that legislation and regulations dealing with conditions and hours, payment, entry and training shall be based upon the nature of the work and not upon the sex of the worker and to secure for a woman, irrespective of marriage or childbirth, the right at all times to decide whether or not she shall engage in paid work, and to ensure that no legislation or regulation shall deprive her of that right.[33]

This was equality feminism with a vengeance; Cicely entirely approved of the Council's position:

> since its aim was to correct the tendency of our legislators to be overkind to women who earn their livelihood, to treat them youth to age as if they are permanently pregnant, and forbid them all manner of trades and callings in case they might injure their health – forgetting that the first need of women like the first need of men, is bread to put in their mouths.[34]

The women who belonged to the Open Door Council were reluctant to concede that child-bearing and motherhood made demands on women different from those that men's lives made on them lest such a concession should in any way jeopardise their demands for completely equal citizenship. In 1929 Cicely's friend Elizabeth Abbott wrote a pamphlet for the Open Door Council on 'Women and the Right to Work in Mines' and the report on the proceedings of the Second Conference of Open Door International in Stockholm asserts that:

> The Open Door International holds that neither marriage, pregnancy, childbirth nor the fact that a woman is nursing the child is a reason for denying to her the same human right as is enjoyed by others (whether men or women) namely the right at all times to decide for herself whether she shall engage in paid work.[35]

The 'equality' feminists were often attacked for their resistance to making special provision for mothers but Elizabeth Abbot in her article in the *Woman's Leader* made the point that until the status of all women was changed the status of mothers would not be valued and in order to be valued women must have the same rights and opportunities as men. Any attempt to raise the status of motherhood until women had won complete equality was bound to fail.[36] These debates are reminiscent of those conducted in the early days of the current wave of feminism and the outcome was just as damaging to women.

A concern with women's biological nature was characteristic of 'new feminists' such as Eleanor Rathbone who argued that in motherhood women fulfilled their 'true nature', and even Cicely at times resorted to biological arguments to refute those of the 'new feminists'. In an article published in the *Daily Mirror* she argued that women were much tougher than men, referring to a couple she had seen riding a motorbike where the man was well muffled up while the young woman was dressed in her usual summer clothes. Men may have better muscles but 'when you have given him the credit for his biceps, you have said about all there is to be said for the superior strength of mere man'.[37] Again the article is not at all unlike many that appeared in the early seventies and to some extent represents a trivialisation of the debate. She did, however, discuss the issue more seriously in an article in *Time and Tide* in which she argued that protective legislation for women was dishonest, since it did not really spring from a concern for women's welfare and was unnecessary since women were anyway stronger than men. The real reason why men want to limit women's work, especially at night, is that 'its justification, conscious or unconscious, is the long masculine tradition that woman is the adjunct of husband and child and, apart from her sexual and maternal functions has no real purpose or place in the social system'.[38]

It is, she says, assumed, erroneously of course, that most women are supported by men and therefore do not need to work, and should stay at home instead. Thinking of this sort has sinister connections, as she points out with 'the doctrines of the Fascist and the Nazi'.[39] Since women live longer than men, despite often being less well fed, Cicely concludes that they are innately tougher and so it is ironic that:

> It is woman, for instance, tough woman, the enduring who is forbidden to work in the telephone exchange after the hour of eight at night; it is man, poor man, with his lesser hold on life, who is forced to miss his nightly rest in the service of the telephoning public![40]

Legislators, Cicely points out, have failed to notice women's need to earn a wage: 'in their intense anxiety to protect the wage-earning woman from unhealthy conditions and over-exertion, her would-be benefactors sometimes overlook her primary need for bread'.[41] Besides, she adds, in the sort of sally reminiscent of her triumphant unmasking of male hypocrisy in *Marriage as a Trade*, they only pass legislation when women are earning a wage; 'No legislation has yet been introduced to prevent the miner's wife from cooking midnight meals for her night-shift menfolk or the growing little girl from injuring her spine by carrying about heavy babies.'[42]

So she takes leave to doubt the genuineness of their concern for women's welfare; it is simply a ploy to keep women financially subservient. It is reassuring to see the old fire and feel the old passion in Cicely's writing, to feel that at sixty she was as sceptical and committed as she had been twenty years before.

As distinguished a feminist as Cicely was presumably frequently asked to participate in campaigns and despite her many other commitments she was treasurer of the Woman's Election Committee which, under the chairmanship (as they described it) of Dr Christine Murrell, had been set up 'to enable approved women candidates of the recognized political parties to come before the electorate with at least as good a chance of success as men have'.[43] The journalists' section of the Lyceum Club – one of the most prominent women's clubs in London – gave a dinner on 13 March

1922 to discuss the Million Shilling Fund which was to help to finance the work of presenting female as well as male candidates for adoption by political parties. Speaking at the dinner, Cicely said that the vote was much more valuable now than it had been when women were first given it and they were struggling to add to the two women MPs. 'Before the war they had to break something, even the masculine monopoly, but they now found it much more difficult to make something. There must be a certain amount of sex resistance in politics but there was no need to assume a bitter sex war.'[44]

Cicely herself managed to maintain a high level of sex antagonism no matter what she said in public and one cannot help feeling how disappointed those campaigners would be by the still-paltry number of women MPs in the early 1990s although some at least would welcome a woman Prime Minister, of whatever political complexion.

As if being a professional journalist were not enough Cicely also wrote letters to the papers, especially *The Times*. In one such letter she argued that women should be allowed to join the diplomatic service since their non-combative instincts would be an asset in settling international disputes.[45] At every opportunity throughout this busy decade she campaigned for women's right to equality. For many women in their fifties and sixties that would have been enough; Cicely had many more strings to her bow.

Cicely's other great campaign in the 1920s and early 1930s was birth control. This campaign was still controversial in the 1920s, even though it had started as long ago as 1877, when the Malthusian League was founded. This was named after Thomas Malthus, an early nineteenth-century theorist who had emphasised the connection between too many children and poverty. The League was concerned to reduce poverty by limiting family size and to improve the quality of the race by limiting the birth of children to impoverished parents. The League held open-air meetings and opened clinics to give contraceptive advice, and was everywhere met with abuse and hostility. Opposition to birth control came from many quarters: from medical men who claimed it was harmful to health; from the clergy who claimed that it would encourage immorality by separating sexual activity from procreation and by protecting women from the consequences of their behaviour; and from some socialists who claimed that it would reduce the numbers of workers available to fight the class war and that population control was offered as an alterntive to social reform.[46]

The Malthusian League changed its name to the New Generation League, and began to publish a monthly journal, *New Generation*. In its first issue, in 1922, the League stated that it stood for 'national birth control to enable children to become happy, healthy and useful citizens'.[47] Cicely's fundamental position on birth control can best be summed up by a point she made in *New Generation*: 'the feminist cause is far from won so long as elected persons, of whatever shade of political opinion, consider that they have the right to force reluctant women into child-bearing'.[48] She believed this so strongly that she was a vice-president of the League for at least ten years and for a long time wrote for every issue of their journal.

In many of her articles Cicely argues for birth control for the unemployed – unemployment was a major problem throughout this period – because women were being forced to feed families on a few shillings a week and were embarking on pregnancy after pregnancy while seriously underfed. 'There are those of us,' Cicely wrote, 'who "feel strongly" that the withholding of knowledge from those who most need it is something like a crime against the helpless.'[49]In her later articles she adduces a variety of economic arguments: that unlimited population growth produces too many workers, or unadaptable ones, and that taxpayers should welcome birth control as a means of reducing the cost of supporting the unemployed. She is also harsh about the sentimentalists who glamorise the idea of childhood without recognising the suffering that large numbers of children cause to a family.

Many of Cicely's arguments are not strictly feminist ones and she was somewhat out of step with many of her fellow equality feminists in her passionate espousal of the cause of birth control; many of them did not regard it as a feminist arena of debate, but simply as a matter of social reform. Apart from her genuine concern for the welfare of women forced to bear too many children too close together, Cicely's stand on birth control is consistent with her belief in a women's right to free herself from the obligation to be a wife-and-mother. By resisting uncontrolled child-bearing women were taking for themselves some measure of self-determination.

It is disappointing that she does not put forward such ideas in her articles in *New Generation*. These are very much in line with the general tone of the journal; Cicely described herself as a Malthusian and played down her feminism. In one article, opposing family allowances, she is true to the equality feminist position but her reason is Malthusian – that with birth control such measures would not be necessary and that such allowances would lead to higher taxation. 'New' feminists, most notably Eleanor Rathbone, a great advocate of 'the endowment of motherhood', argued from the opposite position: that the wrong people were producing children and that payments to mothers would change this:

> It would put an end to the increasing practice among all the more thrifty and far-sighted parents [of] deliberately limiting the number of children while slum-dwellers and the mentally unfit continue to breed like rabbits, so that the national stock is recruited in increasing proportions from its least fit elements.[50]

Many members of the League campaigned for birth control for the working class on the grounds that it would improve the quality of the race. While Cicely never actually puts forward this eugenic argument she hovers quite close at times.

Cicely also linked arguments about birth control to her theories about how to ensure world peace. She argued that constant population growth would lead to war because countries would need more territory for their increased population. In October 1924 she gave a lecture at Caxton Hall for the New Generation League, entitled 'Peace and Population'. Here she argued that given the fact that modern warfare concentrated attacks on civilians as well as soldiers, large populations were a positive disadvantage in time of war. The report of the meeting commented, 'We have, perhaps, never before had so original a lecture or so lively a discussion.'[51] When she explored the same argument in a later article Cicely added that she was pleased that patriotic arguments against birth control – the need to produce plenty of soldiers – would vanish in the face of changes modern warfare had brought about. In this context she does not mention the far graver implications of modern warfare which she was usually so concerned to impress upon her readers; when she wrote or spoke on birth control she often took an uncharacteristically narrow view of the issues. Naturally it was desirable that patriotism could no longer be used as an argument against birth control for it must have been a potent one, but both Cicely and her audience must have felt that the price paid for this change of heart was unacceptably high.

Cicely's concern to free women from the burden of unwelcome motherhood went further than a commitment to contraception. She was also an advocate of abortion. In March 1931 she provoked considerable controversy with her wholehearted approval, in her book *Modern Germanies* of a play *Paragraph 218* which argued in favour of legalised termination so that women did not have to risk their lives at the hands of backstreet abortionists. When Cicely was challenged in *Time and Tide* she replied: 'I will own frankly that there seem to me cases – many cases – where unborn life cannot be held sacred.'[52] Earlier *New Generation* had quoted a letter she had written to Stella Browne of the New Generation League in which she said of the play, 'It is just too awful in *the truth of its misery*' [her emphasis].[53] Like many modern feminists Cicely believed firmly that the mother's health and well-being were far more important than those of her unborn child and that only legalised abortion would ensure that it was safely available to all those who needed it and not only to those who could afford to pay.

Cicely's stand on abortion and her belief that contraception freed women from the sexual double standard shocked many people. A profile of her in *New Generation*, which praises 'the most masculine mind that the feminist movement has produced' (and presumes that is a compliment) says that 'some months ago she exploded a bomb in *Time and Tide* by frankly discussing the future of sexual morals'.[54] In the article she argues that with the advent of birth control, 'Gretchen, like Faust, may take her hidden pleasure and go free as Faust from open penalty.'[55] She claims that this is true equality and suggests that women's sexual morality will be more honest even if it is more 'lax':

> The 'virtue' which was of the body only, not of the spirit, which was only maintained under threat of penalty; this form of virtue, in a freer atmosphere, will probably languish and wither. It will no longer be necessary, in that freer atmosphere, for a woman to be chaste because she dare not be anything else.[56]

Cicely had resented the double standard ever since she read the story of the Rape of Lucrece in her schoolroom, and although she does not say so in so many words she must have welcomed the honesty that opportunities for contraception brought with them. She had spoken out against the double standard before but this was one of the few occasions when she was explicit about what it meant for women to enjoy true sexual equality with men. The crux of her argument is that with contraception women will be able to be more honest and this is very much in line with her arguments stretching back to *Marriage as a Trade* and beyond. In a patriarchal society, so she had always argued, it was impossible for women to live honestly and for them to be true to themselves. The removal of the fear of pregnancy which artificially constrained women's sexual activity was to be welcomed because it meant that whatever decisions women made about their behaviour could now be made honestly. And the chance to make decisions honestly was an essential part of women's moral and social emancipation. Cicely's outspokenness may have been designed partly to shock, but the sentiments of the article are in keeping with all she had ever written about sexual morality. She might have been surprised to learn that it was not until the advent of 'the Pill' in the 1960s that women felt entirely free to please themselves and she would surely not have welcomed the pressure this put on women to engage in extensive heterosexual activity.

Some of this pressure was already there in the 1920s and 1930s and Cicely's involvement in the birth control movement put her in the same camp as people who represented values the very opposite of her own. Many of her colleagues were in favour of 'Sex Reform', which advocated greater freedom for sexual activity, arguing that such activity was 'natural' and healthy while at the same time attacking those who disagreed with them as 'repressed'. One paper given at the 1929 Sex Reform Congress by an R.B. Kerr and entitled 'The Future of Spinsters' argued that all women should have the chance to have sex with a man and that, in view of the greater number of women than men, women should be prepared to share a man. The idea that they might be quite happy without one clearly never entered his head. Such arguments, which denied completely the idea that women might *choose* to live without men, are even more damaging when they are put forward by a woman. Stella Browne, with whom Cicely worked for so many years in the New Generation League, had attacked women who did not enjoy heterosexual intercourse as early as 1912 in an exchange of letters in the pages of the *Freewoman* on the desirability of sexual abstinence.

> It will be an unspeakable catastrophe if our richly complex feminist movement with its possibilities of power and joy falls under the domination of sexually deficient and disappointed women, impervious to facts and logic and deeply ignorant about life.[57]

In her paper 'Sexual Variability Among Women', Browne warns of the dangers, as she sees them, of what she calls 'cold' women within social reform movements making rules 'for more ardent natures'.[58] She also claims that 'No woman has been given her full share of the beauty and joy of life, who has not been very gradually and skilfully initiated into the sexual relation'.[59] Browne's emphasis on the delights of heterosexual love and her insistence that the pursuit of such delights constituted feminist behaviour cut across the arguments of the more radical feminists, like Cicely, who saw sexual relationships as part of the political relationship between men and women. And of course one of the most lucid expositions of this point of view had come in *Marriage as a Trade*.

It seems surprising that Cicely, who wrote in that book that men treated spinsters with neglect and contempt because they bore witness 'to the unpalatable fact that sexual intercourse was not for every woman an absolute necessity',[60] should now be working, apparently contentedly, with a woman who argued that sexual intercourse was indeed essential for a 'real' woman and that those who resisted it were repressed, and often what she called 'artificial homosexuals'.[61] But it should be borne in mind that Cicely positively disliked agreeing with people just because she was working with them on a particular campaign, and that she thrived on controversy. She may have had very different views on many topics from Stella Browne but they agreed on the need for birth control and for the time being that was enough to unite them. Cicely remained resolutely individualistic and would probably not have felt at all compromised by the collaboration.

Throughout the 1920s and 1930s Cicely campaigned unstintingly. Everything she wrote or said on women's issues was concerned with achieving full political, financial and social equality. During this period she seems to have recovered the vigour that World War I had sapped and although she turned sixty in 1932 she remained as radical as ever. The fact that there were so many organised campaigns in which she became involved shows that many others felt as she did – that the vote had been only the beginning – but the originality of Cicely's thinking often put her in the vanguard of radical opinion, on women's issues at least. She continued to connect public and private morality, hence her concern with abortion and contraception, and to stress that there could be no true equality for women without financial independence. When the writer in *New Generation* called Cicely's a masculine mind he was surely acknowledging the range of her ideas and her ability to see the implications of an issue, often long before anyone else did. Her writing about war, which became more pertinent as the thirties progressed, shows how well she understood human nature and how right she had been to doubt the ability of organisations like the League of Nations to prevent war. It can have given her little satisfaction to know she had been proved right.

Eleven

The Good Comrade

All her political activity did not get in the way of another vitally important part of Cicely's life – her friendships. Indeed many of them flourished because she was working with friends on shared campaigns and projects. As always Cicely's reticence and the dearth of personal papers make it almost impossible to know much about the nature of these friendships, but what evidence there is suggests that she was as lovable and loyal a friend as ever, delighting in and reciprocating the affection of other women. She still remained friendly with Chris St John, now a colleague on *Time and Tide*, and with Edy Craig, although Edy now spent more of her time in the country.

In 1931 Edy's brother, Edward Gordon Craig, published a book about his mother Ellen Terry which Cicely declined to review for *Time and Tide*. Called *Ellen Terry and her Secret Self*, it was an extraordinary volume in which Edward Gordon Craig attacked Bernard Shaw for publishing the correspondence between himself and Ellen Terry, and his own sister, Edy Craig, for selling other letters to Shaw. Only he, Craig claimed, knew the true Ellen Terry; Edy did not really understand her and the side of their mother which Craig designated 'Nelly' was revealed to him alone. It is an immensely self-regarding book which patronises Ellen Terry and depicts her as a foolish child. It says far more about the author and his obsessions than it does about his mother. Cicely wrote to Edy to explain that she thought the book was bad and that the fact that she was a friend of hers meant that 'the author might discount any remark of mine by explaining that I was a friend of yours and had been prompted etc.'[1] Edy was apparently worried about the reception the book would receive and Cicely did all she could to make sure that other reviewers knew how untrustworthy Gordon Craig's account was. She lent one woman the letters between Shaw and Ellen Terry as well as Chris St John's *Life* of her so that she would have the other side of the story. All this was at a time when Cicely was, by her own admission, 'horribly busy' and yet she offered to do anything else she could to help. In the same letter to Edy, Cicely mentions that Holtby – as she always referred to her – was going to review the book briefly for *Time and Tide*.

Winifred Holtby was one of the women with whom Cicely had become friendly as a result of working on *Time and Tide*. Nearly twenty-five years Winifred Holtby's senior, Cicely had been an important influence on the younger woman's thinking and when in 1934 – the year before her tragically early death – Winifred Holtby published her book *Women* she dedicated it to Ethel Smyth and Cicely Hamilton 'who did more than write the "March of the Women" '. Despite her short life, Winifred Holtby managed to write seven novels as well as prodigious amounts of journalism for the *Yorkshire Post*, the *Manchester Guardian*, *Good Housekeeping* and the *Schoolmistress*, among others.[2] She was very active in support of the League of Nations and spoke frequently in public on behalf of that and other political and peace organisations. She was a director of *Time and Tide* and wrote for it nearly every week in the 1920s. Writing after Winifred Holtby's death, Lady Rhondda, who was a very close friend, stated that she doubted 'whether *Time and Tide* would be in existence now if it wasn't for Winifred',[3] but it was as a friend that those who loved her celebrated her. By such accounts as exist – Vera Brittain's *Testament of Friendship* and the collection of letters to Jean McWilliam[4] are the main sources – Winifred Holtby was an extraordinarily warm and generous woman with a genius for friendship. She is often referred to as a 'saint' and there seems to have been a strong bond between her and Cicely. There was also a strong sense of political agreement between them. Although Winifred Holtby belonged to a younger generation she was a staunch 'equality' feminist, as she revealed in an article in the *Yorkshire Post*:

> I am a feminist because I dislike everything that feminism implies. I desire an end of the whole business, the demands for equality, the suggestion of sex warfare, the very name of feminist.

> I want to be about the work in which my real interests lie, the study of inter-race relationships, the writing of novels and so forth. But while the inequality exists, while injustice is done and opportunity denied to the great majority of women, I shall have to be a feminist with the motto Equality First.[5]

This statement applied to Cicely too; she had come back from World War I very preoccupied with issues of war and peace, yet once involved again in British society she could not turn her back on the many questions which had in no way been resolved by giving the vote to women over thirty. Cicely's closeness to Winifred Holtby was personal as well as political and for much of the 1930s (and probably the 1920s too although no record of that period exists) they were on the most relaxed and informal terms, with Cicely often dropping in to supper or coffee with Winifred and Vera Brittain. The two women shared a household in Glebe Place while Vera Brittain's husband, George Caitlin, taught at universities in America and made periodic visits to see his wife and two children. It was an arrangement which seems to have suited all the parties concerned very well, not least because it enabled the two women to continue the close and creative friendship which had begun when they were at Oxford and which gave them such support in their work. According to Elizabeth Abbott, who was also a near neighbour, that part of Chelsea was distinctly bohemian in the 1920s and 1930s and certainly a number of artists – Charles Rennie Mackintosh and Alfred Munnings among them – lived in Glebe Place during this period. Vera Brittain's diary for the 1930s records a number of occasions when Cicely dropped in to visit or went with them to the cinema, usually to foreign-language films – Cicely had a low opinion of Hollywood and its products. In July 1932 a rather stiff evening with Lady Rhondda was enlivened by Cicely's appearance after coffee, and later that year Vera Brittain showed some of *Testament of Youth* to both Winifred and Cicely for the first time, when Cicely was there to supper. When the book, Vera Brittain's powerful and moving account of her experiences during World War I, was published in August 1933 Cicely had expected to review it for *Time and Tide*, 'and is very disgusted at not being asked; has now written to ask if she may do it for the *Morning Post* but fears it may be too late'.[6] After Winifred Holtby's death Cicely remained friendly with Vera Brittain, watching the Boat Race with her in 1939.

Even with the sparse information available there is an intimation that of the two women it was Winifred who was Cicely's close friend. When Winifred Holtby was resting in Buckinghamshire in March 1932, desperately trying to reduce the blood pressure which was a result of the kidney disease that was to kill her, Cicely wrote to explain that she had not written before so that Winifred could have a complete rest, but said that she wanted to see Winifred, '& should love a country walk when weather improves',[7] before Cicely set off on the travels to France which formed the basis of her book *Modern France*. The tone of the letter is affectionate and informal; Cicely regrets that Winifred will not be with Cicely and Lady Rhondda on their visit to Alsace. *Testament of Friendship* gives a good indication of the closeness of the friendship between Lady Rhondda and Winifred Holtby, and Cicely, while perhaps not as intimate with either of them, certainly shared parts of her life with both.

Cicely's friendship with Lady Rhondda has already been referred to. No correspondence between them has survived but clearly the friendship was important to both women. Based initially on Lady Rhondda's admiration for Cicely's feminist writing, it ripened into something deeper, a relationship based on working together on *Time and Tide* and a shared perspective on current feminist politics certainly, but with a dimension which caused Cicely to write in her will: 'I desire to place on record my appreciation and thanks for the great kindness which Lady Rhondda has shown to me and also for her friendship.' Cicely never had much money and its seems likely that Lady Rhondda, who was wealthy, sometimes helped her out. Certainly they travelled together in Europe a number of times and in her obituary of Cicely, Lady Rhondda mentions a house party they both attended. Cicely always referred to her friend by her surname only, as she did with Winifred Holtby, which may indicate a particular kind of intimacy – different from that with other friends.

Cicely's finances always gave cause for concern and there were occasions when her friends felt they had to come to the rescue. At Christmas 1932 Cicely wrote to Winifred Holtby thanking her for a present of cutlery:

> That nefarious woman Elizabeth Montizambert, not content with spending a lot of her valuable time and furniture upon me, has now gone around blackmailing my friends on my behalf! Really

> she ought not to but the result is so magnificent that I can't be as angry with her as I ought to be. I never thought to have such knives and forks and spoons – I had Christmas dinner for four and they looked splendid![8]

Elizabeth Montizambert's furniture remained in Cicely's house for the rest of her life and she requested in her will that it be returned to its owner. One possible explanation for Elizabeth Montizambert's need to lend Cicely furniture is that Cicely's sister Evelyn had moved out in 1929 and the house was rather sparsely furnished as a result. Cicely had quite a reputation among her friends for being rather unworldly about money and material possessions, so clearly from time to time they took matters into their own hands.

In 1921 Cicely had engaged in correspondence with the Society of Authors over the fees she was being paid for articles in the *English Review*. She had contributed two articles, and the editor declined to pay her the pre-war rates of four guineas per thousand words for both, offering that fee for only one. The intervention of the Society seems to have won the day for her. After her early mistake over *Diana*, Cicely frequently used the Society to make sure she was never underpaid again. It helped her out in other ways too – by asking her to read and comment on playscripts. She was paid a fee of £2 for each manuscript she read. Characteristically she made no attempt to disguise her judgments. Of one play she wrote, 'I have confined myself to explaining as briefly as possible why – in my opinion – there is no hope of getting any drama out of it. The real reason, of course, is that the author did not put any drama in – I have tried to put it a little more politely.'[9] Her dealings with the Society of Authors were not, however, one-sided. She had been a member of their drama committee since before World War I and, despite a number of attempts to resign, remained one well into the 1930s. On one occasion when her attempts to resign were being politely rebuffed, she replied that she was prepared to stay on 'as long as I can be of service'.[10] She showed the same loyalty to the organisations she supported as she did to her friends.

I have often been forced to piece together an account of Cicely's private life during the 1920s and 1930s from very inadequate information; her friendship with the 'nefarious' Elizabeth Montizambert thus remains something of a mystery. Montizambert's father had been a leading member of the Canadian Red Cross and Elizabeth had been born and educated in Canada. In 1916 she opened the Canada Ward at Royaumont and this may well have been the first time that she met Cicely. After the war she settled in London where she worked as a freelance writer and journalist. She does not seem to have shared Cicely's feminist politics – she certainly did not write for feminist journals – but, like her friend, she published in a wide variety of publications ranging from the *Lancet* to *Queen* so it is safe to assume that she was a serious journalist earning at least part of her living with her pen. In 1921 Women Publishers Ltd had published her book *London Discoveries in Shops and Restaurants* with a preface by Cicely. Although the book is aimed mainly at visitors to the city, Cicely, a lifelong Londoner, claimed that it had pointed out all manner of new delights to her. It seems likely that they were close friends judging from the loan of the furniture and from the way in which Elizabeth Montizambert persuaded other people to give Cicely substantial presents to help with her domestic arrangements. Cicely's letter to Winifred Holtby mentioned that Elizabeth Montizambert expended time as well as property on her – could this mean that Elizabeth Montizambert gave her the kind of support that only close friends can give each other and which Cicely had perhaps never enjoyed before because so many of her other close friends were already in relationships with other women? Sadly we shall probably never know.

We know slightly more about Cicely's friendship with Elizabeth Abbott, herself a redoubtable fighter for women's causes. They first met in 1920 when Elizabeth Abbott called on Cicely to ask her to be press officer for the International Suffrage Alliance Congress in Geneva; they cemented their friendship in the course of the congress. Elizabeth Abbott had been involved in the suffrage campaign before the war and during hostilities had been a fund-raiser for the Scottish Women's Hospitals in India, Australia and New Zealand. In 1926 she founded the Open Door Council and worked for forty years for the Association of Moral and Social Hygiene whose main concern was justice for prostitutes. Her whole life was devoted to women's causes and she was admired and loved by her fellow-workers for her passionate commitment to justice for women and for her refusal to compromise on important issues. After Elizabeth Abbott's death Katherine Bumpus wrote:

> There are perhaps at any time few people who are capable of a sustained and strong emotion – not for individual cases, but on

> behalf of the whole tragic race of man. It is a thing which is apt to frighten people and perhaps also to make them uncomfortable since it disturbs the more pleasant, even and 'reasonable' pursuit of a cause.[11]

It is tempting to suppose that Cicely's friendship with Elizabeth Abbott was based on a shared ardour of temperament and a similar capacity for feeling and sustaining strong emotion on large human issues – one cannot imagine Cicely being either frightened or uncomfortable in the face of such commitment. Both women fought for what they believed in and, despite differences of opinion, especially about the causes of war, enjoyed an 'unshadowed and unbroken friendship'[12] for thirty-three years. Mutual respect and shared politics may help to sustain such a friendship but by themselves they are not enough. Elizabeth Abbott enjoyed Cicely's more energetic side – her passion for long-distance walking and her gifts as a companion on such walks. Cicely loved travelling and with Elizabeth Abbott she tramped great distances in the mountains of Britain and Europe, as her friend remembered:

> She was par excellence 'the good comrade', as such occasions proved. There were no complaints about the weather – but she was one of those who never complained about anything. She took all things as they came and made the best of them. If she had – and indeed she had it – the gift of speech, she had the gift of silence. And what a sense of fun and of the ridiculous she had. Laughter was never far off whatever happened.[13]

Elizabeth Abbott's account shows better than almost any other how much fun it was to be Cicely's friend. Cicely took serious matters seriously but she knew how to enjoy herself and among the pleasures she shared with Elizabeth Abbott were the food and wine of the countries they visited. Apparently Cicely always said, on the subject of drink, 'Water! Well it's all right to wash in.'[14] She always had time for her friends, certainly for Elizabeth Abbott. When they were neighbours, Elizabeth commented, 'I often wandered down to the little cottage with its green gates. There was always a welcome, never that sense of disturbing another which is an afflicting thing.'[15]

Sometimes Cicely escaped from London and stayed in a converted tram she owned on the slopes of the North Downs near Box Hill. It was very rough and ready but she seems to have taken close friends there sometimes – Elizabeth Abbott certainly went there with her on at least one occasion in the 1930s. The information we have about Cicely's friendship with Elizabeth Abbott is very slight but the obituary gives some idea of the latter's feelings; Cicely's may be guessed at by the fact that she left her friend the copyrights of all her literary works and made her her residuary legatee. Although Elizabeth Abbott was married this does not seem to have stopped her from being perhaps the most intimate of all Cicely's friends.

With another friend Cicely shared another aspect of her life, her 'first and most glamorous love'[16] – the theatre. Lilian Baylis had inherited the Old Vic Theatre in Waterloo Road from her aunt Emma Cons, and she dedicated her life to making it the home of some of the finest acting of the day. She was deeply committed to the idea of a National Theatre, a commitment Cicely did not share, and fittingly the Old Vic was the home of the National Theatre Company before it moved to its present home on the South Bank. She also established Sadlers Wells and thus laid the foundation of both the Royal Ballet and the English National Opera.

Cicely became friendly with Lilian Baylis some time in the early 1920s and the introduction may have come through Lady Rhondda and *Time and Tide*. In her autobiography Cicely writes of her 'intimacy' with Lilian Baylis, a stronger term than she uses for any of her other friends. She must have enjoyed her company, since Lilian Baylis was one of those whom she took to her country retreat at Betchworth Hill. As a result Lilian acquired a one-room shack there – known as the Hut – to which she often went in order to escape the pressures of running the Vic. There also seem to have been other people with primitive dwellings on the hill where they all lived the simple life at weekends. Cicely's tram was featured in a press photograph from an Easter weekend during this period. It shows Cicely clad in a smock with her hair tied up gypsy-fashion in a kerchief, pouring tea with a resigned expression on her face for a little girl called Peggy Jones who looks very nervous indeed. Who the child was or why she was there is not explained.

Cicely chose her friends from among women as determined and energetic as herself. Her friends were all busy and committed; half-heartedness had no place in her circle. Lilian Baylis had a reputation for not being an easy woman to work with; she was strong-minded, convinced she was always in the right and brooked no criticism at all of her eccentric methods of running her beloved

Old Vic but, even if there were disagreements, and one feels that there must have been, Cicely and Lilian Baylis found it possible, even agreeable, to work together. Cicely also introduced her to the Soroptimists – an organisation which became a very important part of her life. This is a kind of female Rotary Club in which business and professional women meet, usually once a month for lunch, and listen to a guest speaker. The organisation, which is still in existence, has always provided an important network of contacts for professional women. It was perhaps even more vital at a time when fewer women were in business in their own right.

Since neither Cicely nor Lilian Baylis has left an account we know next to nothing about their friendship. We do know that Lilian Baylis enjoyed the company of a number of the writers from *Time and Tide* and that her friends felt that contact with these women had made her more sophisticated and worldly. But her bond with Cicely may have been very different. Lilian Baylis was a deeply religious woman and her faith was a very visible part of her life: Cicely's faith was quieter but none the less important to her. It is quite possible that this was one of the links between them, but of course not one they would discuss in public.

In 1926 Cicely published a history of the Old Vic with a chapter by Lilian on her aunt Emma Cons. Although Cicely wrote most of the book, it was inevitably a collaboration, since she drew very much on information given to her by Lilian Baylis. It is quite a substantial book and a testimonial to the achievement of two redoubtable women – Emma Cons and Lilian Baylis. Given her friendship with the owner of the Old Vic it is surprising that none of Cicely's play for adults was ever put on at the theatre. Her nativity play, *The Child in Flanders*, was performed there in the winter of 1925–6 in a programme with a pantomime – which seems a rather odd combination. At Lilian Baylis' request, G.K. Chesterton, Cicely's old sparring partner from suffrage days, wrote a link for the two items. The Old Vic touring company also performed another of Cicely's plays for children, *The Beggar Prince*, in the 1940s although it had been performed in London before that, in 1926.

It was on a much more long-standing theatrical association, that with Lena Ashwell, that Cicely mostly relied for performances of the few plays she wrote in the post-war years. After the war Lena Ashwell had continued for some time to take plays round various semi-official bodies and out of this grew an organisation originally called the Lena Ashwell Once-a-Week Players and later known simply as the Lena Ashwell Players. This was a co-operative of professional actors and technicians which aimed to bring 'good' plays to the poorer boroughs of London which had no theatres of their own. They were peripatetic, performing one night in each venue on the same night each week – hence the company's original name. There are still people alive today for whom the Lena Ashwell Players provided their first experience of serious drama. The company put on their plays in whatever hall or other large building was available, rather like the fit-up companies in which Cicely had served her apprenticeship.

The Lena Ashwell Players were always short of money and in the 1920s Cicely managed to obtain a grant for them from the Carnegie Trust, a charity based in Scotland; apparently she had contacts among the trustees. She was very much committed to the company's work, although this did not stop her deploring the fact that in 1926 they began to charge a fee to dramatists who submitted plays to them for consideration. While she recognised the company's need to make money her loyalty, as ever, lay with the writer and her need to have her work read before publication or performance without having to pay for the privilege.

On 23 February 1920 the Lena Ashwell Players gave the first performance of Cicely's *The Brave and the Fair* at the Excelsior Hall, and performed it at the Kingsway in October the same year, when it was reviewed in *The Times*. *The Brave and the Fair* is an interesting play, not least because of its integration of comedy and near-tragedy and because of its rather unusual subject matter.

The plot is simple. Act I opens in a canteen workers' hostel in France during the German advance in March 1918. The main character, Edna, is a beautiful young woman for whom the war is a wonderful adventure which gives her the opportunity to meet a never-ending supply of men. The other women who work with her in the canteen have better reasons for being there and disapprove of Edna's behaviour and her concern with her appearance:

> *Nell: (not looking at her, reflectively)* I expect when the flood began – when the heavens opened and the rain poured down – there was quite a lot of women who fussed about the pattern of their raincoats.[17]

Edna becomes engaged to Amos, who goes away on leave. Enter another suitor, Pollock, who is besotted with her. Edna is extremely coquettish and gets engaged to him as well. Amos and Pollock are close friends and when Amos returns unexpectedly each thinks the other is lying and they quarrel, but in the end the truth comes out. The act evokes very well the chaotic conditions and heightened emotions just before a major 'push' and captures too Edna's total heartlessness, her complete disregard for the feelings of both men. Act II is set a year later in the Devastated Area. Pollock's unit is laying out graveyards and he is drinking himself to death following the death of Amos. The grim, but at times also humorous, tone of the men's conversation – they describe themselves as 'digging up corpses in a desert' – contrasts sharply with Edna's heartless frivolity. By chance a group of women of whom she is one are about to arrive at the camp and the men, who have been desperate for female company, make elaborate preparations for their arrival – this provides some light relief. Pollock sees Edna again and they quarrel, she perfectly sure that she is in the right. Valentine, a friend of both men, is present and determines on revenge.

Back in England a few months later Edna is convinced that Valentine, who is a baronet, is in love with her. She is totally indulged by her mother whose character is fixed by a waspish stage direction about the room setting: 'The general effect is rather showy with a lack of individual taste'; Edna has been boasting to her friends about her conquest. In a very skilfully written scene Valentine asks Edna what she would say *if* he proposed to her. She falls completely for his trick and he then tells her that he is using her own weapons against her and gives her a fierce lecture on her behaviour. Edna's only fear is that she will look foolish in front of her friends; she expresses no remorse for what she has done.

Cicely shows absolutely no sympathy for Edna and it is tempting to suppose that she had had personal experience of women who behaved as her character did. Her depiction of life in France certainly rings true and there is a sense that she is writing out a disgust at the behaviour of some women during the war. In an article published in the *English Review* in January 1921 she had attacked women who had responded to the war by becoming ultra-feminine and remaining indifferent to what was really happening. Cicely's skill as a dramatist, however, prevents the mood from becoming too dark and there is plenty of comic relief. The audience certainly ends by feeling satisfaction at Edna's humiliation, even if she is not fully aware of it herself. The reader for the Lord Chamberlain's department, G.S. Street, commented: '. . . the drawing of the second-rate coquette is bitterly good and the nice people, the canteen girls and so on, are delightful'. He added that Cicely 'takes the minx too seriously'[18] but attributed this, dismissively, to the fact that she was a woman. It is probably true that Cicely did expect a higher standard of behaviour and morality from other women than a man would do: she definitely seems to in this play. *The Times* reviewer called the play 'a bright little comedy', which rather underrates its serious side but he also observed, approvingly, that Cicely was telling some 'vitriolic truths which wanted saying'.[19]

The Brave and the Fair belongs with *William* and *Theodore Savage* as a work which Cicely felt compelled to write despite the lack of enthusiasm in the early 1920s for books and plays about the war. Although by no means as serious as the two novels, it offers another insight into the effect of war on human behaviour and into Cicely's response to such behaviour. The anonymous author of the profile of Cicely in *Time and Tide* commented, of her attitude in general: 'She never misses an opportunity of trouncing her own sex . . . But we have the highest authority for the belief that those whom we love we chasten.'[20] She did feel that women could, and should, behave better than they very often did and that they owed it to their sex to be more, not less, honourable than men. What the journalist's comment does ignore, however, is the extent to which Cicely attacked men and patriarchal society – with no quarter given. Women were by no means her main target.

In her next play, *The Old Adam*, Cicely called male notions of honour, among other things, into question. First performed at the Birmingham Repertory Theatre as *The Human Factor*, the play puts forward in comic terms Cicely's theory that man will always find new ways to fight. Set in the mythical state of Paphlagonia whose government is committed to peace at any price, it contains recognisable caricatures of contemporary politicians which apparently delighted audiences and even Cabinet ministers – Asquith, then Prime Minister, saw the play three times.

When Ruritania, Paphlagonia's near neighbour, threatens war, Paphlogonia is totally unprepared and faced with humiliation but then a scientist offers them a ray which will paralyse all enemy machines and weapons and thus enable them to win a bloodless victory. Barton, the Minister for Foreign Affairs, is afraid that the nation's young men will not like this kind of victory: 'What they want is not only victory – they want a good fight for it first,'[21] and he adds that everyone is clamouring to 'do their bit'.

Despite the recognition that the people want war, the government uses the ray – and all the machines in Paphlagonia itself are immobilised. At first they think it has gone wrong but then they realise that Ruritania has a ray too. When this is discovered the armies, navies and airforces on both sides abandon modern technology and turn to hand-to-hand fighting. The Prime Minister, Shadlock, proclaims:

> What is not paralysed is the spirit of a free democracy. What is not useless is the strong right arm of the man who is filled with that spirit. You have forgotten the human factor, your excellency – the man behind the gun, ship and aeroplane. This war is backed by the courage and will of a nation.[22]

The Bishop comes to plead with Barton to end the war and Barton tells him that his only son has been killed. This leads him to muse on the reason men cannot resist the urge to fight. He believes that men fight because of:

> The love of strife and the need of it. Did you never think that we need our enemies as we need our friends – that there are times when we need them even more? Did you never think that there are gifts that only an enemy can give us? The desire to prove ourselves, to wrestle to the utmost of our strength – who can gratify that but an enemy striking his hardest?[23]

When the Bishop admits that he too has fought for righteous causes, Barton answers: 'Would any man die in a cause that was not righteous? When the sword is unsheathed it is always the sword of the Lord . . . if you want peace on earth, you must abolish the righteous causes.'[24]

The play ends with the ministers watching the first company of volunteers marching off to the Front and the closing tableau reveals their different responses, not least the Prime Minister's 'attitudinizing' as the stage direction calls it. The Bishop, in a complete change of heart, raises his hand in blessing and utters some of the words of the Benediction: 'The Lord make His face to shine upon you.' The irony, as most of the audience would have realised, lies in the words that come next and which he does not speak: 'And give you His peace'.

The Old Adam was well received by audiences and ran for sixty-seven performances at the Kingsway. The critic of *The Times* wrote: 'The play is distinctly "clever", its point is its logic, strictly carried out to extreme conclusions.'[25] This had always been one of Cicely's most successful satirical techniques; she had, for example, used it to great effect in *Marriage as a Trade*. Another reviewer seems to have missed the point somewhat: 'Cicely Hamilton has dealt with her subject a trifle superficially, but with wit and humour. Her types of politicians are well hit off, and gave the players the opportunity for telling character sketches.'[26] The final pages of the play are anything but superficial in their treatment of the subject; perhaps the critic was deceived by the amount of humour, some of it quite broad. The satirical portraits of Cabinet ministers seem to have found their mark, as did the jibes at civil servants and other officials. In keeping with the style of the times the working-class characters tend to conform to stereotype with the exception of Joe Bunting, former skipper of the fishing boat the *Skylark*, who is promoted admiral when more modern kinds of vessel cannot operate because of the ray. Cicely's skill as a dramatist and her gift for comedy had once again enabled her to present a serious, even unpalatable, subject in such a way that audiences could enjoy it and at the same time perhaps absorb some of its ideas.

This was Cicely's last successful theatrical venture. In 1932 she translated and co-produced a play by the German, Carl Zuckmayer, called *Caravan*. She put a great deal of energy into the production, even making a dash to see it in performance at the Residenz Theatre in Munich. But to no avail: the critics were brutal. 'It is one of those mysterious plays for the appearance of which a cause cannot be discerned or imagined. Why was it written? Why adapted? Why produced?'[27] It opened on Wednesday 7 April 1932 and closed on the Saturday – 'in view of the agreement of critical opinion'. For once Cicely's theatrical instinct had let her down. In view of the completeness of the disaster it is perhaps not surprising that after that she entirely gave up writing for the theatre.

Cicely's concern to educate people towards peace by alerting them to what she believed to be the causes of war did not lead her, as it did many ex-suffragettes, to work actively with the League of Nations Union or any of the other organisations working for peace. She was, however, always willing to speak to peace organisations, and in 1922 she addressed the summer school of the Women's International League at the invitation of Helena Swanwick. One of her fellow speakers was Evelyn Sharp, her old friend from suffrage days. Both Evelyn Sharp and Helena Swanwick, who had also been active in the suffrage campaign, were firm adherents of the view that wars were caused by men and that women could act against them as an active force for peace. They had both been pacifists during World War I.

Cicely's point of view – that wars were inevitable and that ways had to be found to minimise their effect – would certainly have met with some opposition at the summer school, but that would not have dismayed her. And she was not totally out of step with the ideas of her hosts: she now believed, as they did, that women were naturally less warlike than men. She was not, however, as confident as some other workers for peace that women would always be able to restrain male violence. We know nothing about the debate at the summer school but it is interesting to see how, throughout her life Cicely's path crossed and re-crossed that of other women, like Evelyn Sharp and Helena Swanwick, who, like Cicely herself, lived largely in a world of women and dedicated much of their energy to women's causes.

One reason why Cicely did not find it easy to enter unreservedly into the work of peace organisations was her deep-rooted pessimism. In order to be able to commit oneself to such campaigns one has to believe in the perfectibility of human nature; that people want to be better than they are and are capable of becoming so. Cicely believed very firmly in original sin and applied that belief to both individual and collective morality. In an interview in 1925 she put forward her familiar claim that all communities are immoral:

> But perfectly good people, once they have resigned themselves to the communal activity, will go out with a gun, or agree to starve opponents; they will in fact, do all manner of things they would be incapable of doing as individuals.[28]

She warned too against idealism:

> When a man is suddenly thrilled with an ideal and says, 'I will sacrifice everything I have to it,' you cannot persuade him that he is not doing a good thing. As an individual he is then at his highest in devotion to his ideal; and he knows it. You come along saying he is desirous of bloodshed, and he will deny it and declare he is only desirous of sacrificing himself.[29]

So, if high ideals lead to bloodshed, what else is there to do but be pessimistic about the future? In answer to the question 'Would you say that pessimism is a more reasonable attitude than optimism?' Cicely replied, 'Yes, pessimism is more reasonable. Especially should a human being be pessimistic about himself. The doctrine of original sin is sound.'[30] Such a view of life goes some way to explaining why Cicely was able to work to improve the lot of others but found it hard to envisage the possibility of bringing about fundamental changes in what she perceived as human nature.

Apart from the difficulty of re-establishing her career after the war, other events in the early 1920s may have contributed to Cicely's feelings of bleakness. In 1921 her aunts Lucy and Amy Hammill died within a few weeks of each other; Lucy was seventy-five and Amy seventy-three. Cicely travelled up and down to Bournemouth to be with them as they were dying and apologised for delays in answering letters to friends because she was feeling 'rather worn out with sleeplessness and sick nursing'.[31] She did not record her feelings at her bereavement but, despite her firm belief in an afterlife, she must have felt it keenly.

In January 1922 Cicely was involved in a motor accident in the Camberwell Road in which she broke her collar bone and tore the muscles of her legs badly. At the time she found the situation quite amusing:

> I can still recall the faces of the crowd as they watched my stretcher being hoisted into an ambulance – the varying expressions by which pleasurable interest was registered. I regretted afterwards that I had not played up to my audience by emitting loud groans or presenting a corpse-like appearance; as it was the ring of open-mouthed delighted boys struck me as entirely comic and I spoilt the situation by laughing.[32]

But it was months before she could walk without a stick. Her account of the accident encapsulates neatly the two aspects of Cicely, the writer and the actress: as a writer she was closely observing the crowd; as an actress she longed to play to the gallery.

The death of her aunts was not the only important bereavement Cicely suffered during the 1920s: in 1927 Jane Wells died of cancer. Jane Wells, née Catherine Robbins, was the second wife of the writer H.G. Wells. She had met Wells when she was taking biology classes from him at a cramming college; she was trying to get a degree in order to become a schoolmistress and support herself and her mother. They had run away together when he was twenty-six, already married and thought he was dying of TB. For reasons of his own H.G. Wells had changed her name to Jane when they married. According to Wells' biographer, Lovat Dickson, the relationship was sexually unsatisfactory because Wells expected too much of it. Jane Wells was a strong woman and was not prepared for her husband always to have his own way and as a result, after 1900, they began to lead rather separate lives. The compromise did not really suit Jane, who wanted a single and complete relationship which Wells was not willing or able to provide. Despite his notorious philandering the marriage survived until her death at the age of fifty-five. When functioning as Mrs Wells Jane was a most efficient woman, shrewd financially and a marvellous gardener, but she also wrote under her real name of Catherine Wells and in that guise seems almost to have been another person.

Jane Wells was a great admirer of the work of Katherine Mansfield, Virginia Woolf and Edith Sitwell and she took rooms in Bloomsbury where she could go alone to do her writing. Wells never went to them. He admitted that the fact that her creative side was excluded from their union was a weakness in the marriage and he did regret it. In his autobiography Wells says of her writing, 'In her dream there was a lover who never appeared.'[33] On the evidence of at least one of her short stories it is possible that the lover of whom she dreamt was a woman. After his wife's death Wells published *The Book of Catherine Wells* – a collection of her short stories which present what Virginia Woolf called 'Moments of Being', significant episodes in people's lives.

The longest and most fully developed story in the collection 'The Beautiful House', deals with a relationship between two women which is destroyed when one of them falls in love with a man. Mary Hastings loves Sylvia Brunton 'with the love that finds no flaw'. There is much emphasis on the intimacy and delight of their relationship and by chance they find a perfect house in the country which seems to have been destined for them. They rent it and Mary, who explicitly says that her feelings for Sylvia are those of a lover, sees it as crystallising their relationship. They arrange to spend a week together at the house each month. Sylvia then meets a beautiful young man who is insensible to the magic of the house; she is delighted when he proposes. At the same time Mary dreams of the destruction of the house, then hears that it has burned down.

When she meets Sylvia and the young man he is depicted as a triumphant horseman who has won a contest. His 'satin-skinned' mount is very clearly a symbol of male sexuality and potency. Unlike stories by men on the same theme – D.H. Lawrence's 'The Fox' for instance – 'The Beautiful House' makes the relationship between the women both convincing and attractive. The connection between the arrival of the young man and the destruction of the house seems to suggest that men destroy much that is beautiful and do not even realise what they are doing.

We do not know how Cicely and Jane Wells became friends, although it seems likely that it was through Jane's husband; he and Cicely moved in similar literary circles and both were vice-presidents of the New Generation League. Cicely makes no reference to the friendship in her autobiography and it is not mentioned elsewhere. In a letter to the Society of Authors Cicely wrote, 'I have been away from London lately, kept by the illness of a friend of mine as she said she would like to have me with her during her illness,[34] and in another letter she identifies the friend as Jane Wells. For Jane to have wanted Cicely with her and for Cicely to have been prepared to spend so much time away from London and her own affairs the friendship must have been important. Cicely had a reputation for generosity and unselfishness where her friends were concerned; this seems to be a good example of her devotion to a dear friend, a woman who, although married, understood and valued love and friendship between women. It is interesting that when he came to write about his wife's final illness H.G. Wells completely failed to mention that Cicely had nursed her. It is by such omissions that women's relationships are rendered invisible.

Cicely was by this time well established in literary and theatrical circles; her famous friends included George Bernard Shaw, with whom she visited the Malvern Theatre Festival in 1933. A well-known public figure, she was considered sufficiently celebrated by newspaper editors for small items about her to appear in the press, stories such as the one about her spending an Easter weekend at her converted tram on Boxhill for instance. In July 1929 a specially commissioned photograph of her was published as one of the *Morning Post*'s 'Portrait Gallery of Distinguished British Women' and other photographs appeared from time to time. On 23 January 1923 *Time and Tide* published an extensive profile of Cicely which explored her ideas and writing in some detail and rather wistfully concluded by regretting that the war had 'turned one of the few wits among women writers into a serious, earnest and rather dry recorder of facts to be faced'.[35] Her inclusion in the column 'Personalities and Powers' put her in the elevated company of distinguished artists and statesmen such as the then newly appointed Governor-General of Canada, Lord Willingdon.

Of all the instances of public recognition, the one which probably gave Cicely the greatest pleasure was the dinner organised by her friend Winifred Holtby in conjunction with the Old Vic in November 1931. Although Winifred Holtby was already ill she did most of the hard work and sent out the press releases – she also managed to attend. The dinner was a recognition of Cicely's achievements in many fields of public life. The actor Sir Nigel Playfair presided, supported by Lilian Baylis and Lena Ashwell from the theatre and Margaret Bondfield and Lady Rhondda from the world of politics; among the guests were representatives from the French and German embassies. This was a certain kind of recognition, the recognition of her peers; in 1937 the award of a Civil List pension marked the nation's recognition of her services to literature.

The dinner in 1931 was timed to coincide with the publication of her new novel, *Full Stop*. This is perhaps the oddest of her novels, exploratory and questioning. Much of Cicely's work seeks to provide answers to public questions or to analyse political or social issues. *Full Stop* is unusual in that it is an inward-looking novel concerned with the hero's individual response to his own situation rather than to larger public issues. In this novel Cicely seems to be working out some of her ideas about death and dying, an unsurprising subject in view of the number of bereavements she had suffered in the preceding decade or so.

The hero of the novel, John Royle, is a dedicated and successful politician whose wife had died many years before, after only six months of marriage. In the forthcoming general election he hopes to lead his party to victory and become Prime Minister; his main rival for the leadership is one Drayton Curtis. He begins to have strange bouts of weakness and fainting and when he finally agrees to see a doctor is told that he has only weeks to live. The rest of the novel explores Royle's response to his impending death.

At first he is angry and frightened and refuses to rest or take it easy, despite his doctor's advice. He decides to go on as before and orders that no one shall be told. The only person who knows is his doctor and Royle notices that he is beginning to treat him differently:

> It flashed into Royle's mind that argument was avoided out of pity. We do not bandy words with those who are sick unto death. Because life was slipping from him he was no longer the equal and fellow of those who had their full health and strength; the living, once aware of the nearness of his end, would humour and bend down to him as they bent and humoured a child. The thought was intolerable and came from him almost as a cry.[36]

Royle plans to ruin Curtis' political prospects by revealing that he is an adulterer but realises that he will not be there to see Curtis' humiliation '. . . he had seen himself living on unaltered, a spectator of that which should happen when the darkness of death had closed over him'.[37] He loses his anger towards Curtis, recognising at the same time that his lack of anger isolates him from the rest of humanity.

Royle begins to think about faith and religion and realises that whether or not one believes in an afterlife affects the whole way one lives one's life. He reads about spiritualism and even attends a spiritualist prayer meeting. The meeting is very vividly described: it is a cheerful, matter-of-fact gathering and at the end, disappointed by the paltriness of the examples of manifestation, Royle realises how much he had been counting on it. Although he had cancelled all his speaking engagements, an oversight means that one constituency is still expecting him so he decides to go there and speak anyway. But Royle is unable to give his prepared speech because it seems ignoble to utter the usual politician's deceptions in the face of death. Instead he tells them that he is dying and that he is now free from all the constraints which have bound him throughout his political career. Nothing is important to him now, not even the kind of funeral he is given. He tells them, 'The same certainty of death that has given me freedom has likewise set me in loneliness. I have no part with you. My world is mine alone – a vastness that has room for me alone.'[38]

Full Stop is a curiously concentrated novel, with only one character and one line of action. There is no sub-plot, very little description and no interaction of character. It explores Royle's experience largely from the inside and is often moving in its intensity of feeling, especially in the portrayal of his sense of isolation. Royle's final speech bears the stamp of Cicely's career as a playwright – it would be marvellous on stage. *Full Stop* lacks the insistent, almost desperate quality of *William* or *Theodore Savage*, but it is important because it is the only time that Cicely explores the spiritual and religious side of life in her fiction. We know that she was herself a deeply religious woman; perhaps she felt that, at nearly sixty, it was time to write about issues which seemed to her more important than ever.

All the novels Cicely wrote after World War I have male protagonists. It seems a little surprising that a woman for whom other women were so important should not have wanted to explore women's experience further in her fiction. It is possible that when she wrote about 'big issues' – war and death for instance – she felt it gave the work greater universality to write about men and she may have recognised too that it reflected the fact that men still held the dominant position in society. If she wanted to write about the effect of private experience on public morality, as she did in *Full Stop*, it was more realistic if the politician involved was a man. Cicely wrote no more novels after *Full Stop* and I cannot help regretting that she never created a heroine in her novels to match Diana Massingberd in *Diana of Dobsons*.

Cicely might have been sixty years old, but she was not yet ready to settle down into retirement. Between 1931 and 1950 she published nine books on modern Europe, including England, Ireland and Scotland, which necessitated her travelling widely all over the continent, usually alone. Perhaps the most interesting volumes are those in which she describes Russia as it functioned under communism; Italy, newly dominated by Fascism, and Germany just before and just after the Nazis assumed power.

The interest of Cicely's account lies, as one would expect, in the idiosyncracy of her approach. When she travelled to Russia in the early 1930s most of those who had written about the country before her had been concerned to prove either how well or how badly communism worked. Cicely had no axe to grind; her book concentrates on those aspects of Russian society which she finds interesting and which she thinks will interest her readers. Thus there is an extensive section on abortion and birth control because she is intrigued by the practicalities of legalised termination. She comments on the minutiae of daily life, using detail with her usual skill to enable her readers to visualise the reality of day-to-day existence. Because she considered it unique to the Soviet Union, she writes at some length about the use of posters as a means of educating the population and also describes her encounters with the bands of homeless, orphaned street children who roamed Russia in the wake of so much social and political upheaval. Cicely remained sceptical about many claims made by the government – as she would have been sceptical about claims made by any government – but recorded life in Russia as she experienced it, bringing it to life for her readers.

Inevitably in Russia Cicely's inability to speak the language and the fact that she was accompanied everywhere by official guides limited her opportunity to go where she liked and speak to whoever seemed likely to prove interesting. In her travels in the rest of Europe she had no such problems. She liked to travel on foot and usually alone, which gave her opportunity to meet people by accident; her French and German were excellent and her Italian seems to have been quite adequate for conversation. Her attitude to her first visit to Italy is typical:

> I had always promised and vowed to myself that when (and if) I entered Italy I would not enter like a rat, through a hole in the ground. I would walk into Italy, as the pilgrims walked; I would follow the road as Napoleon followed it, and Hannibal![39]

Cicely's sense of history was a great asset in her accounts of contemporary Europe; in all the books she refers to elements of a country's past which help to explain current developments. Thus, commenting on the ruthlessness with which the Nazis were pursuing national unity in 1931 and the willingness of the German people to accept such behaviour, she observes how this can be explained by the country's long history of destructive disunity. Her own earlier experiences of Germany as a schoolgirl and at the time of the Allied Occupation enabled her to see clearly how much the country had changed and to interpret the significance of those changes.

Cicely came to some general conclusions about European countries in the 1930s which in some measure applied to dictatorships and democracies alike. She was very aware of the possibilities afforded by a state-controlled education system for the regimentation of the young; she had seen its effects in Italy and Russia and warned that such a system could take hold anywhere. She also wrote extensively about the role played by young people in dictatorships and the way they were manipulated by the authorities in order to produce 'The orthodox, obedient mind of a yes-man [which] is the aim alike of Fascist and Communist education, an orthodox mind, let me add, in a healthy and well-developed body.'[40] The young thus organised could be dangerous, 'where the stress of the national life is heavily upon youth, there you have a combative atmosphere; boys, even small boys, as embryo combatants, with their thoughts set on war and their schoolbooks fiercely chauvinistic'.[41] Cicely's account of England and Scotland, although good on the effects of unemployment and the attempts being made to mitigate these effects, are dull compared to the other volumes. Her nearness to home seems to have restricted the range of issues about which she was prepared to write.

Cicely's accounts of inter-war Europe were widely praised for their honesty and freedom from partisan feeling; but *Little Arthur's History of the Twentieth Century*, published in 1933, is anything but unbiased. This satirical *tour de force* first appeared as a series of articles in *Time and Tide* and is a parody of a Victorian classic, *Little Arthur's History of England*. It purports to be written from a future in which all countries have become part of a world state and its function is to explain to Little Arthur how this came about. The concept gives Cicely the chance to develop and play with some of the ideas about society which she had already discussed elsewhere. Inevitably the question of war and its prevention looms large, and she imagines a version of the prohibition on knowledge which she had depicted in *Theodore Savage* projected into a futuristic society which more closely resembles her own. Here it is called the 'Limitation of Dangerous Knowledge', 'Of course that did not help about the scientific bandits already grown up, but it did prevent another generation of scientific bandits succeeding them.'[42] In this society peace has been bought at a price:

> It was difficult to make these people understand that peace and security had got to be paid for by giving up some of their freedom; they couldn't see at first that, if you want to be quite safe, you have to be guarded by walls, or by men, or by laws; while if you want to be quite free and do exactly as you like, you will have to run a good many risks.[43]

Gradually in this safe, standardised, much-regulated world the Worker is replaced by the machine. Various cures for unemployment are proposed and for one of them, that of removing women from the workforce, Cicely saves a special barb, 'The people who liked this plan said the proper thing for women to do was to marry and have lots of children, and those who didn't care for that sort of life weren't at all the right kind of women – they were what were called abnormal.'[44] With amusing detail, riding many of her familiar hobby horses, Cicely once again reveals her satirical talent, her gift for exposing the limitations of an idea by taking it to its logical conclusion. As she does so she warns her contemporaries of the potential outcome of policies and beliefs which may, on the face of it, seem appealing.

Much of Cicely's writing in the 1930s was on broad political issues but she retained her deep commitment to feminism; one of her greatest objections to Nazism and Fascism was that they were profoundly anti-feminist. Towards the end of the decade she was still addressing meetings on women's issues. In February 1936 she spoke at a conference organised by the Over Thirty Association on the problem of the re-employment of middle-aged women displaced by the demand of employers for younger women. In her speech Cicely welcomed the emergence of the association as marking the end of the post-war preoccupation with youth, something she disliked intensely. She argued that efficiency should be taken into account when employing women. In March 1938 at the AGM of the Open Door Council she turned to discrimination against married women workers and said that the demand for an increased birth rate was being used as a smokescreen to attack women's freedom. In neither speech is there any sign that Cicely was prepared to compromise on women's rights.

With the outbreak of World War II, women were to enjoy greater job opportunities and greater economic freedom than ever before. And Cicely was to see her worst fears about scientific warfare fully justified.

Twelve

An Untamed Old Woman

Cicely's travels were, inevitably, brought to a halt by World War II, although her book on Holland, for which she had done most of the research before the war, was not published until 1950. She did not, however, lose her interest in politics nor her commitment to campaigning for democracy and freedom.

Her most passionate appeal came in *Lament for Democracy*, published in 1940. This book was written in an attempt to understand and then to explain why countries all over the world were turning away from democracy and, apparently willingly, accepting various forms of tyranny: Nazism, Fascism and Bolshevism in particular. Many of the arguments Cicely puts forward in the book had appeared in her earlier writing, most notably in articles in *Time and Tide*.

Cicely opens *Lament for Democracy* by saying she would like to believe that government of the people, by the people and for the people could be a form of government which would always exist but that on current evidence it was hard to imagine that this would be the case. Her argument is that democracy works effectively when things are going well but that it cannot withstand pressure and therefore in times of crisis is extremely vulnerable to overthrow by despotism. Its inherent weakness lies in its non-accountability; voters do not individually take responsibility for mistakes that occur as a result of the way in which they have voted. Cicely goes on to argue once again that collectively human beings have lower moral standards than they have individually and that all real achievement is the work of individuals operating on their own. She warns, as she had done so often before, that democracy is fatally weakened by its need to achieve unity by combining against a common enemy:

> Can cause or community long hold together without the stimulus of hate? On the answer to that question depends the fate of our civilisation, the existence of the world as we know it. With methods of mass murder growing ever more formidable we cannot afford to use hatred and mallice as a means of securing unity.[1]

Even as she was writing these words Europe and the world were plunging into a war brought about by the kind of thinking against which she had so often raised her voice. Although Cicely had seen the changes coming for a long time, warnings from her and many others had not been enough to avert disaster. In his autobiography *World Within World* the poet Stephen Spender observes that the 1930s saw a major change in the relationship of the individual to history:

> The 1930s saw the last of the idea that the individual, accepting his responsibilities, could alter the history of the time. From now on, the individual could only conform to or protest against events which were outside his control.
>
> The 1930s, which seemed so revolutionary, were in reality the end of a Liberal phase of history. They offered Liberal individualists their last chance to attach Liberal democracy to a people's cause: specifically, to the cause of Spanish democracy. The total armament of the civilized world drowned all individual efforts in a rising flood of mechanized power.[2]

Cicely had feared this ever since the night she lay on the hill outside Abbeville and lost her faith in 'progress and the onward march of humanity', and yet she had continued to believe that the individual could 'alter the history of the time' if he or she tried hard enough and she had argued, with every means at her disposal, that the effort was worth making. At this point she must have felt something very like despair.

Despair or not Cicely was never one to shirk what she saw as her duty. Even though she was nearly seventy she took as active a part as she could in war work and became a member of the Chelsea Fire Service. The headquarters of the local ARP was at the Cook's

Ground School in Glebe Place, very close to Cicely's house, and she took her turn fire-watching there throughout the blitz. On the night of 16–17 April 1941 a large number of incendiary bombs fell in the area, including one which set fire to the roof of the school. Normally Cicely was not actively involved in the firefighting; Lady Rhondda recorded that 'it was often her business to persuade frightened people that there was nothing whatever to be concerned about',[3] – an activity which probably required all her talents as an actress since she was, by her own admission, not a brave woman. On this particular night fourteen fires were started and at one o'clock in the morning a gas main caught fire near the Chelsea Old Church, which had itself been hit. The number of fires meant that there were not enough people to put them out and as it was a night of heavy bombing throughout London no help was available from elsewhere in the capital. It was a priority to prevent a gas explosion and if possible to save the church, so the rest of the firefighters raced off to tackle those problems and left Cicely sitting on a rooftop playing a hose on another, more minor, fire. Her stoical willingness to do what was required was typical.

This anecdote comes from Lady Rhondda's obituary of Cicely and is the only account we have of her fire service activities. It would be interesting to know what else she did during the war; there must have been other activities of which no record remains. We do know that she suffered 'a long and tiresome illness' in 1942 which kept her in bed for 'a good many weeks'.[4] This may have been the beginning of a decline in her health but in view of her later activities with the British League for European Freedom it seems more likely that she made a good recovery.

Cicely's commitment to fighting tyranny continued until the end of her life and from 1945 she was an active worker for the British League for European Freedom. This organisation seems to have been among the forerunners in pointing out to the British people the implications of the agreements made between Churchill, Roosevelt and Stalin at the conferences held at Teheran in 1943 and Yalta in 1945. Britain had entered the war against Germany with the avowed intention of protecting Poland from the domination of Hitler and yet Roosevelt and Churchill agreed to allow the country to come under Russian control and endorsed Russia's plan to move Poland's borders westward so that the land to the east became part of Russia. This meant that millions of Poles had to migrate westward and that after the war Poland would be a substantially different country. The minutes of the meeting at which this momentous decision was made suggest a very cavalier attitude to the whole issue, especially on the part of Churchill.

> The Prime Minister said that he liked the picture [the new map of Poland], and that he would say to the Poles that if they did not accept it they would be fools and he would remind them that but for the Red Army they would have been utterly destroyed.[5]

Many people in Britain, Cicely among them were very disturbed by what they saw as this betrayal of Poland and by the subsequent domination of a large number of previously independent countries, such as Estonia and Lithuania, by the Soviet Union. The British League for European Freedom, a non-party, non-sectarian organisation, was set up in 1944 to provide a focus for the expression of this disquiet. In one of its early pamphlets it warned that 'These regions are being organised – psychologically, economically and militarily for Russia's war against the West'.[6] The League urged the forces of European democracy to resist Russian aggression and also drew attention to the many violations of human rights which occurred in Eastern Europe. 'Freedom of thought, press, speech and political association have been destroyed. Religious persecution is growing in severity.'[7]

The League was chaired from its inception by the Duchess of Atholl, a flamboyant figure who had been Conservative MP for Kinross and West Perthshire from 1923 to 1938. She had been a delegate to the League of Nations in 1925 and had opposed both women's suffrage and, later, appeasement. She had been involved with the 100,000 group, a right-wing organisation which had sought to press the government for action against Germany. The work of the League brought together people of all political persuasions: speakers at their meetings had included Bertrand Russell, the philosopher and later campaigner for nuclear disarmament, and Labour MP Eleanor Rathbone, as well as conservative churchmen such as the then Dean of Chichester. Cicely first became involved with the League in 1945 when she offered to type for them, which shows a characteristically self-effacing willingness to do anything she could to help a cause in which she believed. The League soon realised that her talents could be put to better use as editor of the weekly press bulletin in which information was published about all its areas of concern and she edited the bulletin from 1946 until her final illness made such effort impossible.

Cicely also found the energy to wage a vigorous campaign against entertainment tax in 1944. This tax was levied on all plays unless they could be proved to be educational and Cicely wrote numerous letters to the press and worked with the League of Dramatists to oppose it. She claimed that managements' reluctance to pay the tax had prevented children's plays of hers from being performed. The campaign seems to have worked, since the tax was abolished in the Budget of 1945.

She also made at least two radio broadcasts. One of these was on the Empire Service of the BBC in 1941 and was one of a series called 'To Talk of Many Things' beamed out to British troops all over the world. Although the broadcast was made at the height of the blitz it makes no reference to international affairs; it is a commentary on the popularity of British detective fiction from Conan Doyle to Christie and Sayers.

More significant was the other, given on the twenty-fifth anniversary of the granting of the vote to women over thirty in 1943. In this broadcast Cicely said that the world in which she was now living was, in most respects, 'considerably less civilised' than the one into which she had been born over seventy years before, 'but with regard to the position of women I have seen betterment all along the line. Some of that at least we owe to enfranchisement.'[8] Characteristically Cicely also insisted, as she had at the time, that the real significance of the campaign lay in the changes in attitude which it brought about and she gave some of the credit for that to the militants: 'The militants were of value because they proved that a body of women, many of them thoroughly domesticated, were prepared to break with the tradition of decorum.'[9]

In other respects she lived to see all the certainties of her youth shaken and destroyed. The ideals for which she had fought so hard throughout her long life seemed out of place in a world where extermination could come at the touch of a nuclear button. According to Stephen Spender, her old colleague H.G. Wells wrote in an article near the time of his death in 1946 that 'he no longer believed in any of the progressive causes to which he had devoted his life. He had abandoned his belief in the inevitably of progress.'[10] Like Cicely, Wells had been born during the reign of Queen Victoria, the period of British history in which, more than any other, people had believed that progress was inevitable and continuous. All the progressive political and social causes for which they, and thousands like them, had worked for the first forty years of the twentieth century had come into being because progress had seemed a possibility. Cicely had ceased to believe in the inevitably of progress nearly thirty years before, but had still considered it worthwhile to work to alleviate hardship and combat injustice for the human race as a whole and, most notably, of course, for women. One of Cicely's greatest qualities was a dogged determination. Even if she could not remake the world as she had dreamed of doing at the height of the suffrage agitation, she and those she had worked with had significantly changed the lives of women in Britain for the better. The total overthrow of patriarchy might have had to be postponed indefinitely but the vote and all that followed had made important differences.

In the 1920s, Cicely had refused to share the general optimism about the role of the League of Nations and the possibility of world peace. Her scepticism had been justified. The values of democracy, as she had predicted, had proved powerless in the face of mass movements. The individual was now and for ever subservient to the great whole, 'the herd' as she had called it. As Britain elected a Labour government in 1945 and began to assemble the machinery of the welfare state she must have reflected ruefully on her description twelve years before, in *Little Arthur's History of the Twentieth Century*, of the 'Social Service Rebellion' when the people rose up in revolt against being taken care of so completely by the government. Yet again she had seen the way society was developing and had warned her readers of the consequences.

By the late 1940s, Cicely, by then in her late seventies, must have felt out of joint with the time. She was not, however, isolated in her private life. In the year of her death she attended a party to honour Elizabeth Abbott and her twenty-five-year association with the Open Door Council. This grand gathering of the survivors of the suffrage and post-war feminist struggles was probably the last time she saw many of the women with whom she had campaigned for so many years.

Although she lived alone to the end of her life she was not forgotten, and during her long final illness she was nursed devotedly 'by friends and neighbours who counted it an honour to serve her'.[11] She died on 6 December 1952; Elizabeth Abbott tells us that she was drinking champagne to the end. Dorothy L. Sayers wrote, 'Time and trouble will tame an advanced young woman, but an advanced old woman is untamable by any earthly force.'[12] Cicely remained untamed, passionate and loved; after eighty years that is an achievement in itself.

It is hard to sum up a woman as variously talented as Cicely but the impression that remains is of a highly original thinker and a fighter, a woman who never gave up. She saw the world with an often frightening clarity and was bold and compassionate enough to write and speak honestly about what she saw. Her grasp of social and political issues sprang from the profound understanding of, and empathy with, her fellow creatures and this understanding was what made her, at her best, a compelling writer. Above all she was a deeply passionate woman, stubborn at times but with an immense capacity for love and friendship. By choosing to remain a spinster and to live alone she was perhaps freer to use her energy and commitment to the full than she would have been had she channelled all her passion into a single relationship, but this in no way diminishes the importance of the close relationships she did enjoy. She was loving and loyal to her friends and unable to bear a grudge. Experimental and versatile, Cicely was a good entertainer as well as a deep thinker. We, her 'daughters of the spirit', owe her a great debt both for her example and for the vivid and exhilarating picture she has left us of what it meant to be a feminist, a writer and a political activist during one of the most dramatic phases of women's history.

Notes

Introduction

1. Nancy K. Miller quoted in Carolyn G. Heilbrun, *Writing a Woman's Life*, p 11.
2. Ibid., p. 18.
3. Ibid., p. 108.
4. Cicely Hamilton, review of *Savage Messiah* in *Time and Tide*, 13 June 1931.

Chapter 1

1. Cicely Hamilton, *Life Errant*, p. 6.
2. Ibid., p. 3.
3. Ibid., p. 4.
4. Ibid., p. 279.
5. Ibid., p. 6.
6. Ibid., p. 9.
7. Ibid., p. 13.
8. Ibid., p. 15.
9. Lucy Boston, *Perverse and Foolish*, p. 36.
10. Hamilton, *Life Errant*, p. 28.
11. Ibid., p. 29.
12. Ibid.
13. Ibid., p. 27.
14. Eva Moore, *Exits and Entrances*, pp. 14–15.
15. Hamilton, *Life Errant*, p. ix.
16. Ibid., pp. 37–8.
17. Lena Ashwell, *Myself a Player*, pp. 60–1.

18. Hamilton, *Life Errant*, p. 43.
19. Ibid., p. 42.
20. Ibid., p. 47.
21. Julie Holledge, *Innocent Flowers*, p. 16.
22. Hamilton, *Life Errant*, p. 47.
23. Ibid., p. 44.
24. Ibid., p. 52.
25. Ibid., p. 55–6.
26. Margaret Llewelyn Davis (ed.), *Life as We Have Known It*, p. 60.
27. Ibid., p. 48.

Chapter 2

1. Cicely Hamilton, *Life Errant*, p. 57.
2. Ibid.
3. Ibid., p. 58.
4. Ibid., p. 57.
5. Ibid., p. 59.
6. Ibid., pp. 59–60.
7. William Archer.
8. *Votes for Women*, 8 October 1909.
9. A.E. Wilson, *Edwardian Theatre* p. 137.
10. The *Stage*, 24 December 1908.
11. Lena Ashwell, *Myself a Player*.
12. Frank Vernon, *The Twentieth Century Theatre*, p. 61.
13. The *Sphere*, 22 February 1908.
14. Ibid.
15. Ibid.
16. Ibid.
17. The *Era*, 15 February 1908.
18. *Reynolds News*, 16 February 1908.
19. *The Times*, 13 February 1908.
20. *Pall Mall Gazette*, 13 February 1908.
21. Cicely Hamilton, *Diana of Dobsons*, p. 28.
22. Ibid., p. 52.
23. Ibid., p. 51.
24. The *Stage*, 14 February 1908.
25. The *Sphere*, 22 February 1908.
26. The *Evening News*, 13 February 1908.

27. Hamilton, *Life Errant*, p. 63.
28. *The Times*, 16 October 1908.
29. Cicely Hamilton to the Society of Authors, 16 November 1909.

Chapter 3

1. Helena Swanwick, *I Have Been Young*, p. 183.
2. Cicely Hamilton, *A Pageant of Great Women*, Preface.
3. Ray Strachey, *The Cause*, p. 306.
4. Cicely Hamilton, *Life Errant*, p. 66.
5. Ibid., p. 69.
6. *Time and Tide*, 17 May 1923.
7. Hamilton, *Life Errant*, p. 75.
8. Ibid., p. 282.
9. Ibid., p. 283.
10. Ibid., p. 76.
11. Ibid., p. 68.
12. Ibid.
13. Ibid., p. 86.
14. *Votes for Women*, 10 December 1908.
15. Ibid.
16. Ibid.
17. Quoted in *Votes for Women*, 10 December 1908.
18. Hamilton, *Life Errant*, p. 71.
19. Ibid., p. 73.
20. Ibid., p. 78.
21. Ibid.
22. Andro Linklater, *An Unhusbanded Life*, p. 119.
23. Ibid., p. 110.
24. Ibid., p. 123.
25. The *Vote*, 9 December 1910.
26. H.G. Wells, *The New Machiavelli*, p. 293.
27. The *English Review*, April 1912.
28. Hamilton, *Life Errant*, pp. 67–8.
29. Cicely Hamilton in a broadcast made on the BBC 2 April 1943. National Sound Archive.
30. Ibid.
31. Ibid.
32. Hamilton, *Life Errant*, pp. 65–6.
33. Ibid., pp. 61–2.

34. Ibid., p. 65.
35. Ibid., p. 281–2.
36. The *Literary Digest*, 12 August 1912.
37. Cicely Hamilton, *Marriage as a Trade*, p. 31.
38. The *Literary Digest*, 12 August 1912.
39. Ibid.

Chapter 4

1. Cicely Hamilton, *Life Errant*, p. 70.
2. The *Vote*, 23 December 1909.
3. *The Women's Who's Who*.
4. Cicely Hamilton, *Marriage as a Trade*, pp. 130–1.
5. The *Vote*, 23 December 1909.
6. Elizabeth Robins, *Way Stations*, pp. 108–9.
7. Ibid.
8. Ibid., p. 217.
9. Ibid., p. 220.
10. Evelyn Sharp, *Unfinished Adventure*, p. 136.
11. Under this law a married woman ceased to have a legal identity separate from that of her husband. This meant that in civil law they counted as one person and the woman had no right to resist the will of her husband.
12. The *Vote*, 3 June 1911.
13. Cited in Sylvia Pankhurst, *The Suffragette Movement*, p. 278.
14. Much of the information about the marches comes from Lisa Tickner, *The Spectacle of Women*.
15. The *Daily Mail*, 15 June 1908.
16. Lisa Tickner, *The Spectacle of Women*, p. 246.
17. *The Times*, 22 June 1908.
18. The *Stage*, 24 December 1908.
19. Dale Spender and Carole Hayman (eds.), *How the Vote was Won and Other Suffragette Plays*, p. 95.
20. Letter from Cicely Hamilton to Evelyn Sharp, 4 January (no year). Bodleian Library, Oxford.
21. The *Vote*, 12 March 1910.
22. Cicely Hamilton in *Edy. Recollections of Edith Craig*, edited by Eleanor Adlard, p. 40.
23. Ibid.
24. Ibid.

25. The *Vote*, 21 May 1910.
26. See Spender and Hayman, op. cit.
27. The *Vote*, 11 November 1909.
28. Spender and Hayman, op. cit., p. 27.
29. Ibid.
30. *Pall Mall Gazette*, 15 April 1909.
31. *Votes for Women*, 21 May 1909.
32. Cicely Hamilton, *A Pageant of Great Women*, p. 31.
33. Ibid., pp. 47–9.
34. Letter from Cicely Hamilton to Lillah McCarthy. No date (Friday night). Harry Hansom Humanities Research Centre, University of Texas at Austin.
35. *The Times*, 13 November 1909.
36. Adlard, op. cit., p. 43.
37. Ibid.

Chapter 5

1. The *Englishwoman*, February 1909.
2. Ibid.
3. Ibid.
4. The *Nation and Athenaeum*, 22 December 1928.
5. Cited in Elizabeth French Boyd, *Bloomsbury Heritage*, p. 73.
6. *Votes for Women*, 3 September 1909.
7. Cicely Hamilton, *Marriage as a Trade*, p. 17.
8. Ibid., pp. 19–20.
9. Ibid., p. 134.
10. Ibid., p. 81.
11. Ibid., p. 106.
12. Ibid., p. 68.
13. Ibid., p. 44.
14. Ibid., p. 109.
15. Ibid., p. 110.
16. Ibid., p. 33.
17. Ibid., p. 85.
18. Ibid., pp. 54–5.
19. Ibid., p. 61. The Criminal Law Amendment Act of 1885 only raised the age of consent from twelve to sixteen because of relentless public pressure from Josephine Butler and W.T. Stead. Stead was a journalist who revealed in his newspaper

how easy it was to procure a twelve-year-old girl for purposes of prostitution. Ironically he was prosecuted and sent to prison even though his sole intention had been to demonstrate how girls suffered as a result of the low age of consent.

20. Ibid., p. 116.
21. Ibid., p. 135.
22. Ibid., p. 136.
23. For a full discussion of this topic see Rosemary Auchmuty, *Victorian Spinsters*, especially Chapter 4.
24. Cicely Hamilton, *Marriage as a Trade*, p. 141.
25. Ibid., p. 144.
26. Letter from Cicely Hamilton to Elizabeth Robins, 1 August (no year) Harry Hansom Humanities Research Centre, University of Texas at Austin.
27. Minutes of the Women's Tax Resistance League, Fawcett Library.
28. Flora Annie Steel, *The Garden of Fidelity*, p. 265.
29. Cicely Hamilton, *Life Errant*, p. 91.
30. Ibid., p. 92.
31. Ibid.

Chapter 6

1. *Time and Tide*, 26 January 1923.
2. Cicely Hamilton, *Marriage as a Trade*, p. 129.
3. Ibid., p. 127.
4. Ibid., p. 131.
5. Blanche Wisen Cook, ' "Women Alone Stir My Imagination": Lesbianism and the Cultural Tradition,' *Signs* 4, no. 4, p. 738.
6. Ann Ferguson, 'Patriarchy, Sexual Identity, and the Sexual Revolution', *Signs* 7, no. 1, p. 165.
7. Victoria Glendinning, *Vita*, p. 253.
8. Ibid., pp. 250–1.
9. Joy Melville, *Ellen and Edy*, p. 209.
10. Leonard Woolf, *The Journey not the Arrival Matters*, p. 84.
11. Elizabeth Robins, *The Convert*, ed. Jane Marcus, p. vi.
12. Ibid., p. vii.
13. Hamilton, *Marriage as a Trade*, p. 110.
14. Judith Schwarz, *Radical Feminists of Heterodoxy*, p. 85.

Chapter 7

1. Cicely Hamilton to Evelyn Sharp, no date. Bodleian Library, Oxford.
2. The *Vote*, 31 December 1910.
3. Ibid.
4. Ibid.
5. Ibid.
6. The *Vote*, 15 April 1911.
7. Ibid.
8. The *Vote*, 4 June 1910.
9. Ibid.
10. The *Vote*, 14 January 1911.
11. Ibid.
12. Ibid.
13. Ibid.
14. The *English Review*, April 1912.
15. Ibid.
16. The *Vote*, 25 June 1910.
17. The *Stage*, 26 November 1910.
18. The *Era*, 24 November 1910.
19. *Votes for Women*, 26 November 1910.
20. The *Vote*, 26 November 1910.
21. *Stageland*, May 1911.
22. *The Times*, 9 May 1911.
23. *New Statesman*.
24. *The Times*, 10 February 1912.
25. Cicely Hamilton to the Society of Authors, 10 February 1912. British Library.
26. *Votes for Women*, 1913.
27. Cited in Joe Mander and Raymond Mitchenson, *The Lost Theatres of London*, p. 107.
28. Ibid.
29. *The Times*, 9 November 1910.
30. The *Vote*, 19 November 1910.
31. *The Times*, 10 February 1910.
32. *Votes for Women*, February 1913.
33. *The Stage*, 13 February 1913.
34. Cicely Hamilton, *Life Errant*, p. 268.
35. *Pall Mall Gazette*, 12 December 1911.
36. Cicely Hamilton, *Life Errant*, p. 268.

37. The *Star*, 12 December 1911.
38. The *Stage*, 20 February 1913.
39. *The Times*, 17 February 1913.
40. *The Times*, 15 February 1913.
41. Cicely Hamilton to the Society of Authors, 9 December 1910.
42. *Votes for Women*, 8 July 1914.
43. Ibid.
44. Philip Larkin, 'MCMXIV' in *The Whitsun Weddings*.

Chapter 8

1. Cicely Hamilton, *Life Errant*, p. 96.
2. Leila Henry, MS Diary. Imperial War Museum.
3. Eva Shaw Maclaren, *A History of the Scottish Women's Hospitals*, p. 25.
4. Ibid.
5. Ibid.
6. Antonio de Navarro, *The Scottish Women's Hospital at the French Abbey of Royaumont*, p. 118.
7. Ibid., p. 119.
8. Shaw Maclaren, op. cit., p. 32.
9. Henry, op. cit.
10. Hamilton, *Life Errant*, p. 109.
11. Henry, op. cit.
12. de Navarro, op. cit., p. 163.
13. Hamilton, *Life Errant*, p. 116.
14. Ibid., p. 118.
15. D.H. Littlejohn, MS Diary. Imperial War Museum.
16. Marjorie Starr, Letters. Imperial War Museum.
17. Martha Vicinus, *Independent Women*, p. 190.
18. Hamilton, *Life Errant*, p. 111.
19. de Navarro, op. cit., p. 144.
20. Hamilton, *Life Errant*, pp. 106–7.
21. de Navarro, op. cit., p. 144.
22. Hamilton, *Life Errant*, p. 118.
23. Shaw Maclaren, op. cit., pp. 41–2.
24. Cicely Hamilton, *Senlis*, p. 37.
25. Ibid., p. 16.
26. Ibid., p. 126.
27. Hamilton, *Life Errant*, p. 138.

28. Cicely Hamilton to the Society of Authors, 11 November 1917.
29. Ibid.
30. Ibid.
31. Cicely Hamilton to the Society of Authors, 15 December 1917.
32. Hamilton, *Life Errant*, p. 149.
33. Ibid.
34. Hamilton, *Senlis*, p. 34.
35. Hamilton, *Life Errant*, p. 149.
36. Ibid., p. 150.
37. Ibid., p. 153.

Chapter 9

1. Cicely Hamilton, *William, an Englishman*, p. 21.
2. Ibid., p. 27.
3. Ibid., pp. 27–8.
4. Ibid., p. 83.
5. Ibid., p. 95.
6. Ibid., p. 171.
7. Ibid., p. 203.
8. Ibid., p. 199.
9. Ibid., p. 233.
10. Ibid., p. 247.
11. The *Englishwoman*, April 1919.
12. Cicely Hamilton, *Life Errant*, p. 239.
13. Ibid., p. 240.
14. Ibid., p. 241.
15. Ibid.
16. Ibid., p. 242.
17. Ibid., pp. 229–30.
18. Ibid., p. 234.
19. Lena Ashwell, *Modern Troubadours*, p. 197.
20. Ibid., p. 200.
21. Hamilton, *Life Errant*, p. 162.
22. Ibid., p. 105.
23. Ashwell, op. cit., p. 205.
24. Hamilton, *Life Errant*, p. 172.
25. Ibid., p. 176.
26. Ibid., p. 181.
27. Ibid., pp 190–1.

28. Ibid., p. 246.
29. *Time and Tide*, December 1952.
30. Cicely Hamilton, *Theodore Savage*, p. 9.
31. Ibid., p. 18.
32. Ibid., p. 43.
33. Ibid., p. 66.
34. Ibid., p. 56.
35. Ibid., p. 75.
36. Ibid., p. 109.
37. Ibid., pp. 121–2.
38. Ibid., pp. 174–5.
39. Ibid., p. 230.
40. Ibid., p. 234.
41. Ibid., p. 265.
42. Ibid., p. 234.
43. Ibid., p. 307.
44. Ibid., p. 304.
45. Ibid., p. 313.
46. Ibid., p. 158.
47. *Time and Tide*, 12 May 1922.

Chapter 10

1. For further discussion of this topic see David Doughan, *Lobbying for Liberation*, and Sheila Jeffreys, *The Spinster and Her Enemies*.
2. Sheila Jeffreys, *The Spinster and Her Enemies*, p. 154.
3. Elizabeth Abbott, Obituary of Cicely Hamilton in the *WFL Newsletter*, December 1952.
4. The *Englishwoman*, July 1920.
5. The *Englishwoman*, August 1920.
6. Ibid.
7. Cicely Hamilton, *Life Errant*, pp. 199–200.
8. See Dale Spender, *Time and Tide Wait for No Man*.
9. Ibid.
10. Vera Brittain, *Testament of Friendship*, p. 265.
11. Hamilton, *Life Errant*, p. 207.
12. *Time and Tide*, 20 May 1921.
13. *Time and Tide*, 12 June 1925.
14. Ibid.

15. *Time and Tide*, 15 July 1921.
16. *Time and Tide*, 12 August 1921.
17. Ibid.
18. Ibid.
19. *Time and Tide*, 15 September 1922.
20. Ibid.
21. The *English Review*, February 1921.
22. *Time and Tide*, 8 September 1922.
23. Ibid.
24. Ibid.
25. Ibid.
26. *Time and Tide*, 2 July 1926.
27. Ibid.
28. *Time and Tide*, 12 August 1927.
29. Ibid.
30. *Time and Tide*, 19 January 1923.
31. *The Times*, 1 July 1926.
32. Hamilton, *Life Errant*, p. 208.
33. Open Door Council papers. Fawcett Library.
34. Hamilton, *Life Errant*, p. 208.
35. Open Door Council papers.
36. *Women's Leader*, 11 February 1927.
37. *Daily Mirror*, 4 August 1928.
38. *Time and Tide*, 24 December 1932.
39. Ibid.
40. Ibid.
41. Ibid.
42. Ibid.
43. *The Times*, 16 March 1922.
44. Ibid.
45. *The Times*, 28 April 1921.
46. See Sheila Rowbotham, *A New World for Women*, and Audrey Leathard, *The Fight for Family Planning*.
47. *New Generation*, January 1922.
48. *New Generation*, August 1924.
49. *New Generation*, January 1924.
50. *The Times*, 26 August 1918.
51. *New Generation*, November 1924.
52. *Time and Tide*, 7 March 1931.
53. *New Generation*, August 1930.
54. *New Generation*, May 1929.

55. Ibid., May 1929.
56. Ibid.
57. *The Freewoman*, 7 March 1912.
58. Quoted in Sheila Rowbotham, *A New World for Women*, p. 94.
59. Ibid., p. 98.
60. Cicely Hamilton, *Marriage as a Trade*, p. 36.
61. Ibid., p. 102.

Chapter 11

1. Cicely Hamilton to Edy Craig, 1 November 1931. Smallhythe Archive.
2. See Dale Spender, *Time and Tide Wait for No Man*.
3. Margaret Haig, Lady Rhondda, *Notes on the Way*, p. 207.
4. Published as *Letters to a Friend*. Winifred Holtby and Jean McWilliam served together in France during World War I.
5. Quoted in Vera Brittain, *Testament of Friendship*, p. 134.
6. Vera Brittain, *Chronicle of Friendship*, entry for 19 August 1933.
7. Cicely Hamilton to Winifred Holtby, March 1932. Winifred Holtby Collection, Hull Central Library.
8. Cicely Hamilton to Winifred Holtby, 26 December 1932. Winifred Holtby Collection.
9. Cicely Hamilton to the Society of Authors, 3 August 1922.
10. Cicely Hamilton to the Society of Authors, 14 September 1921.
11. The *Catholic Citizen*, 15 November 1957.
12. Elizabeth Abbott's obituary of Cicely Hamilton, *WFL Newsletter*, December 1952.
13. Ibid.
14. Ibid.
15. Ibid.
16. Cicely Hamilton, *Life Errant*, p. 207.
17. Typescript of play, Lord Chamberlain's plays. British Library.
18. Ibid.
19. *The Times*, 30 October 1920.
20. *Time and Tide*, 26 January 1923.
21. Cicely Hamilton, *The Old Adam*, p. 46.
22. Ibid., p. 73.
23. Ibid., pp. 96–7.

24. Ibid., p. 97.
25. *The Times*, 18 November 1925.
26. Unidentified cutting, 18 November 1925.
27. *The Times*, 7 April 1936.
28. *Teachers World*, 24 June 1925.
29. Ibid.
30. Ibid.
31. Cicely Hamilton to the Society of Authors, 14 September 1921.
32. Hamilton, *Life Errant*, p. 206.
33. H.G. Wells, *Experiment in Autobiography*, p. 464.
34. Cicely Hamilton to Society of Authors, 10 July 1927.
35. *Time and Tide*, 23 January 1923.
36. Cicely Hamilton, *Full Stop*, p. 64.
37. Ibid., p. 119.
38. Ibid., p. 211.
39. Hamilton, *Life Errant*, p. 218.
40. Ibid., p. 221.
41. Ibid., p. 224.
42. Cicely Hamilton, *Little Arthur's History of the Twentieth Century*, p. 75.
43. Ibid., p. 53.
44. Ibid., p. 98.

Chapter 12

1. Cicely Hamilton, *Lament for Democracy*, p. 36.
2. Stephen Spender, *World within World*, p. 251.
3. Lady Rhondda, *Time and Tide*, December 1952.
4. Cicely Hamilton to the Society of Authors, 28 December 1942.
5. Mark Arnold Foster, *The World at War*, p. 246.
6. Pamphlet of the British League for European Freedom, no date.
7. Ibid.
8. Cicely Hamilton, speech on BBC April 1943. National Sound Archive.
9. Ibid.
10. Spender, op. cit., p. 251.
11. Elizabeth Abbott, *Women's Freedom League Newsletter*, December 1952.
12. Quoted in Carolyn G. Heilbrun, *Writing a Woman's Life*, p. 124.

Bibliography

Published Works

Adlard, Eleanor (ed.), *Edy. Recollections of Edith Craig*, Frederick Muller, London, 1949.

Arnold-Foster, Mark, *The World at War*, Fontana, London, 1976.

Ashwell, Lena, *Modern Troubadours*, Michael Joseph, London, 1922.

Myself a Player, Michael Joseph, London, 1936.

Bailey, Hilary, *Vera Brittain*, Penguin, London, 1987.

Boston, Lucy, *Perverse and Foolish*, Bodley Head, London, 1939.

Boyd, Elizabeth French, *Bloomsbury Heritage. Their Mothers and Their Aunts*, Hamish Hamilton, London, 1976.

Brittain, Vera, *Testament of Friendship*, Fontana, London, 1981.

Chronicle of Friendship: Vera Brittain's Diaries of the Thirties 1932–1939, edited by Alan Bishop, London, 1987.

Cook, Blanche Wisen, ' "Women Alone Stir My Imagination": Lesbianism and the Cultural Tradition', *Signs* 4, no. 4 (Summer 1979).

Craig, Edward H.G., *Ellen Terry and her Secret Self*, Sampson Low, London, 1931.

De Navarro, Antonio, *The Scottish Women's Hospital at the French Abbey of Royaumont*, Allen and Unwin, London, 1917.

Dickson, Lovat, *H.G. Wells: His Turbulent Life and Times*, London 1969.

Doughan, David, *Lobbying for Liberation*, Vera Douie Memorial Lecture, 1979, Fawcett Society, London, 1980.

Faderman, Lillian, *Surpassing the Love of Men*, The Women's Press, London, 1985.

Ferguson, Ann, 'Patriachy, Sexual Identity, and the Sexual Revolution', *Signs* 7, no. 1 (Autumn 1981).

Findlater, Richard, *Lilian Baylis*, Allen Lane, London, 1975.

The Player Queens, Allen Lane, London, 1976.

Fulford, Roger, *Votes for Women*, Faber, London, 1957.

Glendinning, Victoria, *Vita*, Penguin, London, 1983.

Greville, Frances, *Socialism and the Great State*, Harper, London and New York, 1912.

Haig, Margaret, Lady Rhondda, *This was my World*, Macmillan, London, 1933.

Notes on the Way, London, Macmillan, 1937.

Heilbrun, Carolyn G., *Writing a Woman's Life*, The Women's Press, London, 1989.

Holledge, Julie, *Innocent Flowers. Women in the Edwardian Theatre*, Virago, London, 1981.

Holtby Winifred, *Women and a Changing Civilisation*, Bodley Head, London, 1934.

Letters to a Friend, Collins, London, 1937.

Jack, Eva, *Exits and Entrances*, Chapman and Hall, London, 1923.

Jeffeys, Sheila, *The Spinster and Her Enemies*, Pandora Press, London, 1985.

Larkin, Philip, *The Whitsun Weddings*, Faber and Faber, London, 1964.

Leathard, Audrey, *The Fight for Family Planning*, Macmillan, London, 1980.

Linklater, Andro, *An Unhusbanded Life. Charlotte Despard, Suffragette, Socialist and Sinn Feiner*, Hutchinson, London, 1980.

Llewelyn Davis, Margaret, *Life as We Have Known It*, Virago, London, 1977.

McCarthy, Lillah, *Myself and my Friends*, Thornton Butterworth, London, 1933.

MacLaren, Eva Shaw, *A History of the Scottish Women's Hospitals*, London, 1919.

Mander, Joe and Mitchenson, Raymond *The Lost Theatres of London*, Rupert Hart Davies, London, 1963.

Melville, Joy, *Ellen and Edy. A Biography of Ellen Terry and her Daughter Edith Craig 1847–1947*, Pandora Press, London, 1987.

Montizambert, Elizabeth, *Unnoticed London*, J.M. Dent, London, 1922.

London Discoveries in Shops and Restaurants, Women Publishers,

London, 1924.
Moore, Eva, *Exits and Entrances*, Chapman and Hall, London, 1923.
Nevinson, Margaret Wynne, *Life's Fitful Fever*, AE Black, London, 1926.
Nicoll, Allardyce, *English Drama 1900–1930*, Cambridge University Press, Cambridge, 1973.
Pankhurst, E. Sylvia, *The Suffragette Movement*, Virago, London, 1977.
Robins, Elizabeth, *Both Sides of the Curtain*, Heinemann, London, 1940.
Way Stations, Hodder and Stoughton, London, 1913.
The Convert, with an introduction by Jane Marcus, The Women's Press, London, 1980.
Rover, Constance, *Women's Suffrage and Party Politics in Britain 1866–1914*, Routledge and Kegan Paul, London, 1967.
Rowbotham, Sheila, *A New World for Women*, Pluto Press, London, 1977.
Saint John, Christopher (Christabel Marshall), *Hungerheart. The Story of a Soul*, London, 1915.
Schwarz, Judith, *Radical Feminists of Heterodoxy*, New Victoria Publishers, Lebanon, New Hampshire, 1986.
Sharp, Evelyn, *Unfinished Adventure*, Bodley Head, London, 1933.
Six Point Group, The, *Dorothy Evans and the Six Point Group*, London, 1946.
Spence, Edward Fordham, *Our Stage and its Critics*, Methuen, London, 1910.
Spender, Dale, *There's Always Been a Women's Movement this Century*, London, 1983.
Women of Ideas and What Men Have Done to Them, Ark Books, London, 1983.
Time and Tide Wait for No Man, Pandora Press, London, 1984.
and Hayman, Carole (eds.), *How the Vote was Won and Other Suffragette Plays*, Methuen, London, 1985.
Spender, Stephen, *World within World*, Readers Union, London, 1951.
Steel, Flora Annie, *The Garden of Fidelity*, Macmillan, London, 1929.
Strachey, Ray, *The Cause*, Virago, London, 1978.
Swanwick, Helena, *I Have Been Young*, Gollancz, London, 1935.
Tickner, Lisa, *The Spectacle of Women*, Chatto and Windus,

London, 1987.

Vanburgh, Dame Irene, *To Tell my Story*, Hutchinson, London, 1943.

Vanburgh, Violet, *Dare to be Wise*, Hodder and Staughton, London, 1925.

Vernon, Frank, *The Twentieth Century Theatre*, Harrap, London, 1924.

Vicinus, Martha, *Independent Women. Work and Community for Single Women 1850–1920*, Virago, London, 1985.

Wearing, J.P., *The London Stage 1910–1919. A Calendar of Plays and Players*, Scarecrow Press, New York, 1982.

Wells, Amy Catherine, *The Book of Catherine Wells*, Chatto and Windus, London, 1928.

Wells. H.G., *In Memory of Amy Catherine Wells*, privately printed, London, 1927.

Experiment in Autobiography, Gollancz, London, 1934.

The New Machiavelli, Penguin, London, 1946.

Weymouth, Antony (ed.), *The English Spirit*, Allen and Unwin, London, 1942.

Wilson, A.E., *Edwardian Theatre*, London, 1951.

Woolf, Leonard, *The Journey Not the Arrival Matters: an Autobiography of the Years 1939–1969*, Hogarth Press, London, 1970.

Woolf, Virginia, *Between the Acts*, Penguin, London, 1972.

Unpublished Material

Fawcett Library

Papers of Open Door Council.

Papers of Scottish Women's Hospitals.

Papers of Women's Tax Resistance League.

Australian National University

Auchmuty, R. *Victorian Spinsters*, unpublished PhD thesis, 1975.

Works by Cicely Hamilton

Published Works

Novels

Just To Get Married Chapman Hall, London, 1911.
A Matter of Money, Chapman Hall, London, 1916.
William, an Englishman, Skeffington, London, 1919.
Theodore Savage, Leonard Parsons, London, 1922.
Lest Ye Die (reworking of *Theodore Savage*), Jonathan Cape, London, 1928.
Full Stop, J.M. Dent, London, 1931.

Full-length Plays

Diana of Dobsons, Samuel French, London, 1908.
A Pageant of Great Women, The Suffrage Shop, London, 1910.
Just To Get Married, Samuel French, London, 1914.
A Matter of Money (also known as *The Cutting of the Knot*), Lacey, London, 1911.
The Old Adam (first performed as *The Human Factor*), Oxford University Press, Oxford, 1926.
The Beggar Prince, Collins, Glasgow, 1936.

One-act Plays

How the Vote was Won (with Christopher St John), privately published by Edith Craig, London, 1909; reprinted by Methuen, London, 1985.

Jack and Jill and a Friend, Lacey, London, 1911.
The Child in Flanders, in *One Act Plays of Today*, Harrap, London, 1925.

Other Works

Marriage as a Trade, Chapman Hall, London, 1909; reprinted by The Women's Press, London, 1981.
Senlis, Collins, London, 1917.
The Old Vic (with Lilian Baylis), Jonathan Cape, London, 1926.
Modern Germanies, J.M. Dent, London, 1931.
Modern Italy, J.M. Dent, London, 1932.
Modern France, J.M. Dent, London, 1933.
Little Arthur's History of the Twentieth Century, J.M. Dent, London, 1933.
Modern Russia, J.M. Dent, London, 1934.
Modern Austria, J.M. Dent, London, 1935.
Life Errant, J.M. Dent, London, 1935.
Modern Ireland, J.M. Dent, London, 1936.
Modern Scotland, J.M. Dent, London, 1937.
Modern England, J.M. Dent, London 1938.
Modern Sweden, J.M. Dent, London, 1939.
Lament for Democracy, J.M. Dent, London, 1940.
The Englishwoman, The British Council, London 1940.
Holland Today, J.M. Dent, London, 1950.

Unpublished Material

Full-length Plays

Lady Noggs, 1913.
Phyl, 1913.
The Brave and the Fair, 1920.

One-act Plays

The Sixth Commandment, 1906.
The Sergeant of Hussars, 1907.

Mrs Vance, 1907.
The Pot and the Kettle, 1909.
The Homecoming (also known as *After Twenty Years*), 1910.
The Constant Husband, 1912.
Mrs Armstrong's Admirer, 1920.

Imperial War Museum
Henry, Dr Leila. MS Diary.
Jeffrey, M. MS Diary.
Littlejohn, Dorothy. MS Diary.
Starr, Marjorie. Letters.

British Library
Typescripts of plays by Cicely Hamilton, Lord Chamberlain's Plays.

Harry Hyams Humanities Research Center, University of Texas at Austin
Letters from Cicely Hamilton

Hull Central Library
Letters in Winifred Holtby Collection

Index